Language Program Evaluation

THE CAMBRIDGE APPLIED LINGUISTICS SERIES

Series editors: Michael H. Long and Jack C. Richards

This new series presents the findings of recent work in applied linguistics which are of direct relevance to language teaching and learning and of particular interest to applied linguists, researchers, language teachers, and teacher trainers.

In this series:

Language Program Evaluation

Theory and practice

Brian K. Lynch

The University of Melbourne

CAMBRIDGE
UNIVERSITY PRESS

PUBLISHED BY THE PRESS SYNDICATE OF THE UNIVERSITY OF CAMBRIDGE
The Pitt Building, Trumpington Street, Cambridge CB2 1RP, United Kingdom

CAMBRIDGE UNIVERSITY PRESS
The Edinburgh Building, Cambridge CB2 2RU, United Kingdom
40 West 20th Street, New York, NY 10011–4211, USA
10 Stamford Road, Oakleigh, Melbourne 3166, Australia

© Cambridge University Press 1996

First published 1996
Second printing 1997

Printed in the United States of America

Typeset in Sabon

Library of Congress Cataloging-in-Publication Data
Lynch, Brian K.
Language program evaluation : theory and practice / Brian K.
Lynch.
p. cm. – (Cambridge applied linguistics series)
Includes bibliographical references (p.) and index.
ISBN 0-521-48191-0. – ISBN 0-521-48438-3 (pbk.)
1. Language and languages – Study and teaching – Evaluation.
I. Title. II. Series.
P53.63.L96 1996
418'.007-dc20   95-1719
                                                              CIP

A catalog record for this book is available from the British Library

ISBN 0-521-48191-0 hardback
ISBN 0-521-48438-3 paperback

for my mentor and friend, Russ Campbell,
and to the loving memory of my Dad

Contents

viii   *Contents*

6 **Quantitative data gathering and analysis**   92
Data gathering   92
Data analysis   94
Conclusion   105

7 **Qualitative data gathering and analysis**   107
Overview   107
Data gathering   108
Data analysis   139

8 **Combining positivistic and naturalistic program evaluation**   155
Compatibilist versus incompatibilist perspectives   155
Mixed strategies   156
Multiple strategies   158
Mixed designs   159
Mixed designs and strategies over time   165

9 **Conclusions**   167
CAM step 1 (audience and goals): Determine the purpose of the
    evaluation   167
CAM steps 2 and 3 (context inventory and preliminary thematic
    framework): Determine what is being evaluated   170
CAM steps 4 and 5 (evaluation design and data collection):
    Select a design and collect the data   171
CAM step 6 (data analysis): Analyze and interpret your
    findings   173
CAM step 7 (evaluation report): Communicating the evaluation
    findings   174
The role of program evaluation in applied linguistics research   175

References   178
Author index   188
Subject index   191

Series editors' preface

Program evaluation is important and difficult work in any field, and language education is no exception. The goal is sometimes to evaluate a program's effectiveness in absolute terms, sometimes to assess its quality against that of comparable programs, sometimes both. In ideal circumstances, evaluations receive cooperation from all parties and provide useful information to insiders on how their work can be improved, while offering accountability to outside stakeholders, such as host institutions, governments, and financial sponsors, as well as to students.

Circumstances are often less than ideal, however. Whether insiders or outsiders themselves, evaluators may be expected to employ recognized instruments and procedures, such as standardized proficiency tests and inferential statistics, for gathering and interpreting data. At the same time, they must also adapt to unique local conditions, where, for instance, objective measures yielding quantifiable data may be unwelcome, unusable, or unavailable. Worse, some stakeholders may have incompatible goals, conflicting interests in the outcome of an evaluation, and/or differing views about how it should be conducted. For example, an evaluation requiring full staff cooperation may be commissioned by a host institution, such as a university, with the aim of using the results to justify an already determined policy change with significant potential fall-out for program staff, including job losses. Training in conflict resolution may seem as useful as knowledge of applied linguistics in such cases, and the evaluator can easily end up taking sides or trying to play the role of mediator between warring parties.

Language Program Evaluation deals with these and many other methodological and policy issues, invoking both qualitative and quantitative, or positivistic and naturalistic, approaches in the process. The author, Dr. Brian K. Lynch, of The University of Melbourne, has had extensive field experience in both foreign and second language program evaluation and has made major contributions to theory and practice in this area, including his widely respected *context-adaptive model* for evaluation in applied linguistics. Dr. Lynch's book provides a coherent, rigorous, and comprehensive approach to language program evaluation and also identifies contributions that program evaluation can make to the development of applied linguistics as a research field. It should appeal to a wide range of applied linguists and language educators and is a welcome addition to the Cambridge Applied Linguistics Series.

Michael H. Long
Jack C. Richards

Preface

This book had its beginnings in a motel room in Guadalajara, Mexico. It was there, planning the schedule for the soon-to-be-inaugurated Reading English for Science and Technology (REST) project at the University of Guadalajara, that I rediscovered a manuscript passed on to me by Russ Campbell. The manuscript was a copy of a paper delivered by Michael Long at a TESOL convention (later published in *TESOL Quarterly* [Long 1984]). Reading that paper provided the revelation that led to a preliminary design for evaluating the project, which became the focus of my dissertation, which, in turn, evolved over a six-year period into this book.

Drawing upon the experience of implementing and evaluating the REST project from June 1985 to July 1987 reported on in my dissertation, I constructed the initial outlines of a book designed to provide a thorough theoretical background for the evaluation of language education programs, as well as a guide for putting theory into practice. The earlier drafts of the book made use of insights and feedback gained from teaching a graduate seminar for applied linguistics students at UCLA and from my experience as Academic Director of the ESL Service Courses at UCLA, as well as from supervising graduate student research into program evaluation and serving as evaluator for the California Foreign Language Teacher Preparation Project.

The result of these experiences is a book that presents program evaluation against the historical backdrop of modern language teaching and the development of research in applied linguistics. In particular, the theoretical basis for language program evaluation is discussed in terms of the *quantitative-qualitative debate* in educational measurement, more recently referred to as the *paradigm dialog* (Guba 1990). Validity, the act of determining what counts as evidence for evaluation, is discussed from both the quantitative, positivistic perspective and the qualitative, naturalistic perspective. My goal in presenting this dialog and these, at times, conflicting perspectives, is to present the reader with the necessary range of theory and associated practical techniques that will allow for the most thorough response possible to any language program evaluation context.

The book uses the *context-adaptive model* for program evaluation (Lynch 1990) as an organizing principle for presenting the critical issues facing those who are about to embark upon the evaluation process. As with the context-adaptive model, the book was designed for those involved in language education. The concepts and methods advanced are illustrated with examples from my own experience, primarily ESL and EFL, as well as with vignettes from a variety of second language settings. It will be useful for language teachers who are looking for a systematic way to evaluate the instructional sequences of their classrooms, for language program administrators who need to decide on strategies for evaluating their schools, for language educators who have been asked to provide information on program processes or to make decisions about curricular change, for teachers of graduate level seminars on language program evaluation and research methods, and for a variety of applied linguists conducting research that focuses on, or makes use of, program evaluation data.

Whenever one manages to complete a project such as this, there are innumerable persons who have provided help, vision, encouragement, and advice along the way. Let me try to count and give recognition to at least some of the innumerable. Firstly, to all of those involved in the first two years of the REST project at the Universidad de Guadalajara (UdeG), especially my co-coordinator on the project, Margarita Matte, and the teachers on the project during the formative 1985–1987 years: Lyn Carr, Young Gee, Kathy Lunde, Suzanne McMeans, Carlos Oceguera, and Alfredo Urzúa. My special thanks go to the other three REST teachers from that period who have become lifelong friends: Elizabeth Borkowski, Juan Carlos Gallego, and Shira Smith. All of our students from the Chemical Sciences Faculty of the UdeG deserve recognition for their efforts in the program and as participants in the gathering of evaluation data. My thanks also go to the various officials at the UdeG and UCLA; in particular, Raúl Padilla, Margarita Sierra, Elwin Svenson, and Russ Campbell, whose unwavering support for the project was critical to its success.

I would also like to acknowledge Leigh Burstein, Russ Campbell, Evelyn Hatch, and Harold Levine for their helpful comments on the dissertation from which this book grew. I also wish to give special recognition to Harold Levine, who initiated me into the world of naturalistic research. That experience continues to be one of profound importance in my work. I was saddened to learn that Leigh Burstein passed away months before this book was due to go to press. Much of the knowledge of quantitative analysis that I present comes from my experience in his graduate seminar on quasi-experimental design.

When the book had taken sufficient form to begin the search for a publisher, I received some invaluable criticism on the manuscript from Lyle Bachman, which allowed me to rethink the issues of content and audience in a productive fashion. At the same time, I received important feedback from my students and colleagues at UCLA who attended my seminar in program evaluation for applied linguists; in particular, Patsy Duff, Paul Gruba, Sally Jacoby, Andrea Kahn, Anne Lazaraton, Charlene Polio, and Jean Turner. The final time the seminar was offered, in the spring of 1992, I received helpful reactions to the content and detailed feedback on the manuscript from Bob Agajeenian, Denise Asher Babel, Linda Choi, Tom Griggs, Eric Miller, Micky Safadi, Kim Thomas, Jim Valentine, and Rosa Maria Victori-Blaya.

I would be remiss if I did not mention those who have provided the inspiration, friendship, and support during my years at UCLA, without which this book would never have survived the transition from experience to the printed page. A major expression of gratitude goes to my colleagues in the ESL Service Courses: Donna Brinton, Janet Goodwin, Christine Holten, and Sandy Wallace (also to Jean Turner, for her year as Academic Coordinator). To those in the Department of TESL and Applied Linguistics who were my teachers, I express my sincere thanks: Roger Andersen, Frances Butler, Russ Campbell, Marianne Celce-Murcia, Evelyn Hatch, John Schumann (and to the memory of John Povey). While they did not comment specifically on this manuscript, I owe a debt of gratitude to J. D. Brown, my original mentor who pointed me down the language-testing path and, again, to Frances Butler who took me further down the path with great insight and example. My thanks go also to Fred Davidson, for being such an enthusiastic and conscientious language tester and applied linguist. Most importantly, I want to thank Thom Hudson for his inspiring research and irreplaceable friendship.

In the final months leading up to publication of this book, I have received expert assistance and support from Jane Mairs, Mary Vaughn, and Mary Carson from Cambridge University Press. My thanks also go to Jack Richards, series co-editor, and to the anonymous reviewer of the manuscript for comments that improved the book in significant ways. At the same time, I have been welcomed to a new home in Melbourne, Australia by the students and staff of the Department of Applied Linguistics and Language Studies at The University of Melbourne. I give my special thanks to Gladys Cubberly and Vittoria Grossi for their help in that adjustment process, and to Tim McNamara for his encouragement, advice, and friendship.

During all of these phases I have received the ultimate support that only one's life partner can give. My love and thanks to Buni and to our son, Sam.

Finally, returning to this project's origins in that Guadalajara motel room, I thank Mike Long for inspiring the original concept, and for championing the manuscript all along the way. I will end this lengthy list of thank you's with an acknowledgment of the profound example that has been provided for me and for the field of applied linguistics by Russ Campbell. Russ represents the best qualities of a teacher, administrator, researcher, mentor, and friend. He is the heart of this book.

Brian K. Lynch

1 *Introduction*

It is probably safe to assume that the concept of program evaluation is not completely foreign to most applied linguists, even to those working outside the language education domain. Certainly the words *program* and *evaluation* conjure up reasonably clear mental images, and the notion that a program might need to be evaluated does not seem illogical to most. Language education programs abound internationally, and the majority of applied linguists have most likely, at some stage in their career, been involved in these programs as teachers, administrators, students, researchers, or some combination of these roles. Many, if not most, have been involved in some sort of effort to evaluate a language program. This evaluation may have taken the form of asking students to rate their language course and teacher using a questionnaire, giving achievement tests at the beginning and end of a period of instruction, or having a language teaching expert from another institution visit the program and prepare a report on its strengths and weaknesses. Program evaluation, then, can be seen as relevant to the experience of a wide range of applied linguists, and will be of particular interest to language educators.

Definitions: Applied linguistics, evaluation, program

In order to proceed with a detailed examination of the theory and practice of program evaluation within the broad context of applied linguistics, however, more precise definitions of certain terms are in order. I will focus on three key terms here; others will be presented in Chapter 2. To begin with, *applied linguistics* (AL), as a term defining an emerging academic discipline, has been the subject of recent discussions (Andersen et al. 1990; Pennycook 1990; van Lier et al. 1991). For the purposes of this book, AL will refer to research and practice concerned with the application of knowledge and methods from a variety of disciplines (e.g., anthropology, sociology, linguistics, psychology, and education) to the range of issues concerning the development and use of language.

1

The term *evaluation* tends to be used somewhat ambiguously in relation to other terms such as *assessment* and *testing*. Drawing upon the work of Bachman (1990) and Turner (1991), I will differentiate *evaluation* from these other terms primarily on the basis of its scope and purpose. That is, evaluation can make use of assessment instruments (including tests), but it is not limited to such forms of information gathering. It may include, for example, the use of unstructured interviews. Likewise, assessment instruments (including tests) can be used for purposes other than evaluation, such as to measure individual language ability in order to test a research hypothesis concerning language acquisition. Evaluation is defined here as the systematic attempt to gather information in order to make judgments or decisions. As such, evaluative information can be both qualitative and quantitative in form, and can be gathered through different methods such as observation or the administration of pencil-and-paper tests.

Program is a term that has perhaps been used with less ambiguity than evaluation. In general, it tends to evoke the image of a series of courses linked with some common goal or end product. A language education program generally consists of a slate of courses designed to prepare students for some language-related endeavor. This might mean preparing them to pass a language proficiency exam that, in turn, would allow them to gain entrance to some other program of study. It might also mean preparing them to function, in a general sense, in the context of a second language culture. These types of preparation can, of course, involve a single course (e.g., a Test of English as a Foreign Language [TOEFL] preparation course). In an effort to provide the broadest definition possible, I will use program to refer to any instructional sequence, such as a multilevel English as a second language (ESL) curriculum, a foreign language teacher-training workshop, a teaching unit being tried for the first time in a Japanese-for-business-purposes classroom, or computer-assisted instructional software that is self-accessed by students in a language lab.

Critical issues

The question that arises next, perhaps, is why applied linguists should concern themselves with program evaluation. In part, the answer to this question lies in the perennial need for language education programs to be evaluated, be it motivated by an internal quest for program improvement or by an externally imposed requirement in order to justify program funding. Accepting this, is program evaluation a generalized activity that has no need for a specific articulation within the context of applied linguistics? I believe that evaluation efforts do need to be tailored to the specific concerns of language education programs (Lynch 1990b). Toward that end, I formulated the *context-adaptive model* (CAM) for language program evaluation (Lynch 1990a), drawing upon the historical development of program evaluation in applied linguistics that is discussed in the next chapter. Rather than a rigid model to be tested for validity using experimental research design and appropriate statistical techniques, it is meant to be a flexible, adaptable heuristic – a starting point for inquiry into language education programs that will constantly reshape and redefine itself, depending on the context of the program and the evaluation. I see the adaptable nature of the CAM as a partial antidote to many of the problems that have plagued previous attempts to evaluate language education programs. In the remainder of this introduction, I use this model as a framework for presenting the critical issues for language program evaluation. In addition to elucidating these issues, the CAM provides the basis for arguing for the important contribution that program evaluation can make to the development of applied linguistics as a field of research (see Figure 1.1).

Audience and goals

The first step of the CAM is concerned with identifying the audience and goals for the evaluation. Who is requesting the evaluation? Who will be affected by the evaluation? The answers to these questions help to determine the *stakeholders*, or *clients*, who have an immediate and central interest in the ultimate findings of the evaluation. Common examples of stakeholders are the program staff and the agencies that fund the program. The students of the program, although not clients per se, can also be thought of as an important audience for the evaluation. The concept of an evaluation audience can be broadened still further to include all those potentially interested in the conduct and results of the evaluation. Examples of this peripheral audience are program administrators, curriculum developers, teachers, and researchers from other program settings.

Identification of the evaluation audience leads to determining the evaluation goals, or purpose. Why is the evaluation being conducted? What information is being requested and why? Depending on the evaluation audience, the answers to these questions can be quite varied. Different subsets of the audience may also have different, and even conflicting, goals. For example, a funding agency may want statistical evidence that the program is producing higher test scores than some rival program, in order to justify continued financial support. The program staff, on the other hand, may want more descriptive information about how the instructional objectives are actually being realized in the classroom in order to improve the curriculum. These evaluation goals may

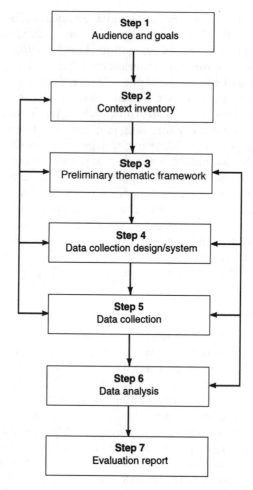

Figure 1.1 The context-adaptive model (CAM). (From B. K. Lynch 1990a:25. Copyright 1990 by TESOL. Reprinted by permission.)

have been stated clearly from the start by the evaluation audience, or they may need to be clarified by the evaluator in preevaluation interviews.

The particular evaluation audience and their goals for the evaluation will to a large extent determine the role of the evaluator. The funding agency, interested primarily in determining whether the program is "successful," may require that the evaluation be carried out by persons external to the program, for greater objectivity. The program staff, interested in improving the curriculum, may elect an internal evaluation, carried out by the program's own teachers and administrators, in order to take advantage of their close understanding of the program context. Of course, the decision to carry out an external versus internal evaluation will often be made based on the ability to find and pay for external evaluators. After being established as either external or internal, the role of the evaluator will be further defined, depending on the audience and goals (and, in certain cases, by the evaluator's preferred style), as someone providing consultation, an expert standing in judgment, a collaborator in program development, or a decision-making facilitator.

Context inventory

Another critical issue for program evaluation is the essential phenomena or features that characterize the program and its setting. The CAM addresses this issue with a checklist, or inventory, of potentially relevant dimensions of language education programs:

1. Availability of a *comparison group* (such as a "traditional" language program in a similar setting)
2. Availability of *reliable and valid measures* of language skills (criterion-referenced and/or norm-referenced tests, with program-specific and/or program-neutral content)
3. Availability of various types of *evaluation expertise* (such as statistical analysis, naturalistic research)
4. *Timing* of the evaluation (when the program begins, ends, and has breaks; how much time is available to conduct the evaluation)
5. The *selection process* for admitting students into the program (random selection, self-selection, selection according to preestablished criteria)
6. Characteristics of the program *students* (native language and culture, age, sex, socioeconomic status, previous education, previous academic achievement, previous experience with the language and culture being taught in the program)
7. Characteristics of the program *staff* (similar to characteristics of students; also, job descriptions, experience, availability, competence, and attitude toward the evaluation)
8. *Size and intensity* of the program (number of students, classrooms, proficiency/course levels, and number of hours per week/term)
9. *Instructional materials and resources* available to the program (textbooks, other instructional media and materials, human resources, basic office supplies)
10. *Perspective and purpose* of the program (notions, beliefs, and assumptions concerning the nature of language and the process of language learning; explicitly stated and informally articulated curricular goals)
11. *Social and political climate* surrounding the program (perception of the program by the surrounding academic and social community, student and community attitudes toward the language and culture being taught in the program, the relationship of the program's purpose to the larger social and political context)

Some of these dimensions will be more relevant in certain contexts than in others. Part of the adaptive nature of the CAM is the recognition that such an inventory will need to be tailored to the particular program setting. This tailoring may reflect practical constraints on the amount of detailed information capable of being gathered in the context inventory as well as the nature of certain dimensions (such as the unavailability of evaluation expertise or instructional materials and resources resulting from budgetary limitations). Along with the information on audience and goals, the context inventory acts as a guide for subsequent steps in the evaluation. It can act as an early indicator of the limits of a particular evaluation, and will inform decisions during subsequent steps in the evaluation process.

Preliminary thematic framework

The amount of information resulting from the first two steps of the CAM can be potentially overwhelming. A critical issue that arises at this early stage is how to focus the evaluation. Where should the evaluator begin? What aspects of the program should the evaluator investigate in detail? A preliminary thematic framework provides a conceptualization of the program in terms of the salient issues and themes that have emerged from the determination of audience and goals and the elaboration of the context inventory. Articulating this framework provides the evaluator with a focus that will guide the collection and analysis of evaluation data. The following is an example of a preliminary thematic framework developed for an English for science and technology (EST) reading program:

1. Effects of focusing instruction on reading only
2. Effects of focusing instruction on reading skills and strategies
3. Effects of using authentic reading texts
4. Feasibility of using Spanish versus English for instruction
5. Availability of classrooms
6. Feasibility of using a "modified adjunct model" approach
7. Feasibility and effects of conducting classroom-centered research
8. Level of student proficiency in English upon entering the program

(adapted from Lynch 1990a)

Data collection design/system

The evaluation audience and goals, context inventory, and preliminary thematic framework combine to suggest questions that the evaluator needs to answer. Another critical issue to be addressed is how best to obtain the information necessary to answer these questions. What type of data will need to be gathered – quantitative, qualitative, or both? What will be the best methods for gathering the data? If the primary evaluation question is "Are the students of this program making significant gains in their language abilities?" then a quantitative design may be most appropriate. Language ability test scores would be gathered before and after participation in the program and analyzed for statistical significance. On the other hand, if the primary question to be answered is "How can we improve this program?" then a qualitative design may be called for. The evaluator(s) would observe program classes, interview students and staff, and try to describe how the program is functioning in order to make recommendations for change. In other evaluation contexts, there may be a combination of questions to answer that require both quantitative and qualitative data.

The context inventory is extremely useful at this stage for determining the feasibility of certain types of data collection design. In particular, the lack of availability of a comparison group will severely constrain the range of quantitative designs that are possible. That is, without a comparison group, the evaluation will not be able to make use of most traditional experimental and quasi-experimental research designs. Dimensions such as the attitude of program staff toward the evaluation and the availability of evaluation expertise will also dictate limits for the data collection design. For example, an unwillingness on the part of the program staff to provide time for evaluation efforts or the lack of available expertise in qualitative data analysis (the evaluator may be untrained in this type of evaluation and may be unable to procure such expertise) may result in the evaluator abandoning plans to collect interview data from program participants. Two examples of the interaction of audience and goals, context inventory, and preliminary thematic framework in the selection of a data collection design are represented in Figure 1.2.

Data collection and analysis

Data collection and analysis follow logically from the type of design chosen for the evaluation. The critical issues that concern the evaluator here have to do with the appropriate conduct of the data-gathering procedures and the interpretation of the results. In the case of quantitative designs, have the assumptions of the design and statistical models been met? In the case of qualitative designs, have the procedures for data gathering been portrayed accurately, and have alternative interpretations of the data been pursued? Like the choice of evaluation design, these are obviously complex issues that are discussed in greater detail in subsequent chapters.

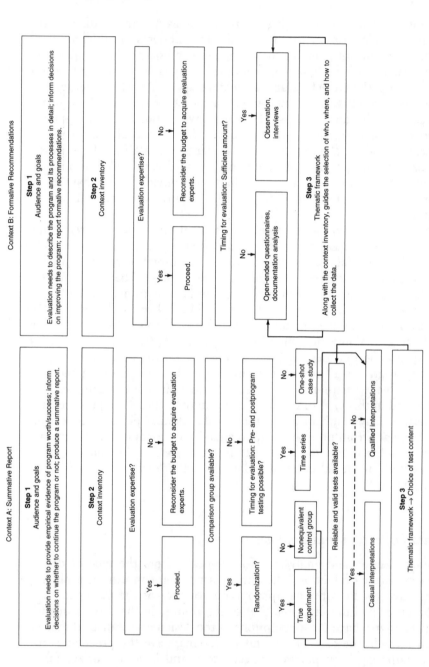

Figure 1.2   Formulation of the data collection design/system. (From B. K. Lynch 1990a:34–35. Copyright 1990 by TESOL. Reprinted by permission.)

Evaluation report

In order to produce a useful final report, the evaluator must be extremely sensitive to the audience and goals of the evaluation. The social and political climate dimension of the context inventory needs to be considered carefully at this stage as well. The critical issue is how to communicate the findings of the evaluation honestly and successfully. The evaluator may find that certain conclusions and the evidence on which they are based need to be omitted from this communication, be it a formal, written document or an informal, oral report. Rather than a covering up or withholding of the truth, this should be seen as a concern for communicating effectively with the audience. Topics that are extremely sensitive or issues that are tied to specific personalities may obscure the intended message and lead to a misunderstanding of the evaluation's conclusions and the evidence on which they are based. The evaluator may find it necessary to provide multiple reports that highlight different types of evaluative information or that express the evaluation findings in different ways, depending on the intended audiences.

Program evaluation and applied linguistics research

I have argued elsewhere that program evaluation can play an essential role in the development of applied linguistics as a field of research (Lynch 1991). Given the critical issue of identifying the audience and goals for an evaluation discussed in the previous section, the work of program evaluation leads to a careful consideration of what counts as evidence. In the literature on program evaluation this has been characterized as the *qualitative-quantitative debate* (Reichardt and Cook 1979; Smith and Heshusius 1986; Howe 1988; Smith 1988), *paradigm wars* (Gage 1989), or *paradigm dialog* (Guba 1990). This debate is summarized in Chapter 2 as part of the historical background for program evaluation in applied linguistics. The point to be made here, however, is that there exists work that has brought knowledge concerning research paradigms from other disciplines to bear on the evaluation of language education programs (Long 1983; Beretta 1986a; Lynch 1988, 1992) and thus adds to the definition of applied linguistics as a field of research. This work has raised the important issue of what we accept as evidence for answering our evaluation questions. Different audiences for a program evaluation force the evaluator to consider the issue of what counts as evidence from different perspectives. As mentioned previously, a funding agency may expect statistics as proof that a program deserves continued support. The program staff as audience for an evaluation may expect a clear description of how the program is actually functioning. Evaluators need to consider these perspectives along with their own requirements for what counts as evidence. I believe that this process strengthens research in applied linguistics by opening the field to different types of knowledge and knowledge validation and by clarifying the bases on which it is built.

In addition to keeping us aware and honest about what counts as evidence in our inquiry, program evaluation can spark investigation across a wide range of research areas that describe applied linguistics. The dimensions of the context inventory, discussed previously as a checklist for gathering the necessary information about a program, involve consideration of such issues as the social and political basis and motivation for language learning and teaching. The concern for reliable and valid measures leads program evaluators into the area of language testing and the application of knowledge and techniques from education and psychology for the improved measurement of language ability. When the evaluation questions to be answered involve a combination of "Has it succeeded?" and "How has it succeeded?" a multiple-research-methods strategy that leads program evaluation into complex qualitative–quantitative designs is called for. For example, in order to investigate the match between program objectives and classroom processes, an evaluator needs to consider a combination of precise quantitative measurement of student achievement and qualitative methods such as an ethnographic description of the classroom, in addition to introspective/retrospective investigation of individual learning processes and their interaction with instruction. If the instructional objectives of a program are based on second language acquisition (SLA) theory, program evaluation can provide a testing ground for SLA research.

What counts as evidence? What are the social and political factors that affect language learning and teaching? How can we best define and measure language abilities? What are the best research designs for our inquiry? How do learners acquire a second language? These questions, which cut a wide swath across the applied linguistics terrain, are all critically related to the enterprise of program evaluation. The chapters that follow attempt to lay the theoretical foundations of this enterprise, as well as provide the practical means for its conduct.

Chapter 2, as mentioned, outlines the differences between the competing research paradigms in program evaluation (the quantitative–qualitative debate). Ultimately, I argue for the use of both paradigms, which I refer to as *positivistic* and *naturalistic*, while maintaining an awareness of the epistemological differences that divide them. Following this discussion of research methodology, I present a history of language education program evaluation from the 1960s to the present. The central focus of this presentation is the shift from essentially quantitative, positivistic studies that look only at end-of-program achievement gains to ones that include an investigation of program process using qualitative, naturalistic methods.

Chapter 3 discusses the issue of validity from both the positivistic and naturalistic perspectives. First I present the classical notions of internal and external validity, as well as some more recent approaches within the positivistic paradigm. Validity within the naturalistic paradigm is then discussed, highlighting the fundamental similarities to and differences from the positivistic paradigm.

Chapter 4 explains the various models or research designs for evaluation within the positivistic paradigm. I contrast true experiments with quasi-experimental design, and discuss the issues of control (or comparison) groups, selection, and measurement.

Chapter 5 presents a variety of models for carrying out program evaluation within the naturalistic paradigm. I present various examples of how certain "metaphors" for evaluation (Smith 1981) might be defined in the language teaching context.

Chapter 6 presents various techniques for collecting and analyzing quantitative data. First, I discuss the issue of the appropriate quantitative instruments, including consideration of norm-referenced versus criterion-referenced measurement and the selection of test content. Using example data from the Reading English for Science and Technology (REST) project evaluation (Lynch 1988, 1992), I present a variety of statistical procedures for analyzing quantitative data. This presentation is accompanied by a discussion of the requirements for using and interpreting the various statistical models in the context of program evaluation.

Chapter 7 begins with a discussion of qualitative data-gathering techniques. It focuses on observation and interviewing, but also considers such techniques as document analysis and journal keeping. I then present techniques for reducing the qualitative data, analyzing it, and forming interpretations. These techniques are illustrated with examples from the REST project evaluation (Lynch 1988, 1992).

Chapter 8 gives examples of program evaluation models that combine features of the positivistic and naturalistic approaches. I discuss various ways of mixing qualitative and quantitative data, analytic techniques, and designs.

In the final chapter, I summarize the theoretical and practical issues presented in the preceding chapters, focusing on the various purposes, contexts, designs, analyses, and modes of reporting results. Finally, I review the potential role for program evaluation in applied linguistics research.

2 Historical background

In order to begin making judgments about how language education programs should be evaluated, it will be helpful to understand how they have been evaluated in the past. Because applied linguistics is itself a relatively young field, the literature on program evaluation within the field is quite scant. There is a body of documented evaluations that can be summarized, however, and this is the focus of the second part of this chapter.

I have defined applied linguistics as a discipline that applies knowledge from other disciplines to language-related issues, and program evaluation in our field has developed within a larger context of evaluation, especially as articulated in the education and psychology literature. Because of this, a historical account of program evaluation in applied linguistics will need to be set against the backdrop of an important "conversation" (Smith and Heshusius 1986) about how evaluation research should be conducted. As introduced in Chapter 1, this is the infamous quantitative–qualitative debate, which more recently has been referred to as the paradigm dialog (Guba 1990a) and is the focus of the following section.

The paradigm dialog

For some time now, there has been a major debate in education and psychology between advocates of positivistic,[1] quantitative research

1 Some people object to the term positivistic, since the discussions in the philosophy of science have clearly moved beyond logical positivism. In recent years, the term *postpositivism* has come into use to refer to modifications of the positivist program (Guba 1990b) or any of the current paradigms, including naturalism/ constructivism (Guba and Lincoln 1989) and critical theory (Schwandt 1990). I use the term positivistic to refer to the variety of modified positivistic positions (e.g., Laudan and Laudan 1989; Newton-Smith 1982; Phillips 1990) and in contrast to naturalistic. Finally, it should be noted that although it has been discredited as a completely accurate program for guiding scientific inquiry, logical positivism continues to provide the basic criteria that researchers in the postpositivistic, quantitative tradition use to validate their knowledge claims (cf. Bechtel 1988).

methodology and advocates of naturalistic,[2] qualitative research methodology. At the core of this debate is a discussion of the epistemological basis for research, which has had parallel discussions elsewhere in the social sciences (e.g., Habermas 1988). What is the relevance of this debate to applied linguists interested in program evaluation? As discussed in Chapter 1, the relevance is in the assumptions that we are making when we insist on one type of evidence over another. In applied linguistics in general, and in program evaluation in particular, there has been a strong tendency to favor a traditional, quantitative experimental approach to conducting research. Regardless of the approach we take, it is important to be aware of the ontological (what can be known) and the epistemological (how we know what we claim to know) bases for our research and how these affect our choice of methodology (Guba and Lincoln 1989:83).

On one side of the debate, then, is the positivistic paradigm:[3] the traditional, experimental approach to evaluation. This approach has identified two major categories of research design: true experiments and quasi-experiments (Cook and Campbell 1979). In a true experimental approach to evaluation, students are randomly assigned to either the program of interest or to a "control" condition, such as an alternative program. The program students are then compared to the control students, usually by testing them for achievement gains, in order to decide if the program is having the desired effect (i.e., that its students are outperforming the control students).

Quasi-experiments can also compare the program of interest to a control group, but the assignment to one or the other of these situations is not random. Usually this means that the students, or schools, self-select into the program of interest or that they are selected by someone else (e.g., a school administrator) for the program in a nonrandom fashion. The problem with nonrandom selection is that we cannot assume that the only systematic differences between the program and control students are the result of being in the program or not. If we compare

2 The term naturalistic is, like positivistic, being used as a general cover term to refer to a variety of approaches to inquiry in the social sciences and humanities. More recently, this term has been relabeled by Guba and Lincoln (1989) as *constructivism*. I will use naturalistic to include the alternative paradigms (to positivism and postpositivism), including constructivism and critical theory (Popkewitz 1990).

3 Although the term paradigm continues to be used in educational research literature, it has been supplanted by other terms in the literature of the philosophy of science. As used here, paradigm resembles Laudan's (1977) *research tradition*, referring to a shared set of ontological as well as epistemological assumptions and their attendant methodological principles concerning how to conduct research. Stated more generically by Guba (1990b:17), a paradigm is "a basic set of beliefs that guides action."

the achievement gains of the two groups after some period of instruction, we do not know if differences in performance are due to the program or to other differences between the students that have nothing to do with the program. For example, the best students may be the ones who self-select into a new program. They may be able to outperform the control students because of their superior ability rather than because the program is superior. Fortunately, there are statistical and design procedures that take the possibility of preexisting differences between students into account (e.g., Campbell and Erlebacher 1970; Cain 1975; Campbell and Boruch 1975; Cronbach et al. 1975; Kenney 1975; Bryk and Weisberg 1976; Boruch and Rindskopf 1977; Cook et al. 1977; Bryk et al. 1980). This is particularly good news for most program evaluators in educational contexts, since the ability to assign students randomly to programs rarely exists. Quasi-experiments tend to be the only choice for those who wish to pursue the positivistic approach to evaluation in language education contexts.

As an alternative approach to inquiry, the naturalistic paradigm has challenged the traditional authority of positivistic research. Naturalistic evaluation generally requires an emergent, variable design, in contrast to the *preordinate*,[4] or constructed before the fact, designs of positivistic research. That is, the design of the evaluation emerges as the evaluator proceeds to investigate the program setting, allowing new information and insights to change how and from whom data will be gathered. In this sense, naturalistic research does not attempt to control conditions or variables in the research setting. The emphasis is on observing, describing, interpreting, and understanding how events take place in the real world rather than in a controlled, laboratorylike setting. This approach views the educational program being evaluated (in experimental design terms, the independent variable, or treatment) as a process that is continuously changing rather than a stable, invariant treatment. The naturalistic evaluator gathers the evaluation data using techniques such as in-depth interviews, participant observation, and journals (see, for example, Bogdan and Taylor 1975; Eisner 1975; Stake 1975; Parlett and Hamilton 1976; Guba 1978; Patton 1980; Smith 1981; Miles and Huberman 1984; Levine 1985; Strauss 1987; Guba and Lincoln 1989).

Rather than just pointing out a difference in the type of data or methods being used in the evaluation, the paradigm dialog underscores important differences in the underlying philosophical traditions that define the two approaches to research. The naturalistic paradigm stems from phenomenology and the interpretive approach to social inquiry that developed in the late nineteenth century. In general, naturalistic inquiry is

---

4 This term, as used by Guba (1978:14), was coined by Stake to contrast with the characteristics of his *responsive model* (Stake 1975).

shaped by the belief that reality is not objective, that there can be no meaningful separation of facts from values, and that "phenomena can be understood only within the context in which they are studied" (Guba and Lincoln 1989:45). The positivistic paradigm stems from logical positivism, which asserts that reality is objective, that facts can and must be separated from values, and that it is necessary for the researcher to "exteriorize the phenomenon studied, remaining detached and distant from it . . . [stripping] context of its contaminating (confounding) influences" (Guba and Lincoln 1989:84).

Some evaluation researchers have argued that the debate between the paradigms is counterproductive. Reichardt and Cook (1979), for example, have pointed out that in the early days of evaluation research it was assumed that programs could be well designed to produce specific, intended results. Under this assumption, the purpose of evaluation was to confirm that the intended effects had taken place. When it was discovered that social interventions were not so easy to accomplish and that there were many unanticipated side effects, evaluators turned to naturalistic research methods to help them discover and describe those effects.

What Reichardt and Cook, along with other evaluation researchers (cf. Cronbach et al. 1980; Howe 1988), argue is that the choice of research paradigm does not predetermine the choice of research methods. You may believe that social phenomena are objective realities that exist independently of individuals' subjective frames of reference (i.e., adopt a positivistic perspective) and still choose to use qualitative methods associated with naturalistic research (e.g., participant observation) to investigate those phenomena. Researchers who ascribe to the naturalistic paradigm will similarly make use of frequency counts and other quantitative methods associated with positivism. On the other hand, choosing to use quantitative methods does not necessarily ensure you of the characteristics of the positivistic paradigm. Quantitative methods are at times "subjective" in the sense of techniques such as opinion polls being concerned with human feelings and beliefs (one definition of subjective). Merely quantifying something does not ensure objectivity.

If there is no automatic linking of a research paradigm with a particular set of research methods, is there any need to choose between the two paradigms? Why not pursue both types of inquiry, letting each inform the other? This idea relates to the notion of *triangulation,* a term introduced by Denzin (1970) for the collection of information from many different sources using different methods in order to avoid the bias inherent in any one particular source or method. Of course, working within both paradigms, using both positivistic and naturalistic methods, can be prohibitively expensive and time-consuming. There is also a general reluctance on the part of most researchers to value both approaches to research equally. As Trend (1979:83) points out, this is influenced by the fact that:

Few researchers are equally comfortable with both types of data, and the procedures for using the two together are not well developed. The tendency is to relegate one type of analysis or the other to a secondary role, according to the nature of the research and the predilections of the investigator.

Are the only arguments against combining positivistic and naturalistic approaches to evaluation ones of cost efficiency and lack of "procedures for using the two together"? The fundamental difference in the philosophical basis for the two paradigms, mentioned earlier, remains for some researchers a compelling argument against the reconciliation of positivistic and naturalistic approaches to evaluation. Smith and Heshusius (1986) claim that such an accommodation obscures the important differences between the two paradigms and stems from confusion over the definition of method. Rather than discussing method solely in terms of the procedures and techniques for conducting research, they are concerned with method as *logic of justification*. Logic of justification defines what counts as evidence in the research being pursued. What counts as evidence is informed by assumptions at the levels mentioned earlier in this chapter – ontological (the nature of what there is to know) as well as epistemological (how we know what we know). Although all of this terminology may seem densely philosophical, it is important to be aware of the way in which it has influenced, and continues to shape, how research and evaluation are done in applied linguistics.

The naturalistic paradigm defines reality, or the nature of what there is to know, as something that depends on mind and interpretation. This means that there is no separation between facts and values, and that knowing is a process of interpretation and consensus. From this perspective, there is no objectivity in the sense of truths about a program, or any other object of social inquiry, that exist independent of our attempts to perceive, interpret, and understand these phenomena. We can not establish validity[5] for our research and program evaluation by appealing to some supposedly neutral set of rules and principles; validity, from this perspective, "is a label applied to an interpretation or description with which one agrees" (Smith and Heshusius 1986:9). In contrast, what counts as evidence from the perspective of the positivistic paradigm derives essentially from positivism, which remains the strongest influence on the way in which applied linguistics research is conducted. From this perspective, the nature of what there is to know is independent of the mind and can be known "as it really is." We can establish

5 Validity is discussed in greater detail in the next chapter.

the validity of our research and evaluation by determining the accuracy of the correspondence between our observation or measurement and this independently existing reality. As Smith and Heshusius (1986:9) critique this perspective:

Moreover, a judgment of validity in this case is conferred only when proper methods or sets of techniques are employed. In fact, procedures properly applied, in that they ensure objectivity and so on, lead to results that are thought to be compelling. Rejection of such results may provoke the criticism that one is being irrational and stubbornly subjective. . . . From the perspective of qualitative inquiry, this line of reasoning is unacceptable.

From the point of view of this critique, it may be possible to mix the procedures and techniques that are typically associated with naturalistic or positivistic research, but it is impossible to mix their logics of justification. Depending on the paradigm, what there is to know and how we know what we know are very different. Smith and Heshusius see the "closing down of the conversation" between naturalistic (qualitative) and positivistic (quantitative) researchers as due partly to an effort on the part of researchers such as LeCompte and Goetz (1982a, 1982b) and Miles and Huberman (1984) "to generate methods for qualitative inquiry that will allow this approach to claim the same objectivity and certitude presumably available to quantitative inquiry" (p. 8). From this view, rather than the two paradigms having reached an accommodation (Beretta 1986a), naturalistic techniques and procedures have been adopted into the positivistic paradigm, retaining its assumptions about the nature of what we are investigating and what counts as evidence.

What makes the positivistic paradigm so attractive to applied linguists? Most likely it is the desire to make certain that our research – what we claim to know, and how we claim to know it – is grounded in clearly articulated methods and criteria for significance. We are rightfully troubled by research that appears anecdotal, subjective, and speculative. The notion that using well-established procedures with predetermined rules for claiming significance will lead us to objective, interpretation-free knowledge claims is extremely appealing. However, the most objective of procedures, such as the construct validation of quantitative measures, can be shown to require subjective interpretations. Furthermore, specific statistical models such as the one underlying the Pearson product moment correlation can be shown to have been chosen because of the social biases of the researchers who were championing their use (Smith 1988). Acknowledging this undermines, somewhat, the authority and comfort we can derive from adhering to the positivistic approach to inquiry. Of course, ultimately the attractiveness of this approach may derive from the training that most applied linguists receive as graduate students. When this training avoids any attempt to include naturalistic research methods, and fails to make explicit the underlying philosophical assumptions of positivistic inquiry, applied linguists are left with the mistaken impression that there is only one valid way to pursue research: some version of positivistic experimentation.

What are the dangers, then, of embracing the naturalistic paradigm? If reality is not objective, if we have no predetermined criteria against which to measure our knowledge claims, what kind of research and evaluation can we expect to conduct? Do we deny the possibility of a meaningful research method (as logic of justification) and abandon any hope of rationality? Feyerabend (1988:19) suggests that research must allow for intellectual anarchism, avoiding any preordinate, fixed notions of method and rationality.

It is clear, then, that the idea of a fixed method, or of a fixed theory of rationality, rests on too naive a view of man and his social surroundings. To those who look at the rich material provided by history, and who are not intent on impoverishing it in order to please their lower instincts, their craving for intellectual security in the form of clarity, precision, "objectivity", "truth", it will become clear that there is only *one* principle that can be defended under *all* circumstances and in *all* stages of human development. It is the principle: *anything goes.*

Naturalistic researchers such as Guba and Lincoln (1989) would agree with the notion that there is no fixed method or theory of rationality, but argue that their alternative approach (constructivism) "does not lead to an *anything goes* posture" (p. 47, orig. emphasis). Like Smith (1988), they advocate the belief that discussion and debate within the research community can be used to make judgments about competing knowledge claims (i.e., resolve the differences in interpretation that are likely to occur in the absence of a predetermined method and criteria for correctness).

Although some would maintain that the paradigm wars (Gage 1989) are over, the paradigm dialog, at least, continues. Guba and Lincoln (1989) have come to distinguish between naturalistic evaluation of the first kind, in which naturalistic methods are used within a positivistic perspective, and naturalistic evaluation of the second kind, which implies a "move away from the basic belief system of positivism" (p. 162). This new belief system is referred to as *constructivism* and embraces a new stage in program evaluation, which they call "fourth generation evaluation." They further assert that "no accommodation is possible between positivist and constructivist belief systems as they are now formulated" (p. 17).

In March 1989, the Alternative Paradigms Conference was held in

San Francisco. The papers and discussions from that conference were edited by Egon Guba (1990a), and the discussion of alternative paradigms focused on three competing "successors to conventional positivism . . . *postpositivism,* on the shoulders of whose proponents the mantles of succession *and* of hegemony appear to have fallen, and two brash contenders, *critical theory* and *constructivism*" (p. 9). The postpositivist voices (e.g., Phillips 1990) seemed to be willing to allow for compatibility between the paradigms, while the critical theorists (e.g., Popkewitz 1990) and constructivists (e.g., Lincoln 1990) argued for recognition of fundamental differences.

Since the Alternative Paradigms Conference, McKerrow and McKerrow (1991) have accused naturalistic researchers of creating false arguments against the positivistic paradigm (which they refer to as rationalistic, following Guba and Lincoln's 1982 use of the term) through their misunderstanding of the Heisenberg uncertainty principle. They point out that this principle was discovered by researchers working with microscopic phenomena in the positivitic paradigm, and that it is not relevant to the macroscopic phenomena-based world of naturalistic research. They define the Heisenberg uncertainty principle as essentially stating the inability for both the position and the momentum of an electron to be measured simultaneously with accuracy. This, they claim, does not support the notion advanced by naturalistic researchers that the observer and the observed cannot be separated.

Miller and Fredericks (1991) have argued that the paradigm dialog is based on assumptions from postpositivistic philosophy that are not always relevant to educational research. In particular, they assert that the paradigms are compatible at a theoretical, conceptual level but become incompatible, or incommensurable, at the level of interpretation. That is, while agreeing on the meaning of key concepts, they disagree in fundamental ways about the interpretation of the consequences of those concepts, for ideological rather than theoretical reasons. Miller and Frederick's conclusions lead them to espouse a form of relativism that, like Guba and Lincoln, they contrast with an "anything goes" approach, in that it is modified by generally agreed-upon criteria for the conduct of research:

. . . one of the absolutes in educational research has always been that there are *no* absolutes, and the conduct of educational research, whether quantitative or qualitative, has always been and continues to be regulated by certain constraints . . . [such as] the ideas of reliability, validity, the "weight of evidence," sampling, the rules of deductive and inductive inference, triangulation, and so on. (Miller and Fredericks 1991:7)

There has been critical response to Miller and Fredericks (Nespor and Garrison 1992); another round of arguments between positivistic and naturalistic researchers has occurred (Schrag 1992a, 1992b; Eisner 1992; Erickson 1992; Popkewitz 1992), and articles continue to appear that seek to justify naturalistic, usually referred to as "qualitative," inquiry to the educational research community (Peshkin 1993; Firestone 1993).

Thus far, then, the paradigm dialog has moved from arguing over which approach is best to arguing that they can be used together because there are no important differences, to arguing for keeping them separate because of important philosophical differences. This seems to leave us with the choice of denying philosophical differences in order to use both positivistic and naturalistic methods, or working within one paradigm or the other. However, a middle ground has been offered by Howe (1988), who argues that a research paradigm (the epistemological level) should not dictate methods (the research practice level). This stance comes from *pragmatism*, which he presents as an alternative non-paradigm that allows for methods to change and develop our notion of paradigm as well as vice versa. From such a perspective, we can admit that the object of our inquiry may not be objective – for example, that the success of a language program is not an external reality existing independent of the participant's and the evaluator's interpretations – and still be allowed to use positivistic methods. Likewise, we can believe that a language program and its success is an objective reality that we should be able to discover without appealing to subjective interpretation and still find naturalistic methods, such as observation or interviews, useful and enlightening. The important difference between this *compatibilist* (also known as *accommodationist*) stance and the one proposed earlier (Reichardt and Cook 1979; Beretta 1986a) is that it acknowledges philosophical differences between the paradigms. Pragmatists such as Howe (also see Cherryholmes 1992) agree with naturalistic researchers in rejecting the positivistic notion that truth is "out there" waiting to be discovered. However, the pragmatist stance puts paradigm and method at the service of practice in order to be able to have something rational and convincing to say about the object of inquiry. To the extent that positivistic methods in practice allow us to have something to say, they are useful. They can also, in turn, lead to changes in the articulation of a naturalistic research paradigm.

The paradigm dialog has raised some important issues for applied linguists to consider both in general and within the specific context of program evaluation. The arguments of researchers such as Guba, Lincoln, Smith, and Heshusius force us to come to a clear understanding of what we will regard as evidence in our research approach to program evaluation. That is, we must articulate a philosophical basis for our inquiry. Even if we adopt the pragmatic stance of Howe, in order to sample from the methods of both positivistic and naturalistic paradigms, we still need to be clear about what we will accept as evidence. From the positivistic perspective, the basis for verifying research findings using naturalistic methods becomes problematic. There is no pre-determined procedure for establishing the significance of our findings within such an analysis. Likewise, from the naturalistic perspective, the traditional reliance on quantitative data and experimental designs is inappropriate. Reporting significant inferential statistics from randomized experiments will not, by itself, establish the validity of our findings. Ultimately, if we plan to mix positivistic and naturalistic methods, our results must be compared with other research findings (findings that may be totally positivistic or totally naturalistic) and establish their acceptability through debate within the applied linguistics community.

This discussion does not presume to resolve the debate between positivistic and naturalistic researchers, nor does it advocate an end to the paradigm dialog. Rather, I propose that we keep the issue in mind rather than blindly combining quantitative and qualitative data and the methods associated with them as if the philosophical assumptions associated with the two paradigms were the same. It is difficult to judge the degree of accuracy in claims such as Reichardt and Cook's (1979: 18) that "most researchers have by now adopted a phenomenological stance" (i.e., the naturalistic perspective). Certainly in the field of applied linguistics it would be difficult to validate this claim. Although most researchers might be open to the proposition that reality is mind-dependent and that "everything is relative," the literature in our field suggests that, until very recently, what was being sought in most research, including program evaluation, remained tied to positivistic notions of what constitutes valid and reliable research. Although I advocate the pragmatic approach of Howe, I am concerned with what I see as a strong bias among applied linguists toward a solely positivistic perspective on research, even when their methods are primarily naturalistic. Accordingly, I will endeavor to make the underlying research assumptions clear in any discussion of positivistic and naturalistic methods and their application to program evaluation in applied linguistics. It is important that we remain conscious of how we determine what counts as evidence in our research and that we understand the naturalistic paradigm as an alternative approach to doing research, with its own way of conceptualizing validity, rather than as merely an alternative form of data. I have more to say on these issues in Chapter 3.

The following section draws upon the issues raised by the paradigm dialog in an effort to provide a historical context for program evaluation in applied linguistics. It begins with the evaluations of second and foreign language programs that were done in the 1960s, as the audio-lingual method rose to the status of most-favored teaching methodology, and ends with more recent developments in language education evaluation.

Evaluation of language education programs in the 1960s and 1970s

In order to provide a sense of the historical development of program evaluation within the field of applied linguistics, I have examined as many of the published studies as I could locate, beginning in the early 1960s. I have tended to concentrate on those studies that focused on evaluating entire instructional programs as they existed or were being implemented, rather than on studies that were smaller-scale comparisons of teaching methods (e.g., Asher et al. 1974). Often, however, the line between program evaluation and method studies blurs (e.g., Scherer and Wertheimer 1962; Chastain and Woerdehoff 1968), and I have also included small-scale ethnographic studies (e.g., Guthrie 1982) in an attempt to present the most complete and representative portrait possible.

Until very recently the focus of program evaluation in applied linguistics was on summative, product-oriented evaluations. Summative, as coined by Scriven (1967), refers to an evaluation designed to determine whether or not a program has been successful. Product-oriented refers to an evaluation that looks at outcomes, such as end-of-the-year student achievement test scores or questionnaire responses. Early applied linguistics program evaluations were also primarily broad comparisons of different teaching methodologies and materials. This approach to program evaluation falls squarely into the positivistic paradigm discussed earlier.

One of the first evaluations involved the language laboratory, which by the late 1950s was being widely used as a component in language teaching programs. The interest in language laboratories can be traced back to the success of the World War II Army Specialized Training Program (ASTP) and the so-called Army method that grew out of it. The Army method was designed to train a large number of adults in a relatively short time to be competent in a foreign language, with a focus on speaking and listening skills. This intensive program made use of the electronic equipment – audio tape recorders, headsets, microphones – of the language laboratory. Although there is some disagreement over the degree and kind of success that the ASTP actually produced (Keating 1963:5–6), it did foster the receptive environment that existed in the 1950s and continued into the 1960s for teaching speaking and listening skills and using the language laboratory.

To evaluate the use of the language laboratory in the public schools, Raymond F. Keating designed a summative experiment. The only prior attempt at empirical validation, according to Keating, was a 1960 study by E. D. Allen, which "would seem to be severely compromised by the conditions under which instruction proceeded" (Keating 1963:8). Keating's criticism of the Allen study centered on its lack of experimental control over such threats to internal validity as the Hawthorne effect (knowledge of being in an experiment) and a demoralized control group (in this case, the nonlaboratory students). Keating's study claimed to avoid these threats but, by his own admission, "cannot be considered an experiment in any proper sense" (p. 24). Clearly, the concern was evaluation research that would conform to the positivistic research paradigm. Using standardized tests of reading, listening, and speaking, Keating found that the nonlaboratory students achieved higher end-of-year scores than the laboratory students. These results were obviously quite controversial at a time when the government was investing heavily in such instructional technology.

Like the Allen study that Keating had reviewed, Keating's own study was criticized for faults in experimental design. Smith (1970:10) claimed that "A careful reading of this study raises serious doubts regarding the validity of the research and the generalization of these results to other foreign-language teaching situations." Freedman (1971:33) similarly criticized the study's lack of validity because "so many variables were left uncontrolled." It is obvious that, at this point in time, what the language teaching field was looking for in evaluation was a tightly controlled, traditional (in the positivistic sense) experiment that focused on product (end-of-instructional-sequence student achievement) in order to make summative judgments.

While Keating was pursuing his language lab study, Scherer and Wertheimer (1962) were also working on a project designed to achieve the elusive experimentally correct (i.e., objective) evaluation. This two-year study became known as the Colorado Project, with the following as its rationale: "A rigidly controlled large-scale experiment which would yield clear-cut data was therefore still needed" in order to be "in a position to draw some definite scientific conclusions about the relative merits of the two methods" (p. I-14).

The two methods being evaluated were the audio-lingual method and the traditional grammar-translation method. Along with the growing interest in the language laboratory, by the mid-1960s there was a methodological revolution in language teaching that saw the displacement of the traditional approach, with its focus on mastery of the syntax and vocabulary of the language, by the audio-lingual approach, with its exclusive focus on listening and speaking skills at the beginning of the language learning process. The two methods were identified with two opposing theories of language learning. The traditional approach was aligned with the cognitive code-learning theory:

The theory attaches more importance to the learner's understanding of the structure of the foreign language than to his facility in using that structure, since it is believed that, provided the student has a proper degree of cognitive control over the structures of the language, facility will develop automatically with use of the language in meaningful situations. (Carroll 1965; quoted in Smith 1970:4)

The audio-lingual approach, on the other hand, was aligned with the audio-lingual habit theory of language learning. This theory asserts that:

From the start the learner plays a dual role in language, first as a hearer, then as a speaker. Only when he is thoroughly familiar with the sounds, arrangements, and forms does he center his attention on enlarging his vocabulary. In learning control of structure, what he may do as a matter of conscious choice, he will eventually do habitually and unconsciously. (Brooks 1961; quoted in Smith 1970:4)

Students being taught German according to these two methods were compared on achievement in the four skill areas (speaking, listening, reading, and writing) in German as well as on various measures of "habituated direct association" (the ability to "think in the language") and on attitudinal measures. The research team was not able to find "suitable" standardized measures of achievement, so the students were given tests constructed by the teaching staff, with the speaking and listening measures constructed by the experimental (audio-lingual method) teachers and the reading and writing measures constructed by the control (traditional method) teachers. The results at the end of the first year showed that the experimental group was better at speaking and listening, and that the control group was better at translating, reading, and writing. In other words, "students tended to learn those skills which were emphasized in the teaching method to which they were exposed" (Scherer and Wertheimer 1962:VI-1). By the end of the experiment, after the second year in which both the original groups received the experimental treatment (and attrition had reduced the group sizes considerably), the only significant differences between them were experimental group superiority on speaking and control group superiority on writing and German–English translation. In addition, the experimental group was superior on most of the measures of habituated direct association, motivation, and attitude.

Given these mixed results, the authors concluded that language teachers should choose the audio-lingual method for instruction in speaking and listening and the traditional method for instruction in reading (if students will be taking only one year of study), writing, and translation (especially German to English). In terms of overall proficiency, the two methods seemed to yield comparable results, whereas the audio-lingual method resulted in better attitudes toward Germans (the target-language group), better attitudes toward self while speaking German, and fewer feelings of "being a different person" when speaking the two languages. Scherer and Wertheimer did not venture to speculate on whether these attitudes are desirable or conducive to language learning.

The Colorado Project received criticisms similar to those received by Keating's study. The major complaint was, again, lack of experimental control (Freedman 1971). In addition, Smith (1970) criticized the study for its relatively small sample size, the creation of special teaching materials, and its investigation of one language only. However, it was seen as "an advance along the road, being a large-scale experiment, controlled to some degree" (Freedman 1971:34). Hilton (1969) also criticized the study for its lack of description of the teaching procedures and language laboratory activities used. This represented the first voice of concern for the investigation of program process as well as product. This concern for description of process might best be addressed with qualitative methods and a naturalistic perspective. However, the major movement in program evaluation in the field of applied linguistics continued to be in the direction of traditional experimental design focused on product and on summative judgments.

Chastain and Woerdehoff (1968), though again using a relatively small sample size ($n = 99$), were able to achieve a more rigorously controlled experimental design than had been previously reported. The major coup for their one-year (1965) study was that they were able to assign students randomly. The equivalence of the two groups was further checked using standardized pretests of aptitude for modern language learning and academic motivation, along with measures of language modality preference and prior language learning experience. The relative merits of the two methods were compared using a standardized posttest covering the four language skills. The students, all first-semester students of Spanish at Purdue University, were tested after one year of instruction.

This evaluation was, again, a broad comparison of teaching methods: the audio-lingual method and the traditional method, referred to in the study as the cognitive code method. In addition to the differences previously mentioned, the authors further differentiated the two approaches in terms of the presentation of new material. The audio-lingual approach was characterized by the inductive presentation of new material, whereas the cognitive code approach presented new material with deductive explanation prior to practice. The authors provided a clear description of the teaching materials and procedures used in the study, and it was evident that the cognitive code-learning method was not entirely "traditional," since it did not rely on a great deal of translation and included a good deal of oral practice.

At the end of one year of instruction, the only significant differences between the two groups were in reading (the cognitive code group was superior) and in imitative ability in speaking (the audio-lingual group was superior). There was also a significant effect for aptitude – the higher-aptitude students did better than the lower-aptitude students regardless of method. Academic motivation and modality preference did not have similar effects. For those students who had never studied Spanish before, all group differences favored the cognitive code group. The authors concluded that the study supported the superiority of the cognitive code method. Again, given their description of the cognitive code method, this was a different methodological comparison than had been made in the Colorado Project.

There is not much discussion of Chastain and Woerdehoff's study in the literature. Levin (1972) mentioned that the conclusions were somewhat surprising and that: "In our view, the statistical evidence rather points in the same direction as that of the earlier studies" (p. 51), where the differences were either nonsignificant or favored the group whose method emphasized the particular language skill that was being tested. That Levin drew conclusions opposite to those presented in the original study illustrates the fact that supposedly objective evidence must still be interpreted, thereby rendering it somewhat subjective. There was no criticism of the basic research design, however, other than the fact that the study lasted only one year.

The culmination of the move toward tightly controlled experiments in the evaluation of language teaching methodologies came with the Pennsylvania Project (Smith 1970). This was a two-year experiment, conducted from 1965 to 1967, with a two-year follow-up study, 1967 to 1969. The research team consciously set out to avoid the lack of experimental control of most of the previous studies. Specifically, they attempted to deal with "unwanted variability in teacher behavior by (1) utilizing large numbers of teachers, (2) teacher testing, (3) employment of teachers with certain experience parameters, (4) teacher orientation and training, and (5) frequent observation of classroom behavior" (p. 14). In addition, "Generalizability of findings was thought to be increased by use of materials and testing instruments of a type widely used and readily available to all schools" (p. 14).

The Pennsylvania Project was not able to use random selection and assignment of students to groups, but the researchers claimed to have approached true experimentation with a nonequivalent control group design (NECG) in which random assignment of intact classrooms to treatment was possible. The study was also large-scale in terms of sample size: 3,500 secondary school students from four major urban centers in Pennsylvania began the experiment, with 2,171 students completing all tests at the end of the first year. The students were beginning students in French and German in grades 8, 9, 10, and 11. There were 104 teachers and intact classrooms: 61 French and 43 German (separate analyses were conducted for each language).

The study was designed to evaluate the effectiveness of three teaching methods: the traditional method (TLM, an eclectic grammar-translation approach following the cognitive code-learning theory), the audio-lingual method (referred to in the study as the functional skills method, or FSM), and a "middle-of-the-road" method that combined functional skills with grammar (FSG). It also examined the effect of the language laboratory at three levels: a tape recorder in the classroom (the control, essentially), a listen-respond language lab, and a listen-respond-compare language lab. The TLM group, given the nature of the method, did not receive any of the language lab treatments.

The methods and the technologies to be used were carefully defined by a select panel of modern foreign language educators. In addition to the previously mentioned attempts to control for teacher effects, teachers were randomly assigned to teaching method (although they were given the "illusion" of preference by being asked for their first and second choice of method). The careful delineation of teaching method and the associated materials meant that "a perversion of the authors of either type of materials would have required an extensive process of rewriting and editing on the part of the individual teachers" (Smith 1970:51). There were also random observations of classrooms in order to detect any deviations from the assigned teaching methodology. Finally, a 28-class, 700-student "confirmatory replication study" was done to ensure reliability of the findings.

In order to provide the necessary quantitative data for the evaluation, the students were tested at the beginning of the experiment with the Modern Language Aptitude Test (MLAT), and at midyear and the end of the year with standardized tests of foreign language achievement (the Modern Language Association Cooperative Classroom Tests). They were also given various attitudinal measures. The quantitative data were analyzed using a multiple analysis of variance (MANOVA) to investigate contrasts and interactions among teaching method, laboratory system, and gender.

At the end of the first year of the study, the researchers concluded that the traditional method (TLM) was the same as or superior to the audio-lingual methods (FSM, FSG) on all measures, that the language laboratory systems investigated had no discernible effect on achievement (including speaking test scores), that there was no meaningful interaction between teaching method and language laboratory system, that student attitudes were independent of teaching method, and that initial attitude was not related to later achievement.

At the end of the second year, there were no significant differences between teaching method groups except that the TLM group was superior on the reading achievement test, and the language laboratory system continued to have no effect on achievement, although there was some evidence that laboratory time may have influenced reading skills. Student attitudes toward foreign language learning continued to be independent of teaching method and language laboratory system.

At the end of the third year of the study, a follow-up study on the few remaining students from years one and two indicated that the TLM group was equal or superior to the FSM and FSG groups on the listening and reading tests. At the end of the fourth year, no significant differences between the method groups were found.

The Pennsylvania Project created a great deal of controversy in the field of applied linguistics. Coming at a time when the audio-lingual method was in such favor with many, if not most, foreign language educators, the implication that the traditional method, or at least its current "eclectic" version, was equally effective or superior was a bitter pill to swallow. Even the research staff itself was surprised and concerned at the results:

... it was covertly assumed that the experiment would reveal advantages in favor of newer approaches to foreign-language learning. . . . Certainly, the conclusions were personally traumatic to the Project staff, deeply committed to a Functional Skills philosophy. (Smith 1970:234 and 271)

However, some foreign language educators did rise to defend the tainted image of the audio-lingual method. Valette (1969:396) criticized the conclusions that were being drawn concerning the audio-lingual method and the language laboratory:

... succinct press releases have proclaimed the superiority of the traditional method and the disgrace of the language laboratory. Such oversimplification of the complex findings of the Pennsylvania Project, however, does a disservice to both the project personnel and the foreign language teaching profession as a whole.

Valette's main criticism of the study itself was the use of what she considered to be inappropriate test instruments for detecting differences between the teaching methods. Specifically, the standardized achievement tests were too difficult for the students being tested at the end of the first year (being designed primarily for high school students who have completed two years of foreign language study). A careful item-content analysis conducted by Valette revealed that, based on the course textbooks, the reading achievement test was extremely biased in favor of the TLM group. Based on this analysis, "the traditional students did much more poorly than one would have anticipated" (p. 399). A similar analysis of the listening test led Valette to conclude that it slightly favored the TLM group, and an examination of the results revealed that both groups performed lower than expected (based on mastery of the respective course materials). Further, the top 5 percent of the FSM (audio-lingual) students outperformed the top 5 percent of the TLM (traditional) students. The writing test was definitely biased in favor of the TLM students because of the difference in textbook content across the methods.

> The failure of the TLM classes to achieve considerably better on these measures than they actually did would indicate that although the audio-lingual classes (FSG and FSM) are presented with less vocabulary and less structure, they are learning the material more thoroughly. (p. 399)

In addition, Valette cited the MLA Cooperative Tests Handbook as stating that the speaking test suffers from scorer unreliability. Thus, the project's results and conclusions, including those regarding the lack of effect of the language laboratory system, are suspect for Valette primarily because of the bias and unreliability of the test instruments.

Although several authors commended the Pennsylvania Project as an exemplary evaluation effort because of its large-scale nature and its sophisticated experimental design and statistical analyses (Carroll 1969; Wiley 1969), others criticized the study for the ex post facto nature of its design (i.e., its failure to randomly assign subjects to treatment groups) and its lack of control over teacher adherence to the assigned method (Clark 1969; Valdman 1969). Freedman (1971:36) pointed out that no classroom records were kept and that the very large-scale nature of the study that others applauded made it impossible to be certain that the teachers were strictly following their assigned methods. Levin (1972: 57–58) further pointed out that the teachers were allowed to choose among four or five (depending on the language) different textbooks and were not regulated as to rate of progress through the material. The TLM group was said to have covered three times the amount of material covered by the FSM and FSG groups.

As an evaluation of an innovative language teaching methodology – the audio-lingual method – the Pennsylvania Project culminated the movement toward tightly controlled experiments that were product-oriented and summative in nature. The major criticisms of the study, other than choice of test instruments, focused more on the need to investigate the process of language education programs. Instead of looking only at student achievement – the product – critics were asking that attention be paid to what was happening in the classrooms. Even the Pennsylvania Project staff recommended:

... that future research include more precise definitions of "traditional teacher" and "audio-lingual teacher" based not only upon texts employed and stated objectives but on detailed physical and verbal interaction analysis. (Smith 1970:166)

To be sure, this concern for classroom process was initially part of the continuing desire for a positivistic approach to program evaluation. This desire led researchers such as Freedman (1971) to conclude that large-scale experiments (used here in the sense of examining entire programs, as they exist in the field) should be abandoned because they cannot be rigidly controlled. She advocated instead a move "toward the small-scale experiment in which it is possible, by virtue of its size, to control effectively" (p. 36). Here, Freedman seemed to be opting for internal validity (certainty about causal relationships within the study) over external validity (the ability to generalize to other populations and settings). Following this model, in an evaluation of the effectiveness of the language laboratory at York University in England from 1967 to 1970 (Green 1975), evaluation researchers were able to attempt control of a variety of variables such as IQ, home background, and teacher effectiveness. For example, they attempted to control for the teacher variable by having the three teachers rotate their teaching assignments so that each group was taught equally by all teachers. Such controls allowed them to make internally valid claims that there were "no detectable differences" between the group using the language lab and those not using it. However, they pointed out that the small-scale nature of the design, which made experimental control feasible, also made generalizing their findings to other settings (external validity) more difficult.

Levin (1972) also pursued tightly controlled, small-scale program evaluation in his documentation of a language teaching project in Sweden. Known as the GUME (Göteborg Undervisnings Method i Engleska; or Göteborg English Teaching Method) project, it represented a series of comparative experiments designed to "assess the relative merits of different approaches to teaching grammatical structures in English as a foreign language" (p. 15). This project, then, was a series of small-scale experiments. As a modification of the previous use of the term, *small-scale* here refers to a focus on particular teaching variables and content, with strict laboratorylike control of potentially confounding variables, rather than to sample size. An example of its strict control was the exclusive use of prerecorded lessons (to control for teacher effect).

Although obviously giving it a more scientific (in the positivistic sense) quality, as in the York language lab study, this strict control limited the ability to generalize to other classrooms and, in so doing, removed this type of research from the traditional concerns of program evaluation. Levin acknowledged this, referring to the study as "conclusion-oriented, instructional research" as opposed to the "decision-oriented" nature of "program evaluation in the ordinary sense" (p. 62). However, he also claimed that the instructional research of the GUME project could be seen as more generalizable than either summative or formative evaluation research. This claim for increased generalizability was based on the argument that decision-oriented forms of evaluation are limited to claims about a particular instructional package, whereas instructional research "is concerned with relationships that hold for large numbers of packages" (p. 63). Thus, in addition to the internal validity that the rigid experimental control of small-scale research brings, Levin seemed to be claiming external validity, or generalizability, for the GUME project as well. Applied linguistics had apparently reached the gold at the end of the program evaluation research rainbow.

However, subsequent program evaluations tended to pursue the large-scale approach. The mid-1970s and early 1980s witnessed several evaluations of immersion and other bilingual programs in the United States and Canada [for an excellent review of these studies, see Genessee (1985)]. In all cases, these evaluations followed the large-scale (examination of existing programs in their entirety), product-oriented approach within the positivistic perspective.[6]

Although they were exceptions rather than a new rule, a few studies during this time began to incorporate a more naturalistic perspective, using information other than test and questionnaire results to evaluate language teaching programs. Marottoli (1973) used his observations as a participant in private language schools in an effort to evaluate these programs in contrast to public school language instruction. Schotta (1973) used data from interviews with foreign language teachers and matched their perceptions of the curriculum and methodology of their courses with the perceptions of their students (gleaned from a questionnaire distributed to those students). McClean et al. (1978), in contrast to the typical immersion program evaluation mentioned above, conducted interviews and analyzed student journals in their evaluation of Ontario, Canada, bilingual programs. Program evaluation in the applied linguistics context, however, continued to be dominated by the positivistic tradition.

---

6 Although it was not a program evaluation or method comparison per se, a five-year research project carried out in the early 1980s by the Modern Language Centre at the Ontario Institute for Studies in Education examining the development of bilingual proficiency (Harley et al. 1990) included a series of "treatment studies" that involved examining process as well as product in the second language classroom. However, process was investigated through observations that collected data with quantitative instruments and analyzed those data from an essentially positivistic perspective.

More recent developments in the evaluation of language education programs

A decade after the GUME project, Jacobson (1982:285) decried what she saw as the lack of "valid and convincing program evaluation information" for foreign language teaching programs. While recognizing summative evaluation as the most powerful and convincing type of evaluation, she also argued for evaluation that would examine the process of language teaching programs. To accomplish this, she suggested the use of other approaches to evaluation, such as needs assessment, implementation evaluation, and formative evaluation. Needs assessment is evaluation designed to examine the match between what is desired for the program versus the actual state of the program. Implementation evaluation is designed to look at the match between the original, stated plan for the program and its actual state. Formative evaluation, the companion term for summative evaluation and also coined by Scriven (1967), looks at a program as it is developing in order to make suggestions for improvement. In all cases the concern is for what is happening inside the program, rather than an exclusive focus on program outcomes. This concern seems to lead evaluators to explore the use of naturalistic methods.

Long (1983:4) specifically criticized the approach to program evaluation taken by the GUME project and other small-scale studies as "a rather extreme form of intervention in normal classroom processes" that "reduces the external validity, or the generalizability of findings." He went on to characterize the decade following the GUME project as one in which there was "a growing body of research designed to describe natural classroom processes, and in a few cases to relate this to second language achievement."

Long (1984) also criticized the positivistic, experimental approach to program evaluation for its sole focus on product or outcome rather than also attending to the process of how the program was being carried out. His argument was that, without a description and clear understanding of the process (i.e., what actually happened in the program as well as what happened in the control or comparison situation), there would be many plausible explanations for the outcomes of product evaluation. For example, the innovative program's students might have outperformed the control group on the outcome measure because the teachers in fact did something other than what was claimed for the program. This, of course, echoed many of the criticisms of the Colorado and Pennsylvania projects as well as Jacobson's concerns and suggestions.

Beretta (1986a) renewed Long's (1984) call for the inclusion of systematic attempts to describe program process as an integral part of the evaluation of language teaching programs. Departing from Long's perspective somewhat, he characterized program evaluation as applied research and cautioned against relying on the methods of basic research (i.e., placing overriding concern on internal validity at the expense of external validity). It was suggested that language teaching programs should be evaluated using information gathered from multiple perspectives via such techniques as historical narratives, focused interviews, and systematic observations. The importance of these field investigations (i.e., large-scale studies, in the Freedman sense), which comes at the expense of the reliability and relative certainty of results associated with controlled experiments, is in the ability to gain information that will be usable by teachers and administrators and relevant to real-world language program settings. The ultimate goal of the evaluation becomes the balancing of internal validity with external validity, reliability with usability, and certainty with relevance. The approach can also be seen as a means of balancing the positivistic perspective with a naturalistic one.

In another article, Beretta (1986b) elaborated the importance of large-scale studies, or field experimentation, in program evaluation. Exploring the relative merits of small-scale and large-scale research, he stated:

Thus, instead of incrementally building up a pedagogic theory through laboratory experiments, it is maintained that a more useful procedure would be to test the effect of a total program, and only then begin the process of analysis. . . . It has been argued in this paper that field experimentation is desirable. The advantage of giving it priority is clear: it fosters a concern for what works in the classroom first, and only then moves on to an analytical stage. (pp. 304, 305–306)

It should be noted that the implied combination of research perspectives mentioned in Beretta's previously cited work is not as clear in this statement. The language used here tends to imply the dominance of a positivistic perspective.

In addition to the three studies from the 1970s discussed in the previous section, a move in the direction of investigating program process – as called for by Jacobson, Long, and Beretta – began to surface during the 1980s. Guthrie (1982) investigated a language maintenance program in California using an ethnographic approach in which she observed the classrooms and talked with students, teachers, administrators, and interested people from the community. She then used her notes from observations and interviews along with program documentation to analyze and interpret the program as a whole. This approach, in essence, involves studying the program as if it were a culture and falls solidly within the naturalistic perspective. It also includes the evaluation of classroom process as an important focus.

Although it was not reported on until 1985, Ullman and Geva conducted an evaluation completed in 1983 of a core French program in Ontario, Canada. These evaluators also broke from the summative, product-oriented tradition and argued for the use of what they call "the broad formative" approach. By this they mean that the program is assumed to be developing and that factors such as the documents on which the program's curriculum is based and the types of teaching strategies actually being used in the classroom are examined as a part of the evaluation. The implementation of the curriculum was investigated through classroom observation using the Target Language Observation Scheme (TALOS) developed by Ullman and Geva (1982).

The results of their evaluation described the nature of the materials and activities used, overall language skill focus, and teacher and student involvement in the classroom. Their findings indicated that the core French classes tended to focus on grammatical form, to be teacher-centered with little student involvement, and to have content that was unrelated to other school subject content areas. They did observe some exceptions to this pattern and "the beginnings of some functional language teaching" (p. 318) in all classes. These observations were used to make recommendations to the Ministry of Education concerning the need for a closer examination and treatment of program content and for more diversified teaching strategies for functional language teaching. Although student achievement, or product, was still of concern, the authors gave a central place to a naturalistic investigation of process, or what happens inside the program.

However, the positivistic, product-oriented approach also continued as the basis for many evaluation designs. Henning (1982) reported on an evaluation of an English as a foreign language (EFL) teaching program in Egypt (the Ain Shams Project). The focus of the report was on a particular evaluation method, called growth-referenced evaluation. This method attempted to evaluate language teaching programs in terms of the comparative rate of growth on the part of the students. The approach was correlational in nature and resulted in information concerning specific program strengths and weaknesses. Henning's approach also required criterion-referenced test instruments in order to measure specific components of the program. Although the concerns of this evaluation could be seen as formative in addition to summative, the focus was still on product, or student outcome.

Beretta and Davies (1985) reported on an evaluation of the Bangalore/Madras Communicational Teaching Project (CTP), another EFL/ESL program (given that English is the official language of government in India, some refer to it as a "second" rather than "foreign" language). Their evaluation, like Henning's, maintained the large-scale, product-oriented approach. Students of the CTP were compared to students receiving "normal instruction," which was referred to as "structural." The two groups were compared on three types of achievement tests: one designed to measure structure and thus favor the structural group (whose instruction focused on a procedural, task-based syllabus), one designed as a CTP task-based test to favor the CTP group, and one set of tests designed to measure general proficiency in a "neutral" fashion.

The results showed that the structural group did better on the structure test, the CTP group did better on the CTP task-based test, and that there was no significant difference between the groups on seven out of twelve of the "neutral" tests. However, the CTP group did outperform the structural group on five of the tests, and in no case did the structural group outperform the CTP group. The authors admitted that the lack of control over variables such as school environment, selection of the groups, or age and social background of the students seriously affected the internal validity of the evaluation. However, they claimed that the sacrifice of such controls by using intact classes in real school settings allowed for greater external validity. Ultimately, the lack of experimental control and the possible bias of the test instruments (which were constructed by the research staff) meant "that the results of the evaluation may constitute a 'probe' of the central CTP hypothesis, but not 'proof' " (Beretta and Davies 1985:126). What was considered evidence, or proof, for this study appears to be ensconced in the positivistic perspective.

The authors pointed out that a more fully documented description of the principles and methodologies employed in the CTP existed in other publications, but the focus of their evaluation, like Henning's, was still on student outcome. Their hypotheses were stated in terms of fairly specific classroom processes that defined the two teaching methods being compared, but the method of the evaluation was product-oriented and summative in nature. No systematic effort was made to evaluate what was actually taking place inside the classrooms (although Beretta [1990] later reported on a retrospective study of the implementation of the CTP).[7]

Palmer (1992) reported on an evaluation of an experimental course in German as a second language conducted at the University of Utah in 1985–1986. More of an attempt to test "a radical implementation of Krashen's theory of second language acquisition" (p. 141) than it was a program evaluation, the experimental group was compared with a classroom receiving "traditional" (eclectic) second language instruction. A variety of language test data (lecture summary, oral interview,

7 Beretta (1992b) also offers a candid explanation for why a more complete investigation of classroom process was not carried out in the original evaluation study.

reading translation, reading summary, guided composition, dictation, cloze procedure, and student self-ratings) were analyzed using multiple analysis of variance. In addition, the "affective domain" of the classroom was investigated using journals and questionnaires. In reporting the results (the traditional group outperformed the experimental "acquisition" group), Palmer and his associates did find it helpful to use the qualitative nature of some of the test data (e.g., examples from student writing) to illustrate the quantitative test results for the evaluation audiences.

At about this same time, an evaluation of the English for Specific Purposes program in Brazilian Federal Universities was being designed and implemented (Alderson and Scott 1992) in Brazil. Wary of the "Jet-In, Jet-Out Expert" (JIJOE) evaluations carried out by outside experts, project members and British Council consultant Charles Alderson began to formulate a participatory model of program evaluation that included people from all levels of the program in the active planning and execution of the evaluation. The role of the outside expert, in this case, was to provide recommendations and feedback on the evaluation's design and data-gathering instruments and to offer comments on the interpretation of evaluation results.

In contrast to the Palmer study, this evaluation relied primarily on naturalistic evaluation. Data came from questionnaires, interviews, reports on class discussions, and statistics on use of the language center. Although most of the information used in the evaluation was thus qualitative, a thoroughly naturalistic investigation was hampered by the inability to conduct classroom observations (due to the fact that the teachers, who were also participant evaluators, did not want observers). The evaluation team attempted to strengthen the confidence they could place in their results by gathering the evaluation data from a variety of sources and by different methods. The program participants tended to avoid quantitative test data, fearing that it would be impossible to find or create tests that were capable of being sensitive to student achievement, but Alderson and Scott argue that such data would have been useful along with the qualitative, "perception" data. Thus, they seem to be arguing for a combination of quantitative and qualitative data, if not for a combination of the positivistic and naturalistic perspectives.[8]

Also during the mid-1980s, an evaluation of a bilingual (English and Scottish Gaelic) project in Scotland was conducted (Mitchell 1992). The continuing dominance of the positivistic paradigm for evaluation is indicated by the fact that the primary evaluation audience, the Scottish

8 It is not completely clear whether Alderson and Scott (1992) accept the naturalistic paradigm as a basis for evaluation evidence. They refer to the need for test data in order to provide "independent evidence" rather than solely "reported opinions" (p. 54).

Education Department, had originally requested an experimental–control group design. This audience was reportedly dissatisfied with earlier efforts at providing evaluative information concerning the bilingual project, which were naturalistic and case study in nature. Given that the project (which lasted from 1975 until 1981) was being evaluated retrospectively, the evaluators were forced to rule out an experimental design and used, instead, "systematic, quantitative methods . . . for the observation of bilingual teaching and learning" (Mitchell 1992:105), along with a sampling procedure that attempted to control for individual student differences. Some qualitative data were also gathered, in the form of interviews with teachers designed to elicit aspects of the classroom that had not been captured during the observational visits.

Using this evaluation approach, Mitchell and her colleagues were able to report that the project's original goals were being met where bilingual students were in the majority. Where bilinguals were a minority, English-speaking children had less of an opportunity to become fluent in Scottish Gaelic. Because of the amount of time the evaluation took, these findings were apparently not used by the Scottish Education Department to inform their policy decision making.

Even though this evaluation could not use an experimental design, and even though observation was the primary data-gathering technique, Mitchell's study falls squarely within the positivistic perspective. It should be noted that the quantitative observational instruments were deemed successful at providing a useful description of such program features as "overall distribution of curricular time" and "patterns of activities." However, Mitchell claimed that they were *"not* an effective means of judging the quality of classroom experience" (p. 119; emphasis added).

In the late 1980s, Lightbown and Halter (1989) conducted a three-year study of ESL learning in four school districts of New Brunswick, Canada. Like Beretta and Davies, their evaluation was a comparison of an experimental program with a traditional program, using posttest scores as the measure of program effect. Also like Beretta and Davies, they compared the two programs using tests measuring the skills and content taught in the experimental program, tests measuring skills and content taught in the traditional program, and tests that were judged to be "neutral" in terms of skills and content. In addition to the straight posttest comparisons, the evaluators also investigated the relationship of variables such as student academic ability and degree of parental bilingualism with posttest scores.

Although the interpretation of their results was obscured somewhat by differences across school districts and a larger number of traditional, or control, classrooms in one district, the authors concluded that there were few significant differences between the two programs on the posttest measures. Where they were significant, the differences favored the program group whose skills and content were being tested. The results of the correlation of other variables to posttest scores indicated that, at first, there is a strong relationship among three variables: preinstructional ESL knowledge, parental assessment of ESL ability and contact with English outside the classroom, and posttest scores. This relationship became less important after the first year and, by the end of the third year, classroom learning variables were more strongly related to posttest scores than were preinstructional knowledge or out-of-school exposure to English.

Although their central concerns were with student achievement, or product, the authors did recognize the need for an examination of classroom process:

Current views of program evaluation emphasize the necessity to supplement pre-test/post-test data with information about what actually happens in the experimental and control classroom. Such information is often an indispensable aid in interpreting test results. (Lightbown and Halter 1989: Vol. I, p. 10)

Because of time and resources limitations, this investigation of program process was limited to "informal observation" during the first year, student and teacher questionnaires during the second, and interviews during the third. The informal observation and questionnaires enabled the authors to characterize the experimental and traditional classrooms in a minimal fashion as having "independent students" and "teacher-centered students," respectively, and to make comments on teacher and student perceptions of materials, activities, and degree of learning. The interviews proved to be "a very rich source of information about the students' understanding of their ESL experiences" (Vol. II, p. 20). Lightbown and Halter's interpretation of these data was that the students in the experimental program tended to work and find solutions to problems on their own – rather than ask the teacher – more often than did the students in the traditional program. The authors were also able to identify specific materials and activities that the students either liked or disliked. This research, then, appears to have elements of both the positivistic and the naturalistic perspectives.

A combination of positivistic and naturalistic approaches in a field experimental setting was utilized to investigate both product and process in the evaluation of the Reading English for Science and Technology (REST) project during 1985–1987 (Lynch 1988, 1992). This program was designed to teach English for Science and Technology (EST) reading skills to chemical engineering undergraduate students of the chemical sciences faculty at the University of Guadalajara. To investigate program product, I used a nonequivalent control group (NECG) design. REST student performance on a variety of posttests was compared to the performance of a group of students in another major of the same faculty who did not receive EFL instruction. After analyzing the data using several statistical techniques, I concluded that the REST students had outperformed the control group. This, admittedly, amounted to saying that the REST program "was better than nothing."

To investigate the process of the program, I used a naturalistic approach. The data in this case were student and teacher interview transcripts, classroom observation notes, teacher and administrator journal entries, and program documentation and correspondence. After analyzing this information, I concluded that the program was not an unqualified success, primarily because of a mismatch between the design of the program and the expectations of the students. Several areas in the curriculum and in the facilitation of the program were identified for change. Thus, this evaluation was both summative and formative, in addition to combining the positivistic perspective with a more naturalistic one.

Along similar lines, Brown (1989a) described the framework used in the ongoing evaluation of the University of Hawai'i ESL program. As in my study, the extreme version of summative evaluation was rejected in favor of a combined summative-formative approach. The need for information concerning both product and process was also recognized and incorporated into the evaluation framework. Although both quantitative and qualitative data were recommended, the notion of combining paradigms was not discussed.

Summary

The history of program evaluation in applied linguistics can be seen, thus far, as a move away from a concern with tightly controlled experiments focusing on the analysis of product, or student achievement, to a concern for describing and analyzing the process of programs as well. This move has paralleled the paradigm dialog in educational evaluation, and is beginning to bring ontological and epistemological questions into the research literature of applied linguistics. Specifically, the concern for investigating process as a part of program evaluation has encouraged the use of naturalistic methods. These methods ultimately derive from a research paradigm that I have described as naturalistic and that has fundamental differences with the positivistic paradigm in terms of what counts as evidence.

Rather than forcing a choice between the two paradigms so that the methods available for program evaluation are limited to either positivistic or naturalistic ones, I have argued for the pragmatic stance of allowing the combination of methods from the two paradigms. This does not, however, free us from the responsibility of articulating clearly what we will consider as evidence in our research and why. This notion of how we establish the veracity of our findings is usually discussed as validity, and the categories of internal and external validity have been introduced in summary fashion in this chapter. In order to be clear about our claims for validity, however, we need to examine carefully the assumptions concerning what counts as evidence that underlie the methods we are using. The following chapter, therefore, elaborates the concept of validity from both the positivistic and naturalistic perspectives. In a sense, this also entails a further elaboration of the paradigm dialog, and it informs the presentation of positivistic, naturalistic, and mixed strategies for program evaluation in the subsequent chapters. Ultimately, it will provide us with a means for answering the following questions:

What kind of evidence do I need in order to evaluate a program?

What am I assuming about what is necessary to feel confident about my conclusions?

Whether we choose positivistic or naturalistic methods (or a combination), we should be able to articulate answers to these questions and, thus, be able to define explicitly what counts as evidence for our evaluation.

3 *Validity*

In Chapter 2, validity was referred to as "the notion of how we establish the veracity of our findings" and was linked to the task of determining "what counts as evidence" in the evaluation of language education programs. In this chapter, the concept of validity is developed along both theoretical (What is it?) and practical (How do I know when I have it?) lines. As mentioned previously, this will also involve an elaboration of aspects of the paradigm dialog. That is, to the extent that a determination of what counts as evidence differs from one research paradigm to another, the concept of validity is formulated differently, depending on the paradigmatic perspective chosen.

The first section of this chapter presents validity from the positivistic perspective. I first use Cook and Campbell's (1979) typology and discuss the classic threats to validity. Then I present other conceptualizations of validity from an essentially positivistic perspective. After that, I consider validity from the naturalistic perspective, offering various criteria and techniques for enhancing and assessing those criteria.

Validity from the positivistic perspective

It should be reiterated that the use of the term *positivistic* is meant as a general label for a variety of current stances in relation to the philosophy of science. It should also be pointed out that although there are few, if any, who would refer to themselves as positivists or logical positivists these days, the philosophical assumptions of logical positivism continue to provide the rational basis for what counts as evidence in most scientific inquiry (Bechtel 1988). As an example, Cook and Campbell (1979) admit to certain beliefs held in common with classical positivism, and refer to their philosophical position as *evolutionary critical-realism*. This perspective

... enables us to recognize causal perceptions as "subjective" or "constructed by the mind"; but at the same time it stresses that many causal perceptions constitute assertions about the nature of the world which go beyond the immediate experience of perceivers and so have objective contents which can be right or wrong (albeit not always testable). The perspective is realist because it assumes that causal relationships exist outside of the human mind, and it is critical-realist because it assumes that these valid causal relationships cannot be perceived with total accuracy by our imperfect sensory and intellective capacities. And the perspective is evolutionary because it assumes a special survival value to knowing about causes and, in particular, about manipulable causes. (Cook and Campbell 1979:29)

For the purposes of the present discussion, however, this position will be thought of as a variant of a general paradigm that I continue to label as positivistic. A hallmark principle of this paradigm is the notion that the reality that we seek to know is objective, existing independently of our minds. Although few researchers working within this perspective still cling to the notions that complete objectivity can be achieved and that reality can be perfectly perceived, objectivity as a "regulatory ideal" and the existence of an independently existing reality remain as key philosophical assumptions. Another key notion is that of *causal relationships*. Cordray (1986:10) summarizes the requirements for these relationships as: "First, the purported cause (X) precedes the effect (Y); second, X covaries with Y; third, all other rival explanations are implausible." The other defining principle of this paradigm is that we arrive at an approximation of reality through the test of *falsification*. This means that "at best, one can know what has not yet been ruled out as false" (Cook and Campbell 1979:37).[1]

The traditional validity typology

This view of what there is to know and how we can go about knowing it leads to a particular way of defining and assessing validity. The classic typology, formulated by Campbell and Stanley (1966), divided validity into internal and external. I mention it here in part to pay tribute to its ongoing influence – positivistic and naturalistic researchers alike discuss validity in reference to this original typology – and in part to provide the necessary historical background for understanding more recent formulations of validity. My discussion of the threats to validity within this typology will attempt to contextualize the concepts of internal and external within the field of applied linguistics. However, those readers who are already familiar with Campbell and Stanley (1966) and with Cook and Campbell's (1979) reformulation may wish to skip over this section.

---

1 It should be pointed out that there are divisions and debates within this paradigm. For example, Phillips (1990) discusses the differences between *realists* and *antirealists*: Both groups believe in an independent reality, but they disagree over the status of theoretical entities.

The Campbell and Stanley (1966) conceptualization of *internal validity* had to do with the degree to which observed relationships between variables could be inferred to be causal. In the case of program evaluation this amounts to asking the question: How strongly can we infer that the program being evaluated caused the observed effects (e.g., significant increases in achievement test scores)? *External validity* referred to the degree to which the inferred causal relationship could be generalized to other persons, settings, and times. For program evaluation, the question is: To what extent can the effects caused by the observed program be expected to occur in other program contexts?

Cook and Campbell (1979) later revised this typology by differentiating internal and external validity into four dimensions. What had previously been labeled internal validity was now divided into *statistical conclusion validity* and *internal validity*. Statistical conclusion validity refers to the degree of certainty with which we can infer that the variables being observed are related. For program evaluation this can be thought of as asking: How strongly are the program (the independent variable) and the measure of program effect (the dependent variable) related? This relationship is expressed statistically as covariation, or the degree to which variation in the dependent variable goes along with variation in the independent variable. For example, does the variation in achievement test scores go along with whether the students are in the program or not? Cook and Campbell's revised conceptualization of internal validity has to do specifically with whether or not the observed relationship between the dependent and independent variables can be inferred to be causal. For program evaluation, this is the question of whether the program caused the effects that were measured in the evaluation.

Under the revised typology, Campbell and Stanley's external validity is divided into *construct validity* and *external validity*. Construct validity concerns the degree to which we can use our research findings to make generalizations about the constructs, or traits, that underlie the variables we are investigating. These constructs, for the purposes of this discussion, can be considered as labels that assign meaning to the things we are measuring. The labels, and their ascribed meanings, are derived from current theory. In the case of language program evaluation, this attempt at generalization amounts to asking: To what extent can the observed effects of the language program being evaluated generalize to theoretical constructs such as communicative language ability (Bachman 1990), or to more practical, methodological constructs such as content-based instruction (Brinton et al. 1989)? The revised conceptualization of external validity refers to the degree to which we can draw conclusions about the generalizability of a causal relationship to other persons, settings, and times. For program evaluation, this can be formulated as follows: To what extent can the conclusions reached in this evaluation be generalized to other program contexts? Another way to frame this question is: To what degree can we claim that this program will work equally well for another group of students, in another location, at another time?

Assuming, then, that these definitions of internal (and statistical conclusion) and external (and construct) validity represent the "What is it?", how do we know whether we have it or not? Traditionally, this question has been addressed with reference to the threats to validity. Each type of validity has specific threats associated with it, and these threats must be ruled out in order to make claims for the veracity of research findings – that is, in order for us to "know that we have it."

Threats to validity

Following Cook and Campbell's (1979) typology, the specific threats to statistical conclusion validity are as follows:

1. *Low statistical power*   If a small sample size is used, if the alpha level for statistical inferences is set too low, or if the statistical tests being used are not powerful enough, we increase the chances of type II error. This means that we may incorrectly conclude that there are no significant differences when they do, in fact, exist.
2. *Violated assumptions of statistical tests*   If particular statistical procedures with restrictive assumptions are used, we may be left with research findings that are uninterpretable. For example, the use of analysis of covariance (ANCOVA) assumes that the covariate is measured without error. Because most measures that are used in applied linguistics research are less than perfectly reliable, this assumption is likely to be violated and therefore limits our claims to validity when using a procedure such as ANCOVA.
3. *Making multiple comparisons*   When we use several different measures in a research study such as a program evaluation, a certain proportion of the comparisons we make (for example, comparing students in the program of interest with those in a rival program) will turn up statistically significant differences that are due purely to chance. This is referred to as type I error, or the failure to accept a true null hypothesis (no significant differences between groups).
4. *Unreliable measurement*   In addition to being a specific assumption of certain statistical tests, the lack of reliability in the measures we use is a general problem for the validity of our research findings.

For certain of these threats, addressing them is as simple as showing that they do not exist. For example, we can show that we have selected a large sample, that we have set our alpha level at a reasonable level, that we have chosen statistical tests with sufficient power, and that we have not violated the assumptions of those tests. For other threats, we may need to do more. For example, if we have made multiple comparisons, we will need to adopt an experiment-wide error rate or use procedures that control for this threat (e.g., multiple analysis of variance and conservative multiple comparison tests). If we have unreliable measures, we may need to consider correcting them for attenuation. In all cases, these are statistical problems with statistical solutions.[2]

Again following Cook and Campbell's (1979) typology, the specific threats to internal validity are as follows:

5. *History* Factors external to the research setting can affect the research results. For example, events in the community in which the program exists may affect the students in a way that makes it impossible to assess how much the program itself was responsible for the measured effects (e.g., end-of-program test scores).

6. *Maturation* Normal growth or change in the research subjects may account for the research findings. For example, end-of-program test scores may be shown to have improved significantly, but this may be due solely to the fact that the students have become older and more experienced, independently of the program.

7. *Testing* The measurement conducted as a part of the research can have its own effect on the results. For example, if a great deal of testing is done over the course of a program evaluation, the results may be due to increased familiarity on the part of the students with the tests and testing procedures.

8. *Instrumentation* When the testing instruments used have particular properties that may affect the test results, the validity of the conclusions drawn from these measures is threatened. For example, the test being used as the end-of-program measure may behave differently at different points along the test scale – it may fail to measure accurately those students who are at the high or low end of the scale.

9. *Statistical regression* Test scores tend to regress toward the group mean over time when the tests are less than perfectly reliable; that is, high scorers on a pretest tend to score lower on the posttest, low scorers tend to score higher, *as a group phenomenon*. The result is that real differences between groups may be obscured.

10. *Mortality* This rather grim-sounding threat refers to the fact that research subjects sometimes leave the research setting before the study is concluded. When the characteristics of those who remain in the research setting versus those who leave are systematically different in some way, the research conclusions become less than straightforward. For example, a majority of the students who left the program before the evaluation was finished may have been from the lower ability levels. A higher score for the program group at posttest time might thus be due primarily to the absence of these lower ability students.

11. *Selection* The way in which subjects are selected for a research study may have a significant effect on the results. For example, if the students in the program to be evaluated were selected from a particular socioeconomic

---

2 Hatch and Lazaraton (1991) and Brown (1988) provide excellent discussions of these problems and solutions.

group, this might explain the evaluation results independently of the program, especially if the students are being compared with another group who were selected based on some other criteria.

12. *Interaction with selection*   Selection may interact with other threats to produce problems in interpreting the research findings. For example, maturation may combine with selection in that the group of students selected for the program of interest may be growing (cognitively) at a different rate than the group of students to which the program group is being compared.

13. *Diffusion or imitation of treatments*   When the research is comparing two or more groups, the treatment (the independent variable, or the experience that differentiates the groups) intended for one group can reach the other groups to some degree. For example, an evaluation of an innovative language teaching program may be conducted by comparing it to a more traditional curriculum. If, during the course of the evaluation, the students in the traditional curriculum are given elements of the innovative program (because, for example, their teacher is aware of the new program's methods and wants her students to be able to benefit from them), then any claims about the success or failure of the program in comparison to the traditional one will be difficult to make.

14. *Compensatory rivalry*   Similarly, if two (or more) groups are being compared, the ability to keep the treatments associated with each group from affecting each other may be impaired. With this threat, knowledge of the group comparison can lead the "traditional" group to try harder, knowing that it is the underdog (the "John Henry effect").

15. *Resentful demoralization*   This threat is the opposite of compensatory rivalry. In this case, the "traditional" group makes little or no effort to perform well because it believes that it is receiving an inferior program.

Threats 5 through 12 are difficult to avoid unless there is random selection and assignment to the program and comparison groups. This is an issue of research design and will be discussed in Chapter 4. For the present discussion, it should be noted that when it is not possible to select and assign students randomly, these threats, as well as threats 13 through 15, should be investigated and documented as descriptively as possible in order to assess their potential effects on the evaluation results. It should also be noted that even without the use of randomization in the evaluation design, these threats will not always manifest themselves.

For construct validity, the specific threats are as follows:

16. *Inadequate theory*   There may be insufficient theoretical basis for the constructs that we are trying to operationalize in our research. For example, our understanding of some component of language ability may lack sufficient detail and accuracy for us to specify what the research subjects should be able to do in order to demonstrate their language ability.

17. *Monooperation bias*   If we have only one way of operationalizing the constructs of interest, our ability to make claims involving that construct is limited. In program evaluation, this applies when one is examining only one representation of the program being evaluated and only one way of

representing the program's effect (e.g., one task that indicates language ability) – which is usually the case.

18. *Monomethod bias*   This threat is related to monooperation bias, and exists when there is only one method for measuring the constructs of interest (e.g., using only multiple-choice, pencil-and-paper tests).

19. *Hypothesis guessing within program group*   This threat has also been called the *Hawthorne effect*, and refers to the situation in which research subjects respond with behavior they think they are supposed to demonstrate because of their awareness of being in an "experiment." There is little evidence of this threat in the literature involving field experiments, which includes most program evaluation studies.[3]

20. *Evaluation apprehension*   When people involved in research know that they are being "tested," there is a tendency for them to modify their behavior because of a desire to be favorably evaluated by the researcher, who is presumably an expert. To the extent that this occurs, it can confuse the interpretation of research findings.

21. *Experimenter expectancies*   In most research, there is danger that conclusions will be colored by what the researcher expects to find.

22. *Interaction of testing with treatment*   The number of tests and when they are given can have a systematic effect on the research results. For example, giving a pretest and a posttest may have an enhancing effect on student performance in a particular program context. This could make the program look better than it actually is when compared with another context where the pretest and posttest do not interact with the program to produce the enhancing effect.

Threats to external validity are as follows:

23. *Interaction of selection and treatment*   The success of a treatment can be the result of a certain type of subject having been chosen. For example, evaluation results may indicate that a program is improving student achievement test scores, but this may be true only for a particular subset of students who were selected for the program.

24. *Interaction of setting and treatment*   This is basically the same type of threat as the previous one, in that the success of a program may depend on a combination of a program feature and the particular setting in which it is offered.

25. *Interaction of history and treatment*   When this threat exists, certain aspects of the program are combining with certain events that occurred external to the program to produce the observed evaluation results.

The threats to construct validity need to be considered and ruled out with theoretical arguments (e.g., by showing that there is sufficient theory on which to base the research and that the constructs have been reasonably operationalized). Threats to external validity can be minimized by selecting representative program contexts for evaluation or,

3 An exception can occur when the measures being used in the program evaluation are attitude questionnaires – for example, regarding the importance of English (e.g., Coleman 1992).

when multiple program settings are available, by selecting several, diverse contexts for evaluation. The interaction threats can also be addressed through careful investigation and documentation of the program setting, including relevant events external to the program.

Table 3.1 summarizes the threats to validity in this conceptualization.

Other positivistic validity typologies

As noted previously, I believe that the Campbell and Stanley/Cook and Campbell typology remains the strongest influence on our thinking with respect to validity. There have been other attempts to conceptualize the issue, however. For example, Cronbach (1982) proposes an alternative framework for validity in his writings on program evaluation. His typology begins with identification of the "elements in an evaluation design," which are:

U, the population or domain of *u*nits from which subjects will be drawn, and about which a conclusion is sought
T, the *t*reatment domain; the plan for the program and its installation
O, the admissible procedures, or *o*bservations and conditions for obtaining data
S, the *s*etting, or large social context in which the study takes place

In his notational system, uppercase letters – $UTOS$ – refer to the domain about which decisions will be made. Lowercase letters – *uto* – refer to the sample; for example, u refers to the actual participants in the evaluation study, t to the actual procedures applied to any u, and o to the particular form of observations taken with respect to u and t. The setting, S, the particular times and cultural conditions under which the study is made, is not considered to be capable of "sampling." That is, the setting is always considered as its own, irreducible domain, and is always given the capital letter notation. An asterisk in front of the notational string – *$UTOS$ – refers to a situation or set of conditions that is different from the original class of domains, UTO, about which a conclusion is wanted. *$UTOS$ is also referred to as "the domain of application," and may include the original UTO, overlap with it, or be completely separate.

It is further testimony to the lingering power of Campbell and Stanley's (and Cook and Campbell's) formulation of internal versus external validity that Cronbach refers to these concepts when discussing his typology. However, a critical difference is his insistence on recognizing validity as a property of our inferences, rather than our research designs, and his claim that "external validity does not depend directly on internal validity" (1982:107). In Cronbach's scheme, then, internal validity refers to the confidence that we have concerning inferences made from *utoS* to *UTOS*. External validity is the trustworthiness of infer-

TABLE 3.1 THREATS TO VALIDITY

Type of threat	What to do
Internal validity	
Statistical power	Use large sample, appropriate alpha level, tests with power
Statistical assumptions	Check for violation; choose appropriate tests/procedures
Multiple comparisons	Use MANOVA, Scheffe or Tukey multiple comparisons procedures
Unreliable measurement	Check reliability; consider correction for attenuation
Testing, instrumentation	Choose test instruments and timing of administration carefully for the intended students
Statistical regression	Use reliable instruments; do not compare groups from different statistical populations
History, maturation, mortality, selection, interaction with selection	Randomization; describe the setting and the potential for these threats to explain evaluation findings
Diffusion or imitation of treatments, compensatory rivalry, resentful demoralization	Describe and document the potential for these threats in the evaluation setting
External validity	
Inadequate theory	Review the literature extensively
Monooperation, monomethod bias	Use multiple representations of the variables and multiple test instrument formats and task types
Hypothesis guessing, evaluation apprehension, experimenter expectancies	Describe and document these threats and their potential effect on the interpretation of results
Interaction of testing with treatment	Describe and document; difficult to deal with in field experimentation
Interaction of selection and treatment or setting, interaction of history and treatment	Describe and document; choose evaluation sites based on representativeness or diversity

ences made from *utoS* to **UTOS*. This is the distinction that removes some of the tension between external and internal validity:

> Internal and external validity are not emphatically different. The distinction comes down to whether a conclusion refers to a domain that was deliberately and systematically represented in *utoS* or to some other domain. . . . Methodologists, myself included, have hitherto written as if internal validity "comes first," as if, in other words, a conclusion is first established as true of *UTOS* and then extended. That is not always the case. My present conception is that a conclusion about a **UTOS* extrapolates the evidence on *utoS* in the light of other experience. The extrapolation is best made from the facts, not from the synoptic conclusion about *UTOS*. (pp. 107–108)

Cronbach seems to be saying that external validity, or external inference, is not a question of how well a conclusion from an evaluation of one program can be "generalized" to another program setting, but the degree to which the specific information from the original evaluation – the particular subjects, the particular implementation of the program, the particular operations for data collection – can be extrapolated, or relevantly applied, to another situation. The challenge of Cronbach's approach to validity, as I see it, is to describe the evaluation setting adequately and to portray the evaluation data and findings in sufficient detail that other researchers are able to determine for themselves the degree to which the evaluation has external (or internal) validity. In this sense, validity is less an inherent property of the research design than it is a property of active inferencing by various researchers (the original evaluator or other researchers reading the original research report). As will be seen, this also puts Cronbach's perspective on validity closer to that of naturalistic evaluators.

In the examples that I have presented thus far, validity has been defined in terms of typologies. Rather than trying to replace one of these typologies with another, Mark (1986) presents an attempt at synthesizing the various conceptualizations of validity from the positivistic perspective. He finds that the typologies of Cook and Campbell (1979), Cronbach (1982), and others all include a generic statement of the form: "The treatment causes the effect for persons (or units) X in conditions Y" (p. 50). Recognizing Cronbach's emphasis on elements of inference as the basis for conceptualizing validity, Mark provides an expansion of this generic statement to include the level of generalization and the certainty of inferences. The *level of generalization* corresponds to the internal versus external validity and *UTOS* versus **UTOS* concepts discussed previously. *Certainty of inference* refers to both statistical estimations of the range of "effect sizes"[4] witnessed in the quantitative data

---

4 Effect sizes are discussed in Chapter 6.

and the "subjective confidence" that can be placed in a particular statement of inference.

Instead of a checklist of threats to validity, Mark proposes three "principles" that require assessment. The first is the *similarity principle*, which can be summarized as the ability to predict outcomes from like instances. If the evaluation findings are to be judged valid, then we should be able to predict what will happen if the same program is implemented under similar conditions in a similar setting. A second principle is *robustness*, which can be assessed by the degree to which an outcome is observed over diverse circumstances. If our evaluation of a particular program is carried out such that we observe its functioning in several different school settings, and we find that it is successful across those differing settings, our findings can be said to exhibit robust validity. This type of check on validity might be done within one evaluation study with multiple settings, or across several evaluations with differing settings. Mark's final principle is *explanation*, which he draws primarily from the work of Cronbach. This principle is assessed by the ability to describe relationships among the various levels of a program, its effects, and the responses of evaluation audiences. In this sense, our evaluation findings are valid if we are able to be specific about *why* the program is successful. Our validation efforts would need to pinpoint the specific combinations of program objectives, curricular principles, teaching materials, and individual instructional styles that result in particular achievement outcomes or changes in attitude. We would also want to relate these combinations to how the outcomes are received in particular ways by those who have a stake in the evaluation results. Mark ends his synthesis with the important reminder that validity typologies should be used to improve the quality of evaluation design and analysis rather than to rationalize evaluation findings or to avoid the exercise of critical analysis.

Summary of validity from the positivistic perspective

One way of summarizing the discussion of validity from the positivistic perspective is to focus on its two major concerns: *certainty* and *generalization*. Internal validity, or internal inference, is concerned primarily with certainty. In program evaluation, this means being concerned with making accurate inferences about whether the program as it was implemented *caused* the effect that was measured with the specific program students in the particular program setting being evaluated. The trade-off for such certainty is that these inferences are generally difficult to generalize to other students and settings. This occurs because internal validity requires control: We need to control as much as possible about the students in the program and the surrounding context in order to be certain that it is the program, and nothing else, that is causing the observed effects. This control results in a relatively artificial, unrepresentative set of conditions under which the program is being evaluated. However, it allows us to make strong claims about what was observed in that program setting with a high degree of certainty that those claims are valid.

External validity, or external inference, is concerned primarily with generalization. In program evaluation, this translates into a concern with generalizing from the specific instances of one evaluation to other students and other settings. It has already been mentioned with respect to internal validity that a highly controlled program evaluation will impose a high degree of artificiality and lack of representativeness. This, in turn, limits generalizability. Suppose, for example that we conduct an evaluation of a program that is implementing a new language education curriculum. In order to be certain that we are able to assess the effects of the program accurately, suppose that we randomly select and assign students into the program classrooms, keep them sheltered from outside events by having them live in isolated dormitories, give them prerecorded lessons to control for teacher variability in the presentation of the curriculum (cf. Levin 1972), and basically maintain the environment as a closed system laboratory. Although the internal validity of our evaluation would thus be strengthened, it would be highly unlikely that we would be able to generalize our findings given the improbability (if not undesirability) of finding a similarly controlled program elsewhere.

It should be pointed out, however, that there are researchers who disagree with this portrayal of the conditions necessary for external validity. Berkowitz and Donnerstein (1982), for example, feel that the generalizability of results is governed by more than the type of representativeness of setting noted to be lacking in the preceding example. They argue that "demographic representativeness" and "surface realism" are not as important for generalization as is the meaning assigned by research subjects to "the situation they are in and the behavior they are carrying out" (p. 255). What this type of approach to external validity seems to focus on is a concern for research that will help to develop theory. The authors point out that laboratory experiments are designed to "test a causal hypothesis . . . , not to determine the probability that a certain event will occur in a particular population" (p. 255). Although this type of generalization may be of interest to researchers working on certain theories, it may not be relevant to researchers such as program evaluators seeking to apply their findings to areas such as decision making in uncontrolled, field program settings.

For Cronbach, this apparent tension between internal and external validity is a misconception. Perhaps the key difference between what might be termed the Cronbachian and the Campbellian approaches to validity is the conceptualization of causality. In the Campbellian typology, causes are seen as separate elements in the evaluation design, whereas in the Cronbachian view they are better expressed as the proper "labeling" of relationships between a sample (*utoS*) and its larger domain of interest (*UTOS*), or *utoS* and a different domain of interest (**UTOS*). That is, Campbellian causality is seen as a clear and certain statement about the program as cause. Cronbachian causality is expressed as the complex interactions among units, treatments, and observations, which require the researcher/evaluator to make use of prior knowledge and to rely on the rhetorical as well as the logical in forming evaluation claims. As I mentioned before, this conceptualization of causality and validity moves beyond the traditional, positivistic perspective and closer to the naturalistic perspective, discussed in the next section.

Validity depends not only on the data collection and analysis, but also on the way a conclusion is stated and communicated. Validity is subjective rather than objective. (Cronbach 1982:108)

Validity from the naturalistic perspective

As was the case with the term *positivistic*, I am using *naturalistic* as a convenient label to refer to a variety of perspectives. In Chapter 2, the naturalistic perspective was defined as a research paradigm that differs from the positivistic paradigm in that it does not hold with the notion that the reality that we seek to know is objective, existing independent of our mind. Instead, reality is seen as relative to our mind and the particular historical and cultural settings within which we are attempting to make our knowledge claims. In other words, knowledge claims are made and judged in relation to:

. . . a given conceptual scheme, language game, set of social practices, or historical epoch. There is a nonreducible plurality of such schemes, paradigms, and practices; there is no substantive overarching framework in which radically different and alternative schemes are commensurable – no universal standards that somehow stand outside of and above these competing alternatives." (Bernstein 1983:11–12; cited in Smith 1987:354).[5]

As with the positivistic paradigm, one can take various positions within naturalistic research. Although I do not wish to diminish the

5 It is interesting that Smith quotes Bernstein to define relativism. The philosophical debate becomes too complex to accomodate here, but I should point out that Bernstein argues against both objectivism and relativism.

importance of the differences that exist between, for example, critical theorists (Farley 1987; cf. Pennycook 1990, 1991), constructivists (Lincoln 1990), and interpretivists (Pearsol 1987), I do see them as united in opposition to the positivistic paradigm in terms of a key naturalistic principle. That principle is the assumption of the inherent subjectivity of our inquiry: that values always mediate our understanding of reality.

This difference in principle between positivistic and naturalistic research and evaluation unavoidably plunges us into some fairly dense philosophical terminology. It seems necessary to introduce some of it here, in order to pursue the notion of what counts as evidence. One naturalistic researcher, Egon Guba (1990b), has articulated the philosophical differences in what I hope is an interpretable fashion. He characterizes the current state of affairs between what I am referring to as positivistic (represented by "postpositivism") and naturalistic (including "critical theory" and "constructivism") in terms of "assumptions." Critical theory, but not constructivism, shares *ontological assumptions* with the positivistic paradigm – both postpositivism and critical theory being "critical realist" in perspective, in that they allow for objects of inquiry that are independent of our perceptions, or constructions, of them. Both critical theory and constructivism differ from the positivistic paradigm in their *epistemological assumptions* – postpositivism being "modified objectivist: objectivity remains as a regulatory ideal, but can only be approximated, with special emphasis placed on external guardians such as the critical tradition and the critical community" (Guba 1990b:23), whereas critical theory and constructivism are "subjectivist, in the sense that values mediate inquiry" (p. 25). This means that although a constructivist and a critical theorist may disagree over the existence of objects in the world that are independent of our mind (the critical theorist, like the positivist/postpositivist, will allow for the existence of these independent objects), they will agree that our ability to understand those objects depends on our subjective, value-laden interpretations.

This distinction, involving objectivity versus subjectivity, will be worrisome to many. Does this mean that by adopting a naturalistic perspective we are forced into a situation where our knowledge claims are reduced to purely aesthetic judgment or matters of opinion? I think not. Even extreme relativists such as Smith (1987, 1988, 1990) hold reason and rationality as critical to our inquiry. We are required to put forward the best argument possible for any conclusion we draw in our evaluations and in our research, and it is understood that the argument will reflect our particular theoretical, social, political, and personal interests and purposes. In other words, "facts" cannot be separated from "values," but this does not doom us to irrationality.

Establishing naturalistic validity

A NATURALISTIC TYPOLOGY

The basic validity question that remains is: How do we choose rationally between competing knowledge claims? Many naturalistic researchers seem to answer this question in ways parallel to the typological approaches that define positivistic validity. For example, Maxwell (1992) has outlined an approach that is consciously similar to the Cook and Campbell typology. In this scheme, types of understanding and inferences replace design features and research procedures as the key elements. Validity is seen as the correspondence between the researcher's "account" of some phenomena and their "reality" (which may be the participant's constructions of the phenomena). Internal and external validity are replaced by descriptive, interpretive, theoretical, generalizable, and evaluative validity.

In Maxwell's typology, *descriptive validity* refers to the "factual accuracy" of the research account – basically, making certain that what is said or heard or seen by the researcher is not distorted or invented. *Interpretive validity* refers to the accuracy with which the account captures what the phenomena mean to the participants. *Theoretical validity* refers to how well an account provides an explanation of the phenomena. This explanation is in reference to some theory and as such depends on agreement between researchers concerning "the terms that are used to characterize the phenomena." *Generalizability* is used in a slightly different fashion than in positivistic discussions; Maxwell differentiates generalizations within the community, group, or institution being studied (internal generalization) and generalizations to other communities, groups, and institutions (external generalization). He points out that this is parallel to Cook and Campbell's statistical conclusion validity and external validity, respectively. The final type of validity defined by Maxwell is *evaluative validity*, which pertains to the accuracy of value judgments assigned to the phenomena in the research account. Although he has less to say about this type of validity, he points out that critical theory raises the question of value judgments implicit in any account.

Maxwell's conceptualization of validity introduces some important notions for naturalistic research and evaluation. For example, suppose that our evaluation study makes use of interview data. We may be able to make statements about those data that are valid on certain levels – descriptive, interpretive, and even theoretical – but those statements may be valid only for the interview situation and thus generalizability. That is, we may have accurately accounted for what was said in the interview and what that meant to the participants, and there may be agreement in the research community about our use of terms to describe and explain what was said in the interview. However, despite all this accuracy and agreement, we may not be able to generalize those conclusions, even for a specific interviewee, beyond the interview setting. What is required, in this case, is an understanding of the effect of the roles of interviewer and interviewee, and the relationships in the interview setting to the phenomena being studied. Ultimately, Maxwell's typology, like the positivistic ones, functions as a checklist of the kinds of threats to validity that need to be considered when drawing research conclusions. Unlike positivistic approaches to validity, this typology (and naturalistic approaches to validity, in general) is used after or during the conduct of the research rather than as an a priori guide to research design.

TRUSTWORTHINESS CRITERIA

Naturalistic researchers and evaluators Guba and Lincoln (1989) have also presented a typology that parallels those of the positivistic paradigm. They refer to their conceptualization as *trustworthiness criteria*, and present techniques for increasing the likelihood of meeting those criteria. Instead of internal validity, they refer to *credibility*, or "the match between the constructed realities of respondents (or stakeholders) and those realities as represented by the evaluator and attributed to various stakeholders" (Guba and Lincoln 1989:237). Where positivists speak of external validity, naturalistic evaluators such as Guba and Lincoln look for *transferability*, or the degree of similarity between sending (the original evaluation or study) and receiving (the context to which generalization is desired) contexts. *Dependability*, parallel to reliability in the positivistic paradigm, refers to "the stability of the data over time" (p. 242). *Confirmability* is as close as naturalistic researchers will come to attempting objectivity. Like Maxwell's descriptive and interpretive validity, it is "concerned with assuring that data, interpretations, and outcomes of inquiries are rooted in contexts and persons apart from the evaluator and are not simply figments of the evaluator's imagination" (p. 243).

Techniques for assessing naturalistic validity

The trustworthiness criteria provide an answer to the "What is it?" question of validity. In order to answer the "How do I know when I have it?" question, Guba and Lincoln (1989:233–43) provide the techniques listed below. Actually, these techniques can be thought of as increasing the validity of the evaluation findings, as well as providing the means of verification.

For credibility, the techniques are the following:

- *Prolonged engagement*: the immersion of the evaluator in the evaluation setting, establishing rapport and trust with program participants in order to understand their perceptions
- *Persistent observation*: in part, as a consequence of prolonged engagement, the evaluator's attempt to identify the most relevant elements of the evaluation setting on which to focus during the observation periods
- *Peer debriefing*: an extensive discussion between the evaluator and a "disinterested peer" concerning the evaluation findings, conclusions, and tentative hypotheses
- *Negative case analysis*: the search by the evaluator for instances in the evaluation data that do not fit the "working hypotheses" and revision of the hypotheses accordingly
- *Progressive subjectivity*: the recording of the evaluator's initial "constructions," or what is initially expected to be found, and the continuing recording and comparison of the developing constructions against these initial expectations (The goal is to avoid giving too much "privilege" to one's initial constructions.)
- *Member checks*: the repeated checking (done formally and informally) of developing constructions, or evaluation findings, with the members of the evaluation setting who provided the data from which those constructions were drawn

The technique for transferability is

- *Thick description*: the provision of "an extensive and careful description of the time, the place, the context, the culture" (Geertz 1973:241) from which the evaluation findings and hypotheses were drawn

The technique for dependability is a

- *Dependability audit*: the documentation of decisions made by the evaluator over the course of the evaluation concerning the methods for gathering and analyzing data

The technique for confirmability is a

- *Confirmability audit* (normally carried out in conjunction with the dependability audit): the attempt to trace the evaluation conclusions back to the original sources (This technique assumes that the data and the process by which the conclusions were drawn are available for inspection by an outside reviewer.)

One of these techniques, negative case analysis, is elaborated by Patton (1980, 1987). I shall characterize his approach to this technique with the following vignette. Suppose that an evaluation of a new language teaching program is being carried out from the naturalistic perspective. Let's say that the evaluator finds that most of the students in a program are reporting that the curriculum has greatly improved their language ability. In this case, it is important to examine closely those students who report that they have *not* been helped by the curriculum. The explanation that the curriculum was having a positive effect on most students would be tested by finding an explanation for why the deviant cases do not fit the trend. The evaluator's claims to validity would be strengthened by presenting these negative cases and demonstrating how they relate to the explanations being offered in the evaluation conclusions.

Patton also discusses a concept related to Guba and Lincoln's progressive subjectivity: *reactivity*. This phenomenon refers to the changes in what is being observed that are due to the presence of the researcher or evaluator, as well as the changes that occur in the researcher or evaluator as a result of being in the evaluation setting. It should be noted that reactivity was included among the threats to positivistic validity, as well (e.g., the Hawthorne effect, evaluation apprehension, experimenter expectancies). The suggested procedure for addressing this threat is to record in the data collection and analysis stages any observations of this effect that can be made and to include a discussion of the potential reactivity effects in the analysis and reporting of evaluation conclusions.

Patton discusses another technique for enhancing credibility, which could also be used as part of a dependability or confirmability audit: the *search for rival explanations*. This technique can be applied as the evaluator begins to interpret the evaluation data. At this stage of the evaluation, preliminary conclusions about the nature of the program, critical forces inside and outside the program, and key relationships among program factors begin to emerge. Rather than working with scores on a test and preordained statistical procedures, the naturalistic evaluator is using words, descriptions, and procedures that attempt to order these data in a systematic fashion so that logical arguments can be made for one interpretation over another. The validity of these interpretations resides in the strength of the arguments presented to the evaluation audience. In a very real sense, the evaluator is a part of that evaluation audience: The evaluator, too, must be convinced that the interpretations are well founded.

The strength of interpretations is tested by formulating alternative explanations to the ones that have emerged preliminarily. Let me try to illustrate this technique further with a continuation of the previous vignette. Suppose that after considering the evaluation data, the evaluator begins to notice a recurring theme: The teachers in the program perceive the students as intensely disliking them and the curriculum. Probing further, it is discovered that there are numerous references in the data to unhappiness on the part of the students over the lack of time spent in the program on oral skills. A reasonable interpretation, at this stage, might be that the lack of oral skills practice is having a negative effect on the relationships between students and teachers and on student attitude toward the curriculum. The evaluator would then test the strength of this interpretation by considering rival explanations. Perhaps there are other references in the data that portray negative reactions on the part of the students and that would also explain their relationships to the teachers and curriculum. It can be instructive to formulate seemingly outlandish explanations – ones that are perhaps the exact opposite of the one being tested. For example, a rival explanation to explore might be that the students, in fact, love the curriculum, but the teachers themselves are unhappy with it, causing negative relations with the students and the perception that the curriculum is disliked. This interpretation would need to be seriously considered, by looking for support in the data and examining their ability to account for such things as the students' unhappiness over the lack of oral skills practice.

In my illustration of this technique, I have begun to touch upon issues concerning the analysis of qualitative data. This problem is dealt with in greater detail in Chapter 7. Questions of validity from the naturalistic perspective are intimately tied to questions of data analysis, in much the same way that questions of validity from the positivistic perspective are tied to issues of research design and the choice of statistical tests. However, naturalistic data analysis is much less fixed and preordained than the designs and statistical tests used in positivistic research. In naturalistic analysis there are no established probability levels or score distributions to refer to, and validity becomes an issue of reasoning and argumentation. This is not to say that positivistic analysis does not also include reasoning and argumentation; it just tends to be embedded in preordained designs and methods to a greater degree than is possible with naturalistic analysis. Naturalistic evaluators need to build their case for validity more explicitly. As Patton (1980:328) says: "Reporting on what alternative explanations were considered and how those alternatives were considered in the formal evaluation report lends considerable credibility to the final set of findings offered by the evaluator."

TRIANGULATION

The techniques we have discussed for assessing the validity of an evaluation can be thought of as strategies for increasing validity as well. That is, techniques such as negative case analysis and member checks are not carried out as a separate exercise for validation, but are normally pursued as an integral part of the data-gathering and analysis stages of naturalistic evaluation. *Triangulation*, a term introduced by Webb et al. (1966) and developed further by Denzin (1970, 1978), deserves special consideration in this dual role of validity check and analytic strategy. Triangulation refers to the gathering and reconciling of data from several sources and/or from different data-gathering techniques. For example, this can be accomplished by combining observational field notes with interview transcripts, or think-aloud protocols with multiple-choice test scores. The triangulation may also be among different persons who have collected the evaluation data. For example, the evaluation may provide for the same classrooms to be observed by several different people, or notes from meetings to be gathered by several different participants. Multiple sources for data collection is another avenue that triangulation can take. The evaluator can gather data from program participants of different perspectives (e.g., teachers, students, administrators), from different settings (e.g., in the classroom, outside of the classroom), and from different times (e.g., before examinations, after examinations).

At first glance, triangulation seems like an obvious strategy for strengthening the validity of evaluation findings. Since there is always the possibility of bias in any particular source or technique of gathering data and since one source or technique's weakness is often another's strength, the argument can be made that triangulation will cancel out the bias inherent in any one source or method. However, there has been disagreement in the literature over the meaning and value of triangulation. In part this controversy stems from the way in which the metaphor of triangulation is perceived. For example, McFee (1992) perceives triangulation through the navigational metaphor of locating a position in relation to other, fixed points of reference. In evaluation, this sought-after position is the valid conclusion we are seeking, and the fixed points of reference are the multiple sources of data mentioned above. When viewed from this perspective, McFee argues, triangulation can lose its explanatory force. If the data are collected from different persons – say, from teachers, students, and administrators – in hopes of locating a "position" (the valid evaluation conclusion), the triangulation metaphor breaks down because the data from these different persons do not truly represent independent, fixed points of reference. Basically, the navigational metaphor fails for McFee because it assumes that there will be different data points that are all equally valid, which taken together help us to define another, valid point: the evaluation conclusion. If program students, teachers, and administrators all have the same perspective on an evaluation issue, then there are no differing reference points to triangulate. If our program students, teachers, and administrators have different perspectives on the same issue, there is no principled way to decide among the equally valid positions to locate a valid evaluation conclusion.

This is, perhaps, why Greene and McClintock (1985) define triangulation using the characteristics of *congruence* and *complementarity*. The goal of triangulation according to their view is to find agreement and support for a particular conclusion from different perspectives. If the student, the teacher, and the administrator all report the same perception of some aspect of the program, then these viewpoints converge on a conclusion whose validity is strengthened. However, triangulation still breaks down if there is disagreement or contradiction. Greene and McClintock, for example, attempted to use triangulation across different methods and paradigms – with one evaluation team using a survey questionnaire from a positivistic research perspective, and another team independently using interviews from a naturalistic research perspective. Their efforts at triangulation were judged "successful" (i.e., they produced convergence or complementarity) across the method/paradigms when examining their "descriptive results," or specific evaluation findings concerning such things as program participant characteristics, interpersonal perceptions among program participants, but these efforts were judged "unsuccessful" (i.e., they produced divergence) when examining their "major findings," or the conclusions that the independent qualitative and quantitative research teams reached. Ultimately, Greene and McClintock concluded that the failure to find convergent or complementary results for the major findings using the positivistic and naturalistic approaches derived from the fact that triangulation across paradigms is impossible.

Taking triangulation as a navigational metaphor and insisting that it achieve convergence in order to be considered successful, then, seems to create problems for the use of triangulation as a strategy for increasing the validity of evaluation efforts. However, there is an alternative way of looking at triangulation that solves some of these problems. Pointing out that the origins of this technique lie in the multitrait-multimethod work of Campbell and Fiske (1959), Mathison (1988) questions the assumption that inherent bias is automatically canceled when multiple methods, data sources, and investigators are used. That is, differences across sources and methods do not necessarily result in strengths and weaknesses that balance each other, nor should this be seen as the only value in pursuing them. Mathison also suggests that the navigational metaphor – that we use multiple reference points to locate the "truth" about social phenomena – reflects a particular assumption about the nature of inquiry (presumably, a positivistic one) and suggests that it may be profitably replaced with another metaphor for triangulation, such as "detective work." Denying the automatic bias-canceling effect and seeing triangulation from a detective perspective allows for useful outcomes other than convergence – specifically, those of inconsistency and contradiction. In this mode, the previous examples of disagreement among students, teachers, and administrators, and Greene and McClintock's contradictory survey and interview findings are turned into additional evidence that can strengthen the evaluation conclusions – triangulation becomes the search for an explanation of contradictory evidence. As Mathison (1988:15) summarizes:

The value of triangulation is not as a technological solution to a data collection and analysis problem, it is as a technique which provides more and better evidence from which researchers can construct meaningful propositions about the social world.

It still needs to be kept in mind that there are no clearly defined procedures for turning contradictory or inconsistent findings into valid conclusions. Validity can be enhanced through the inclusion of multiple data sources and perspectives, but only to the degree that the evaluator can reasonably construct meaningful conclusions from these data. As Fielding and Fielding (1986) have pointed out, triangulation, in itself, will not guarantee validity, and as Pearsol (1987) claims, credibility is defined in terms of the evaluator, not the methodological technique of triangulation. This technique, as with the others suggested here, needs to be accompanied by a clear elaboration of the process that the naturalistic evaluator followed in triangulating the data and in deciding on interpretations. How does the evaluator reconcile contradictory evidence across sources? How did the triangulated data increase the evaluator's confidence in the conclusions presented to the audience? Rather than giving the evaluation some sort of privileged status, just because multiple data sources were used, triangulation should be a tool for providing the evaluation audience with richer and clearer information.

MULTIPLE PERSPECTIVE NEGOTIATION

Another technique for assessing the validity of naturalistic evaluation involves addressing something that Greene (1987) refers to as the "expression and legitimation of multiple value claims." What I will refer to as *multiple perspective negotiation* represents a combination of this concept together with triangulation, member checks, and Stake's (1975) "responsive model" for evaluation (discussed in Chapter 5). The main idea is to arrive at evaluation conclusions as a result of a consensus among persons from different perspectives in relation to the program. This means having the reconciliation of data from multiple sources and data gatherers negotiated among those persons. As an example, the evaluator may have assembled data from several teachers about the program that suggests a divergence in views on its success. The next step would be to assemble these teachers to discuss these views and attempt to arrive at a consensus. If no such consensus is forthcoming, the evaluator must take the lead in the negotiation, perhaps ultimately deciding on an interpretation or perhaps simply reporting the lack of consensus. The important point is that the preliminary analysis be shared with different people involved with the program and that their reactions become a part of the analysis.

Another method of multiple perspective negotiation is to provide program participants and evaluation audience members with some of the assembled data (e.g., observation notes) and ask them to provide their own interpretations. This can be done before, during, or after the evaluator examines the data, and serves as the basis for what Guba and Lincoln (1989) call a negotiation session. During the negotiation session, the various interpretations are presented and discussed. Again, these discussions become another layer of data for the evaluation. It is also instructive to either schedule or allow "branching sessions" to evolve (Patton 1980, 1987). This amounts to identifying an issue in one negotiation session that could be enlightened by pursuing it with another group of people (e.g., the students) or with another set of data (e.g., interview transcripts).

Again, the discussion of validity has moved into a discussion of qualitative data analysis. The important point here is that validity from the naturalistic perspective concerns an overt establishment of credibility. In the absence of clear-cut rules for drawing inferences from qualitative data, the evaluator needs to make what was done in the evaluation extremely clear to the evaluation audience. This requires a thorough reporting of how the data were gathered and how they were analyzed. This also means that the evaluator is responsible for a disciplined investigation of the data: returning to it again and again, sifting through it and searching for meaningful trends and explanations, and exposing those trends and explanations to alternative ones and to multiple perspective negotiation. The more that this thoroughness and discipline can by demonstrated and documented as a part of the evaluation process, the more the evaluation conclusions will be seen as credible and valid.

THE UTILITY CRITERION

In addition to the trustworthiness criteria, pragmatists such as Greene (1987) would add the criterion of *utility* when considering the validity of naturalistic evaluations. Utility is also discussed by Patton (1986) and refers to the degree of usefulness the evaluation findings have for administrators, managers, and other stakeholders in terms of the decisions they need to make with respect to the program. When we evaluate a program, we want to know whether it works or not. Similarly, the utility criterion asks whether or not the evaluation "works": Does it provide the information that decision-makers need concerning issues such as the appropriacy of future funding for the program, aspects of the program that need improvement, and so forth? Techniques for assessing this criterion, like most of the other techniques already presented, are bound up with the act of carrying out naturalistic evaluation – being responsive to stakeholders' needs and perceptions, allowing evaluation issues and hypotheses to emerge from the data – and are developed in greater detail in Chapters 5 and 7. Techniques such as the member check can also be used to address this criterion.

THE AUTHENTICITY CRITERIA

Guba and Lincoln, who crafted the trustworthiness criteria discussed above, continue to champion naturalistic evaluation and to distinguish it from its positivistic counterpart. An important contribution to this effort is their articulation of a new stage in program evaluation, fourth generation evaluation (Guba and Lincoln 1989), referred to in the previous chapter. A hallmark of this articulation is a set of criteria that, unlike the trustworthiness criteria, are *not* parallel to the positivistic validity typology. They refer to these as the *authenticity criteria*: fairness, ontological authenticity, educative authenticity, catalytic authenticity, and tactical authenticity. These criteria differ from previous naturalistic efforts in that they "could have been invented by someone who had never heard of positivism or its claims for rigor" (p. 245).

Fairness refers to making certain that the multiple perspectives, or constructions of meaning, of the various evaluation stakeholders and program participants have been taken into account in a thorough and representative fashion. "The role of the evaluator is to seek out, and communicate, all such constructions and to explicate the ways in which such constructions – and their underlying value systems – are in conflict" (p. 246). Making use of techniques discussed in the section on trustworthiness criteria, the evaluator attempts to create a "permanent audit trail" that documents the various stakeholder constructions, and conducts an open negotiation session to generate recommendations and an agenda for subsequent action. Guba and Lincoln describe a set of rules, taken from the literature on labor arbitration, to guide this session, including the accessibility for all participants to skilled negotiators.

Ontological authenticity refers to the degree to which the evaluation process results in its participants gaining information and the ability to use that information. This might seem like a difficult criterion to verify, as well as achieve, but Guba and Lincoln advise us to seek "testimony from selected respondents" and keep the audit trail as documentation of these testimonies and those of the evaluator's. The proof of this criterion, then, is in the ability of the participants to communicate their increased understanding and appreciation of the broad range of issues informing the program being evaluated.

Educative authenticity is similar to ontological authenticity in that it represents the degree to which understanding and appreciation are increased. In this case, it is the participants' understanding of the perspectives of those outside their own stakeholding group. For example, an evaluation could be said to achieve educative validity if its process resulted in teachers understanding the program better from the point of

view of the administrators, administrators understanding the program
better from the point of view of the students, and so on. This criterion
can be demonstrated with the same techniques – testimony of selected
respondents and audit trail evidence – as are used for ontological authenticity.

The final two authenticity criteria – catalytic and tactical – clearly
distinguish this set from the parallel, trustworthiness criteria. *Catalytic
authenticity* refers to the degree to which something is actually done as
a result of the evaluation. This criterion harkens back to that of utility,
in the sense that the evaluation findings are considered valid only if they
can actually be put to some use. If evaluation findings need to be judged
by how well they suggest and facilitate some form of action, then they
also need to be judged in relation to how well program stakeholders
and participants are actually empowered to take that action: *tactical
authenticity*. The techniques that demonstrate the attainment of these
criteria are the aforementioned testimony from respondents (all groups),
the articulation of formal resolutions from the negotiation sessions, and
systematic follow-up assessments in which the evaluator and participants make judgments about the degree to which action was taken and
participants were empowered. These criteria give an activist stance to
program evaluation:

The purpose of evaluation is some form of action and/or decision-making.
Thus no fourth generation evaluation is complete without action being
prompted on the part of the participants. (Guba and Lincoln 1989:249)

Summary of validity from the naturalistic perspective

For the most part, naturalistic validity has to do with the degree to
which the evaluator and the evaluation audience place trust and confidence in the evaluation analysis and conclusions. In comparison to the
positivist notion of validity as a congruence between evaluation findings
and some objective reality, this perspective on validity emphasizes the
degree to which the evaluator and evaluation audience can agree on,
and feel confident about, an interpretation of the evaluation findings.
For naturalistic evaluation, the practical validity problem of "How do
I know when I have it?" does not reduce to a list of threats that must
be ruled out or overcome. In fact, the distinction between "What is it?"
and "How do I know when I have it?" tends to blur, as both validity
problems, definition and verification, become integrated into the process
of naturalistic evaluation. In other words, when we do naturalistic evaluation, our attempts to uncover the multiple perspectives, to reconcile
or explain conflicting judgments, and to articulate clear and usable
plans for action, all serve both to define our validity goals and to dem-

onstrate how well we have reached them. However, there is still a need for explicitly stated standards for judging the validity of naturalistic evaluation. The accumulated standards from Guba and Lincoln, and others, expressed as techniques, are presented in Table 3.2 as a summary of this perspective.

Conclusions: Validity from the two perspectives

From the positivistic perspective on validity, there is an objective truth that can be known, at least approximately. Validity, from this perspective, "is understood to be an imperfect approximation to truth about a real world that exists independently of human knowers" (Shadish et al. 1986:33). We can improve the accuracy of that approximation by designing and conducting our evaluation so that it rules out factors that threaten our ability to determine that correspondence objectively. This is the essence of experimental and statistical control: to establish the conditions that allow us to be certain about our conclusions concerning, in the case of program evaluation, the relationship between the program and our observations of its effect. This was discussed earlier as internal and statistical conclusion validity.

The naturalistic perspective on validity concentrates on investigating the research setting without attempting to manipulate or control for anything. Rather than pursuing a correspondence between research findings and an objective truth, validity from this perspective refers to an interpretation that cannot be considered "independently of human knowers" but, rather, is embedded in and shaped by people's experience. In the case of program evaluation, this means reaching a consensus on the nature and value of the program. I have discussed multiple perspective negotiation as a technique for enhancing this sense of validity as well as Guba and Lincoln's related techniques such as member checks and open negotiation session

Positivistic evaluation has the tendency to value internal validity at the expense of the representativeness needed for external validity. This was discussed in Chapter 2 as a hallmark of a certain stage of early program evaluation efforts in applied linguistics. However, in addition to Berkowitz and Donnerstein's (1982) opposition to this criticism, presented earlier in this chapter, Fielding and Fielding (1986) pointed out that artificial experiments are not necessarily incapable of representing other contexts, and naturalistic settings are not necessarily representative of other contexts to which we might wish to generalize. Both of these criticisms seem to reflect a predominantly positivistic view of validity and generalization. That view relies on sampling – random or representative – as the key to generalizability. If proper sampling is

TABLE 3.2 TECHNIQUES FOR NATURALISTIC VALIDITY

- *Prolonged engagement:* immersion in the evaluation setting, establishing rapport, trust, and understanding of program participants

- *Persistent observation:* identification of the most relevant elements of the evaluation setting

- *Peer debriefing:* discussion of evaluation findings, conclusions, and tentative hypotheses by the evaluator and a "disinterested peer"

- *Negative case analysis:* using "nonfitting" data to revise evaluation hypotheses

- *Reactivity:* documenting the changes in what is being observed that are due to the presence of the researcher or evaluator, as well as the changes that occur in the researcher or evaluator as a result of being in the evaluation setting

- *Search for rival explanations:* formulating alternative explanations to the ones that have emerged preliminarily, such as logical reversals

- *Progressive subjectivity:* recording of initial evaluator interpretations and understandings ("constructions"), and subsequent constructions, to avoid giving too much "privilege" to evaluator expectations

- *Member checks:* checking the developing evaluation findings with the members of the evaluation setting

- *Thick description:* providing an extensive and careful description of the evaluation context

- *Triangulation:* gathering, reconciling, and explaining of data from several sources and/or from different data-gathering techniques

- *Multiple perspective negotiation:* arriving at evaluation conclusions as a result of a consensus among persons from different perspectives in relation to the program

- *Permanent audit trail:* documenting the decisions made by the evaluator, the connection of evaluation conclusions back to the original sources, the identification of stakeholder constructions of the meaning of the evaluation, the degree to which their understanding of their own and others' constructions is increased, and the extent to which action is taken and program participants are empowered

- *Open negotiation session:* conducting a formal negotiation of evaluation recommendations and agendae for action with all stakeholders represented equally by skilled negotiators

- *Follow-up assessments:* judging the degree to which evaluation-prompted actions are taken

carried out, and if internal validity allows us to be certain about the conclusions of our experiment, then those conclusions will be generalizable to the population our sample represents. Naturalistic evaluation, in contrast, tends to focus on an in-depth understanding of its setting as "representativeness," and to generalize on a case-by-case basis. Unlike positivistic external validity, this sense of generalization lies in the naturalistic notion of transferability.[6] In the positivistic approach to validity, then, the responsibility for generalization lies with the evaluator or evaluation designer. Naturalistic validity assumes that the responsibility for generalization lies with the various evaluation audiences who may wish to transfer the findings of the evaluation to their own settings. Of course, as Guba and Lincoln's criteria indicate, the naturalistic evaluator is responsible for providing the thorough documentation necessary for such transfer attempts.

Another key feature of positivistic validity is the concept of causality. The traditional notion of cause as an objective entity, existing outside the human mind but capable of being perceived by it, albeit imperfectly, remains central to positivistic validity. Although some may allow that naturalistic evaluation can enhance our understanding of the context in which these causal relationships exist, positivistic certainty about cause is tied to experimental evidence. As Campbell (1986:71) puts it, "[naturalistic methods], while improving the validity of our research, nonetheless provide less clarity of causal inference than would a retreat to narrowly specified variables under laboratory control." A naturalistic conceptualization of causality is somewhat different from this account. I believe that constructivists,[7] as well as critical theorists, would for the most part agree with Erickson's (1992:9) definition of causality:

> . . . an interpretive notion of cause is the sense or meaning an action or set of actions has to those who act that way. In trying to discover how an action makes sense to the persons doing it, the interpretive researcher is trying to identify something like cause.

Likewise, House et al. (1989) refer to Searle's (1983) "intentional causation" and point out that the traditional positivistic concept of the program as the cause and student achievement as the effect may not be sufficient for the kind of information necessary in program evaluation. When attempting to apply this notion of causality to evaluation research, it is impossible, at least in field settings, to reach conclusions about the value of a program based purely on experimental evidence, and it becomes critical to include the validity of the inferences that are

6 Firestone (1993) presents an additional approach to generalization in naturalistic research, involving extrapolation from sample to theory.
7 For comparison, see Guba and Lincoln's (1989:97–98) discussion of causality as mutual simultaneous shaping.

drawn by teachers from their classroom experiences. This would seem to be especially true from the naturalistic perspective.

Although the positivistic and naturalistic perspectives on validity do differ in these critical ways, some similarities can also be identified. Fielding and Fielding (1986), for example, draw a parallel between how naturalistic evaluation makes use of negative case analysis and the inclusion of the random error term in positivistic analysis. That is, positivistic analysis assumes a certain amount of error, or negative cases, and assigns it the status of being "random." In naturalistic analysis, since negative cases are not presumed to be random, this "error variance" is dealt with explicitly, with all exceptions being used to revise the hypothesis concerning the relationship between program and effect until all of the data fit the hypothesis.

Another similarity they find between the two perspectives with respect to validity concerns the problem in positivistic analysis of statistically significant results that are not *meaningful*. This is parallel to the situation, in a naturalistic evaluation, in which there are no negative cases but there is only a small amount of evidence to support the interpretation being drawn.

Despite these similarities, I think it is clear that important differences remain between positivistic and naturalistic perspectives on validity. The key notion that this chapter has put forward is that validity is establishing what counts as evidence. We have seen that the criteria for doing this can differ depending on the research perspective being used. Acknowledging these differences, some researchers (e.g., Howe 1988) nonetheless feel that the paradigms can be combined. This approach, at least in the sense of combining evaluation methods that appear to be linked primarily with one paradigm or the other, is discussed in Chapter 8.

The next two chapters present models, or designs, for conducting program evaluation. Chapter 4 presents positivistic designs – experimental and quasi-experimental – that will be illustrated with brief vignettes from language education contexts. Chapter 5 presents designs that follow from the naturalistic paradigm, with vignettes parallel to those illustrating the positivistic designs.

4 Positivistic designs

In Chapter 2 I discussed the quantitative–qualitative debate, or paradigm dialog, and in Chapter 3 I outlined the differences between the two perspectives in terms of what counts as evidence, or validity. This chapter presents a series of models, or designs, for carrying out a program evaluation from the perspective of the positivistic paradigm. By the term *paradigm* I mean, as indicated in Chapter 2, more than just a particular type of evaluation data and a particular set of ways to collect and analyze it. In addition, this choice of data and analysis implies the philosophical basis and conceptualization of validity discussed in Chapters 2 and 3 as positivistic. For the most part, the following discussion recapitulates the classic research designs of Campbell and Stanley (1966) and Cook and Campbell (1979), which still form the basis for positivistic evaluation (cf. Fitz-Gibbon and Morris 1987). Readers who are already familiar with these designs may wish to skip ahead to the final design presented in this chapter, labeled here as structural models.

When the evaluation audiences and the evaluation goals require evidence of whether, or how well, the program is working, the traditional choice of a design for gathering and analyzing information is one of a set of experimental or quasi-experimental designs originally presented and discussed by Campbell and Stanley (1966). These designs all involve the gathering of quantitative data (i.e., a measurement of some kind) from what is traditionally referred to as the experimental group and, if possible, from what is traditionally referred to as the control group. The experimental group receives what is traditionally referred to as a treatment; the control group either receives nothing or receives a different type of treatment. Both groups, when there are two groups, are measured in some way, generally with some type of test. This measurement can occur at different time periods: before and after the treatment, after the treatment only, or at several times before, during, and after the treatment. Measurements taken before the treatment begins are traditionally referred to as pretests; those taken after the treatment are traditionally referred to as posttests.

In the case of program evaluation, the treatment is the program, the experimental group is the program students, and the control group is

TABLE 4.1 DESIGN 1: TRUE EXPERIMENTAL WITH PRETEST

	Pretest	*Treatment*	*Posttest*
Program group	Test A	Program	Test B
Control group	Test A	Comparison	Test B

the group of students to which the program students are being compared. The measurements that are taken generally involve pencil-and-
paper tests of achievement in the content being taught by the program.
In the case of language education programs, these may be language
proficiency tests, whose content is related to the program curriculum in
a general way, or they may be language achievement tests, whose content is taken specifically from the program curriculum. The choice of
test or tests to use in the evaluation is an important and complex matter,
especially when the control group is receiving a curriculum that is significantly different from the experimental, or program, group. These
issues are discussed further in Chapter 6.

I will present three main factors that distinguish positivistic designs:
whether or not there is a control group, how students are assigned to
a group, and how many measurements are taken. These designs will be
illustrated with brief vignettes describing contexts relevant to applied
linguistics.[1]

True experimental designs

The *true experimental* design has a control group and has randomly
assigned the students either to the experimental, program group or to
the control group. There are two types of true experimental designs,
distinguishable by the presence or absence of a pretest (see Tables 4.1
and 4.2).

As an example of Design 1 in the context of applied linguistics, consider the following description.

An ESL institute is considering a new computer-assisted instruction (CAI)
module for teaching reading skills. Since the module is rather expensive, the
company selling it has agreed to let the institute try it out over a 15-week
instructional term. Students from the level that receives a traditional reading
skills component are given student identification numbers. The students are

1 The formulation of these designs and vignettes is patterned after Fitz-Gibbon and
  Morris (1987), who discuss program evaluation in a more general educational
  context.

TABLE 4.2 DESIGN 2: TRUE EXPERIMENTAL WITHOUT PRETEST

	Pretest	Treatment	Posttest
Program group	No	Program	Test A
Control group	No	Comparison	Test A

then assigned to either the CAI module (the program group) in the computer lab or the traditional reading skills curriculum (the control group) in the normal classroom. The company that produces the CAI software also provides a test of reading skills that has two equivalent, reliable, and valid forms for pretest and posttest.

Design 2 has the same description as Design 1, except for the following:

Although the CAI module company is able to provide the software for reading skills instruction, it does *not* have any test instruments. The institute decides to develop its own test, to be given at the end of the instructional term.

Notice that in these designs, the students have been randomly *assigned* to either the program being evaluated or to the control group. For true randomization, the students would also have to be randomly *selected* from the population of interest. That is, if we are interested in making claims about the potential success of this program with university-level ESL students in a large, metropolitan area, we would need to randomly select the students to be assigned to either the program or the control group from all of the possible university ESL students in that area. This, of course, is generally unrealistic as an expectation for evaluation and research within existing language education program contexts. Although it is more within the realm of possibility, random assignment is also a luxury that is rarely available in field settings (i.e., naturally occurring programs).

Another consideration when attempting random assignment is the *unit of analysis*. Classrooms can sometimes be more readily assigned in a random fashion than can students, and it may be that the evaluator is interested primarily in results at the classroom level rather than at the individual student level. Large scale evaluations sometimes randomly assign schools or even school districts to the experimental program or control group. When randomly assigning these units, however, care needs to be taken that there are no characteristics that differentiate the representative units before the evaluation takes place. That is, perhaps the classrooms being considered for random assignment are for one reason or another different in their level of proficiency prior to assignment. In this case, care needs to be taken that "blocking" (see

Kirk 1982), or some similar design precaution, is taken before assigning classes to groups. For example, the classrooms could be blocked into high-proficiency, mid-proficiency, and low-proficiency (perhaps on the basis of pretest scores) groups, and then one or more classrooms from the high-proficiency block would be assigned to the program, and the same number from that block would be assigned to the control group.

Assuming that pretests and posttests are available, is there any reason to choose Design 2 over Design 1? The answer is yes. A posttest-only design allows the evaluator more time to find or develop a test that will be both valid and appropriate for the particular evaluation context. The use of this design also prevents the possibility of the pretest sensitizing the students to the measure of program effects. This was discussed as the testing threat to validity in Chapter 3. Sensitizing the students to the measure of program effect can be especially problematic with attitude assessment, where clues to "what the evaluators are looking for" can be given to the students who take the pretest.

Although the use of random assignment improves the evaluation from an experimental point of view, objections can be raised. For example, some program participants and audiences may object to the chance nature of determining who receives a program that may affect the students' lives in important ways. There are solutions to the various objections to the use of randomization, however. If it turns out to be beneficial, the program can be given to the control group at a later date. Another solution has been termed the *borderline control group* (see Fitz-Gibbon and Morris 1987). In this case, a determination of the students at the lowest level of proficiency – those most in need of an improved instructional program – is made, and all of those students are given the program. Those "on the borderline" of need are randomly assigned to the program or control group for the evaluation experiment.

Quasi-experimental designs

In the other extreme situation with respect to the control group factor, no control or comparison group is available for the evaluation. This results in a *quasi-experimental* design, in which all students receive the program along with a pretest and posttest, as presented in Table 4.3. The following vignette presents a context for the use of this design.

An ESL teacher at a community college has developed a typology for the English article system that she feels will improve her students' ability to self-correct for article errors in their final drafts of academic essays. She compares the number of article errors on the final drafts of two essays, one written before the 10-week module on the article system and one after.

TABLE 4.3 DESIGN 3: QUASI-EXPERIMENTAL WITH PRETEST AND POSTTEST

	Pretest	*Treatment*	*Posttest*
Program group	Test A	Program	Test B

With this design, it is impossible to make a statement about what would have happened to the students without the effect of the program being evaluated. The evaluator can state only that there was, or was not, an effect on the students. It cannot be claimed that the program *caused* the effect, and the relationship between the program and the measure of student gains between pretest and posttest can not be estimated.

There are situations, such as the one depicted in the vignette, when being able to conduct some sort of a study is better than doing nothing at all. There are also ways in which this design can be strengthened in order to make qualified conclusions possible. One method is to use reliable and valid *norm-referenced tests*[2] (NRTs) of language proficiency. These tests are useful in comparing the results of the program group with established results on the same test for a sample of students representing a similar level of language ability over a similar amount of instructional time. There are potential problems with this approach, however, which have to do with the very nature of NRTs. Such tests tend to be insensitive to the achievement of instructional objectives and may, in fact, mask significant gains in achievement. This is primarily a result of the fact that NRTs are designed to work with a *normal distribution* (the famous bell-shaped curve), where one-half of the students taking the test score "below average." The use of NRTs for quantitative data collection and analysis is discussed at greater length in Chapter 6.

An alternative type of test that can overcome some of the problems associated with NRTs is the *criterion-referenced test*[3] (CRT). These tests, by design, are more sensitive to the effects of instruction than are NRTs and help to define what is being measured in the evaluation with greater precision (cf. Bachman 1989). Using this approach, Design 3

2 Norm-referenced tests are designed to measure a student's ability in relation to other students taking the same test. They are developed in order to exhibit certain statistical properties and are valued primarily for their ability to "spread out" the distribution of the scores on the test. For a more complete discussion, see Popham (1978), Hudson and Lynch (1984), and Brown (1989b).

3 Criterion-referenced tests are designed to measure a student's ability in relation to a behavior or skill that is defined in detail. They are developed in order to be sensitive to the effects of instruction, even at the expense of certain statistical properties such as internal consistency estimates of reliability. For a more complete discussion, see Popham (1978), Hudson and Lynch (1984), and Brown (1989b).

TABLE 4.4 DESIGN 4: NONEQUIVALENT CONTROL GROUP WITH PRETEST AND POSTTEST

	Pretest	*Treatment*	*Posttest*
Program group	Test A	Program	Test B
Control group	Test A	Comparison	Test B

could be further strengthened by developing a variety of tests to measure the various components of the program's curriculum. The most important aspect of using CRTs in program evaluation is that it leads to an investigation and detailed description of the instructional goals of the program as an integral part of the test development process.

Another method is to take advantage of the fact that there is only one group of students to investigate and attempt multiple measurements during the evaluation. This could be supplemented by a more descriptive look at the program, asking such questions as "Is there a good match between the theoretical basis for the program and the way in which it is actually implemented?" Student achievement tests could be supplemented with measures of "perceived importance" of the program goals by students and teachers. The effect that the program is having on different types of students (e.g., looking at gender, native language, previous experience with the language being studied) could also be investigated. To the extent that these approaches involve qualitative data and analysis in a quantitative design, the evaluation makes use of a mixed strategy or mixed design. These types of approaches are discussed in Chapter 8.

Between the true experimental, randomly assigned control group and the quasi-experimental, no-control group is the *nonequivalent control group* design. Given the fact that most program evaluations are carried out in field settings and cannot use true random assignment to program and control groups, this design is extremely useful for evaluators. It is the same as Design 1 except that the students are in preexisting, intact groups, such as naturally occurring classrooms, and these groups have not been randomly assigned to the program and control conditions (see Table 4.4). As an example of this type of design, consider the following.

The Spanish Department at Serendipity College has decided to implement the "natural approach" in their beginning-level classes. They convince the other major university in the city (which remains committed to a program using a more traditional, grammar-based textbook) to give a test of proficiency in Spanish as a foreign language to their beginning-level students before and after the instructional term. The same test is given as a pretest and posttest for the natural-approach program at Serendipity.

TABLE 4.5 DESIGN 5: TIME SERIES WITH PROGRAM GROUP ONLY

	Time 1	*Time 2*	*Time n*	*Treatment*	*Time n + 1*	*Time n +2*	*Time n + ...*
Program group	Test 1	Test 2	Test *n*	Program begins	Test *n* + 1	Test *n* +2	Test *n* + ...

In this design the pretest plays a crucial role: It is used to attempt a statistical adjustment of potential preexisting differences between the program and control groups. Recall that an important effect of randomization is that it results in groups that have (theoretically) no systematic differences other than the treatment (program versus control) that they will receive. With the nonequivalent control group design, the program and control groups may have systematic differences other than the treatment (e.g., one group might be more proficient than the other prior to the evaluation) that will confound the interpretation of the evaluation results. Specific statistical techniques for removing this confounding effect are presented in Chapter 6.

A design similar to Design 3 is the *time series design* with a program group only. This design allows for stronger interpretations, however, because of the amount of pretest and posttest administrations. That is, we can establish the trend (over multiple test administrations) of student growth prior to the program and examine whether this trend is altered by the program, or whether the program merely continues the preexisting trend (see Table 4.5).

The following vignette describes a context for Design 5.

A high school EFL teacher in Japan is interested in trying a "project-based syllabus" with his students. The principal will allow him to try it out with one class only and wants some convincing evidence that it works better than the textbook approach used in the rest of the school. The teacher gives his students a test of their EFL proficiency (the one used by the high school to place students into EFL classes) three times, every 2 months, before beginning the project-based syllabus. He then administers the same test three times, every 2 months, after beginning the syllabus.

With this design it is difficult to say with certainty that the observed results would not have occurred without the program. It is a good design, however, for monitoring students' progress over time and for making qualified conclusions concerning the effect of the program on this progress. If, for example, there is a marked increase in test scores from time n (before program implementation) to time $n + 1$ (after program implementation), as compared with the increase from time 1 to time 2 or time 2 to time n, one reasonable conclusion would be that the pro-

TABLE 4.6 DESIGN 6: TIME SERIES WITH NONEQUIVALENT CONTROL GROUP

	Time 1	Time 2	Time n	Treatment	Time n + 1	Time n +2	Time n + ...
Program group	Test 1	Test 2	Test n	Program begins	Test n + 1	Test n +2	Test n + ...
Control group	Test 1	Test 2	Test n	Comparison	Test n + 1	Test n +2	Test n + ...

gram was at least in part responsible for the "jump" in scores. Another indication that the program was having a positive effect on student achievement would be an increase in the *rate* of increase from test to test (e.g., test $n + 1$ to test $n + 2$) following implementation of the program.

The addition of a nonequivalent control group results in the combination of Design 4 and Design 5 (see Table 4.6). The following vignette illustrates Design 6.

IBM has been preparing sales representatives and technicians for assignment in China; the preparation includes a language program for nonproficient speakers of Chinese. Their San Francisco branch has contracted with an applied linguist who wants to use a language teaching program based on the principles of "suggestopedia." IBM wants to compare how this approach will work in comparison to its previous program and hires an evaluator who proposes to gather interview data simulating business discussions in Chinese with the trainees before and after the introduction of the new program. Interviews will be conducted at both the San Francisco branch (suggestopedia) and the Los Angeles branch (traditional) twice before and twice after the introduction of the suggestopedia program in San Francisco. The interview data will be rated for proficiency in Chinese by native Chinese-speaking businessmen, who will be trained to use the interview rating scale.

Rather than coming up with new designs per se, evaluators in the positivistic paradigm instead work on refining analytic techniques such as the use of structural models (Cordray 1986). This results in a quasi-experimental design that remains, in essence, like that of Design 4 or, possibly, Designs 5 and 6. The difference is that this design includes data gathering in addition to pretest and postttest (or time series observations). Multiple measures (on different variables, using different instruments) of the subjects at posttest time are taken; exogenous factors, variables other than the program that influence the outcome measures, are also quantified; factors that may influence how the students experience the program while it is being implemented are measured;

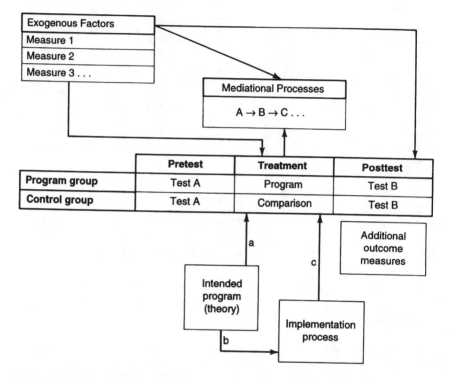

Exogenous factors: variables that influence the outcome, beyond the treatment

Mediational processes: factors that influence the receipt of the treatment and processes that mediate within the treatment as delivered

Path a: theoretical basis for the treatment

Path c: treatment as implemented

Path b × c: relationship between the intended (theoretical) treatment and the treatment as delivered

Figure 4.1   Design 7: structural modeling. (Adapted with permission from Cordray 1986:18.)

and the match between the program as intended and its actual implementation is monitored. Figure 4.1 depicts this design.

A vignette for Design 7 would be exceedingly complex; most likely it would deserve a chapter of its own. However, I offer the following as an "add-on" to the vignette for Design 4.

In addition to the pretest and posttest given to the natural-approach program at Serendipity College and the traditional, grammar-based textbook approach at their neighbor college, the Spanish Department at Serendipity College hires an external team of evaluators to review the program documentation for the natural approach and to monitor its implementation. They also gather background data on the students at both colleges on variables presumed to influence and define their Spanish proficiency. They also hire a team of specialists in Spanish as a foreign language to measure and analyze variables that their expertise and knowledge of current theory identify as potentially intervening in the process of instruction in both settings. Student achievement at posttest time is measured using a variety of test instruments.

In addition to the increased complexity of the design, the analysis of the resulting data becomes much more complex as well. Because of the statistical complexity, structural modeling is beyond the scope of this text, but I discuss a related analytic technique, value-added analysis, in Chapter 6.

These positivistic designs, then, are intended to provide a preordained structure for the gathering of evaluation data. As I have tried to illustrate with the vignettes, the data gathered may be qualitative in nature (e.g., the interview data in Design 6), but the analysis of those data will ultimately involve quantification for the purposes of making a comparison between the program group and the comparison group, or between pretest and posttest.

Techniques for data analysis in these positivistic designs are presented in Chapter 6. The next chapter discusses various designs for evaluation using the naturalistic perspective.

5 Naturalistic designs

As applied linguists begin to accept the naturalistic paradigm as a legitimate and viable approach to research in their field, they can draw upon various models that have been developed in the educational literature on naturalistic program evaluation. In this literature, *model* is sometimes used interchangeably with *design*. When a distinction is made, model tends to be seen as the more grandiose of the two terms and refers not only to the plan for collecting the information on which the evaluation will be based, but also to its theoretical basis and purpose. I will continue with the terminology of the preceding chapter, using design to refer to specific plans for collecting and interpreting data to evaluate language education programs. These designs have, in most cases, been given names or labels and, in addition to specifying steps to take and considerations to make, represent particular motivations, both theoretical and practical, for doing program evaluation.

The responsive model

As early as 1967, Stake was advocating an approach to program evaluation that has been characterized as *transactional* (Patton 1980). Originally referred to as the *countenance model* (Stake 1967), it was refined into the *responsive model* (Stake 1975). The model is transactional in the sense that it responds to the requirements that various audiences have for information concerning the program. The basic steps that define this design are:

- Establish an overview of the program activities.
- Discover the purposes and concerns of the program.
- Conceptualize the issues and problems found in the program.
- Select observers and instruments (if needed) for the evaluation.
- Thematize the findings of the observations and measurements (if taken).
- Prepare a formal report (if necessary).

Underlying these steps is an essentially naturalistic perspective and methodological approach toward evaluation. The evaluator investigates the program as it exists in the field and arrives at an understanding of its process and objectives through observation and interaction with program participants. That is, the understanding of the program comes from ideas and themes that emerge from the collection of information about the program, rather than from concepts and hypotheses formulated prior to the evaluation. As the evaluator arrives at an understanding of the program, these findings are shared with the evaluation audience(s) in the form of brief narratives, case studies, or displays of program outcomes. This interaction further guides the information gathering and helps to refine the description of the program. The information that is gathered from the various observers is always presented to both program participants and the evaluation audience(s) in order to have them assess its accuracy. This is basically the same idea that was discussed as multiple perspective negotiation in the section, "Validity from the naturalistic perspective," in Chapter 3.

It should be noted that this design allows for the possibility of measurement and quantitative data. However, quantitative data gathering, as well as the production of a formal written report, takes place only if this type of information is needed by the evaluation audience(s). As an essentially naturalistic design, the key features of the responsive model are its attention to program process, its acceptance of and reference to different value perspectives when interpreting the information being collected, and its responsiveness to the needs of the various audiences for the evaluation.

The following vignette illustrates one possible realization of this design in an applied linguistics context.

The American English Institute at State University has been asked by the Dean of Humanities to evaluate its program. Knowing that the program is a dynamic one, involving a complex interaction of administrators, teachers, and students, the institute staff selects an evaluator who specializes in naturalistic, qualitative evaluations. The evaluator plans to begin the evaluation by setting up a series of meetings with the program participants and the dean, recording these sessions on audiotape and taking notes. The focus of the meetings will be to discover why the evaluation is needed from their different perspectives. After reviewing the recordings and notes, the evaluator plans to formulate a list of preliminary issues and themes that seem to characterize the program and the purpose of the evaluation. It is anticipated that some of these themes will suggest the need to gather more detailed information in the language classrooms. For example, it may be that the use of academic material taken from other courses offered at the university (the institute is using something it calls a content-based instruction approach) may warrant closer investigation to discover how this is perceived by the participants and the dean. The evaluator then plans to check her interpretations in a meeting with a selected group of administrators, teachers, and students.

Based on the reactions of these people, she will revise the framework and write a report to be submitted to the dean.

The illumination model

Another design, which is sometimes referred to as transactional because of its focus on multiple audience perspectives and program process, is the *illumination model* of Parlett and Hamilton (1976). This design is characterized by an in-depth investigation of the program and its surrounding context.

The aims of illuminative evaluation are to study the innovatory program: how it operates; how it is influenced by the various school situations in which it is applied; what those directly concerned regard as its advantages and disadvantages; and how students' intellectual tasks and academic experiences are most affected. It aims to discover and document what it is like to be participating in the scheme, whether as teacher or pupil, and, in addition, to discern and discuss the innovation's most significant features, recurring concomitants, and critical processes. In short, it seeks to address and to illuminate a complex array of questions. (Parlett and Hamilton 1976:144)

One way of describing the role of the illuminative evaluator is as a social anthropologist investigating a unique subculture – the program. This is especially evident in the attempt to provide a participant's perspective on the program. An illuminative evaluation is carried out in three phases:

1. An initial period of observation in which the evaluator seeks to become acquainted with the day-to-day reality of the program in its entirety
2. A gradual focusing and more intensive look at specific program issues, themes, and events
3. A synthesis of the findings in an attempt to describe and explain the program in terms of its general underlying principles

Following this design, the evaluator starts with the broad context of the program, looking at it holistically, and then proceeds to select from the issues and events that emerge from the program those that will provide the focus for a more thorough and intensive investigation. Parlett and Hamilton refer to this move from the holistic perspective to selected issues and events as progressive focusing. An important benefit of this approach is that unusual and unpredicted occurrences or aspects of the program can be discovered and given appropriate attention.

A variety of data-gathering techniques are advocated within the illuminative model: observation, interviews, questionnaires, tests, and program documentation. Observational techniques are critical to the first phase of this design. The evaluator keeps an ongoing record of observed events such as the day-to-day activities within the program, faculty and student meetings, and special events such as "open houses." These observations take the form of recorded discussions with and between program participants, and are designed to capture the actual language that characterizes these interactions. Other observational notes are taken concerning such things as patterns of attendance and student and teacher behavior in the classroom.

The other major data-gathering technique, interviewing, is employed to gain an understanding of the various perceptions of the program. One important question that confronts an evaluator attempting to make use of interviews is "Whom do I interview?" From the illumination model perspective, those persons who may offer special insight into the program or who are in unique or important positions are prime interview candidates. This approach to sampling, *theoretical sampling*, might result in the selection of students who are especially successful or those who have failed, newly appointed teachers, the persons who developed the program's curriculum, and the program director for interviewing.

Although observation and interviewing occupy key positions in the illuminative evaluator's data-gathering strategy, questionnaires and tests can also provide useful information that supports or qualifies interpretations that come from the more qualitative data. This design does not, however, make use of quantitative data from questionnaires and tests in isolation. Questionnaires present several difficulties that are not always discussed, such as the possibility of ambiguity when attempting to interpret the tallied responses. This problem exists with open-ended, qualitative questionnaires as well as more quantitative ones, of course, underscoring the difficulty of designing such instruments. Questionnaires are also, at times, regarded as impersonal and frustrating by respondents who are trying to express complicated perceptions or attitudes. Tests, such as multiple-choice exams, are similarly difficult to design and interpret and, using the illumination model, are useful only within the larger context of evaluation information.

Documentation and background information on the program provide further data for the illuminative evaluation. Minutes of meetings, funding proposals, consultant reports, example program materials, and registrar's office files can be examined in order to obtain a historical perspective on the program. These information sources can also lead to new evaluation questions, such as "Why were certain features of the original program proposal abandoned?"

Because it allows for the use of quantitative data and analysis as well as qualitative, it might be argued that the illumination model is a mixed design rather than a naturalistic one. However, the quantitative elements of Parlett and Hamilton's design are given such a secondary role and the authors argue so vehemently against the use of the traditional experimental design for evaluation that their model must be seen as championing the naturalistic perspective. It is, perhaps, better thought of as a mixed strategy (to be discussed further in Chapter 8).

The following vignette illustrates the illumination model as a potential design for program evaluation in applied linguistics.

A team of consultants from Applied Linguists Incorporated (ALI) is hired to evaluate a program that is training elementary school teachers to become users of American Sign Language (ASL). The team decides to participate in a regular 6-week summer training session (along with the elementary teachers). During the initial 2 weeks the ALI team will keep journals and field notes independently. They will then have a session in which they will decide upon the most important issues and events that have been identified in this initial period. These issues and events will then guide their investigation during the remaining weeks of the program. The team will begin to informally interview the elementary school teachers in the program, recording these interviews as field notes. They plan to have one team member attend the weekly staff meetings of the program administration. The recordings from these meetings and existing documentation concerning the objectives and rationale for the program will be reviewed and discussed by the ALI team. These sessions will suggest a further narrowing of the original guiding issues. For example, one feature of which they are already aware may prove to be critical: the absence of "native signers" from the program. The team is also interested in examining the data from the exit exam that is given at the end of each session. They plan to examine these data after taking the exam themselves. They also plan to schedule a certain number of observations of trained elementary school teachers who are assigned to classrooms using ASL. After completing their training, the ALI team will have a series of sessions in which they arrive at a portrait of the program and how it relates to the elementary school context.

Goal-free evaluation

Both the responsive model and the illumination model attempt at one point or another to gather information on the stated goals and objectives of the program being evaluated. Although this information may be gathered qualitatively, it nonetheless represents an investigation of the a priori goals of the program being considered. Scriven (1972) proposed an alternative vision, which he labeled *goal-free evaluation*. The accepted wisdom of the positivistic approaches to evaluation is that there can be no evaluation of a program without explicitly and clearly specified goals for that program. Goal-free evaluation challenges this notion in a fundamental way, proposing that an evaluation should be conducted by someone who is external to the program and that this evaluator should make every effort to avoid learning about the stated program goals. With this design, the evaluator does *not* meet with the program staff to discuss the goals of the program, and program documentation is similarly avoided. Instead, the goal-free evaluator attempts to discover the actual effects of the program and to match these against demonstrated needs within the context of the program. The focus is not on what the program is trying to accomplish, but on what is actually happening.

In order to accomplish the task of goal-free evaluation, the evaluator must rely almost exclusively on observational and interview techniques for data gathering. The information needed to ascertain actual effects and demonstrated needs requires a detailed description of what is observed and a great deal of direct contact with the program and its participants. Somewhat like the illumination model, goal-free evaluation is inductive and holistic, allowing an understanding of the program to emerge from the data rather than trying to fit the data to some preexisting blueprint for the program. If the evaluator focused on stated program objectives, certain effects or characteristics might be overlooked or left unanalyzed. Goal-free evaluation allows these unexpected aspects of the program and its processes to surface and be given their appropriate importance and value, rather than being seen as secondary, side effects, or ignored. The goal-free evaluator is also arguably less biased in his or her perceptions of the program and can perhaps make greater claims for objectivity and independence.

An example of goal-free evaluation in applied linguistics might be the following.

The Cultural Association in Montreal is offering a new language instruction program in Spanish as a foreign language. An arts educator who will be visiting the association on a fellowship has been asked to include an evaluation of this program as part of her duties. She asks not to be told anything about the program prior to arriving. Upon arrival she plans to enroll in a beginning-level Spanish class (she speaks English and French, but Spanish will be a new second language). Her initial observations will suggest certain of her classmates with whom she will schedule interviews to discuss their perception of the class and their reasons for taking it. At the end of an instructional module, the evaluator will present a verbal report of her findings to the association staff.

The judicial model

Certain evaluation researchers have used other professional and academic disciplines as metaphors (see Smith [1981] for more recently proposed naturalistic designs. Owens (1973), Levine (1974), and Wolf (1975) used the law profession to develop an approach to evaluation known as the *judicial model*. The evaluation basically follows the pattern of a trial hearing. First, the evaluator generates the important issues for the program through a series of interviews with a sampling of program participants. Next, the evaluator limits the number of issues to be considered and prioritizes them for the hearing. Advocates are then appointed by the chief evaluator to argue the opposing sides of each issue. These advocates, like trial lawyers, prepare formal arguments for the hearing, gather evidence (documents or exhibits, depositions from witnesses), and identify persons who will testify for the hearing. During prehearing sessions, the advocate teams review the hearing process and agree on ground rules. The hearing is patterned after actual courtroom processes and includes an administrative officer and a jury that review the information presented by the advocate teams and carry out the tasks that the chief evaluator assigns.

The main purpose of this process is to arrive at a consensus concerning what can be labeled the "truth" in each evaluation issue. With both advocate teams presenting the strongest cases they can for each side of an issue, the design presumes that a clear understanding of what is taking place in the program will emerge. The end result will depend on what the jury is asked to do – normally they will decide on which argument they find most convincing and make recommendations for program change based on those decisions. Other jury tasks and evaluation goals are, of course, possible.

This approach to evaluation might take the form of the following vignette.

The French department at a major U.S. university has implemented a new instructional program using the "Silent Way" approach. There is less than universal agreement among the faculty on the value of this approach, so the department chair has asked a member of the applied linguistics faculty to conduct an evaluation. The evaluator proposes a version of the judicial model and assigns himself the role of judge. Proponents of the Silent Way are assigned the role of advocates for the program; faculty who favor the previous curriculum are made advocates against the program. A preliminary meeting with the department is held to agree on procedures for eliciting and presenting evidence, and to decide on additional roles needed for the "trial." After considering the evidence presented during the trial, the judge/evaluator writes a formal decision on the program. The department then holds a meeting with the evaluator to discuss the decision before putting the fate of the program to a departmental vote.

The connoisseurship model

Another proposed evaluation design uses art and literary criticism as its metaphor. Eisner's (1975) *connoisseurship model* takes the notion of *critical guideposts* (values and concepts that have come to be identified and accepted in a particular discipline) as the basis for an evaluation. These guideposts are assumed to be accessible by *connoisseurs*, who have training and experience in the discipline and who, therefore, are considered to be the appropriate instruments for measuring the qualities and effects of a program related to that discipline.

With this design, as with the illumination model, the evaluator acts as a social anthropologist, using his or her training and experience to arrive at perceptions and interpretations of what is happening in the program. In this case, however, the training and experience are related to the values of the subculture being investigated. The evaluator is already a member of this subculture and uses his or her familiarity with its values (the critical guideposts) to make interpretations and judgments. In this sense the model is less inductive than designs such as the illumination model or goal-free evaluation, because the critical guideposts provide a predetermined framework against which the program is evaluated. However, this framework is not so much a formulation of what the program is supposed to look like as it is a set of sensibilities for interacting with the program in order to arrive at an accurate description of it.

The connoisseurship model also allows for differences in interpretation across connoisseurs and even for a given connoisseur, depending on how they choose to interact with the program. Different connoisseurs may apply a different selection of critical guideposts and arrive at different evaluations of the same program. Normally this would seem to provide problems for addressing the issue of validity, for if more than one evaluation is possible, then which evaluation is "the truth"? However, from the naturalistic perspective of this design, there are many different ways to view a program, and all of them have their own claims to the truth.

In an applied linguistics context, this design might appear as the following vignette.

The English for Specific Purposes (ESP) project at the University of Technology in Mexico has been asked by the government to provide evidence of the program's value. The project decides to hire a well-known expert on ESP from a leading British university. This expert agrees to undertake an evaluation of the program, on the condition that she not be forced into the "jet-in, jet-out" mode (see Alderson and Scott 1992). It is agreed that the evaluator will spend a year with the project, at the end of which time she will submit a report to the government, in order to meet their evaluation deadline. The evaluator interviews program participants, observes classes, attends project meetings, and participates in the general activities of the university. Her report will evaluate the project in relation to a model for ESP that she has developed in numerous scholarly publications.

Other metaphors for naturalistic evaluation

Besides law and art criticism, several other disciplines have been explored as metaphors for evaluation. Smith (1981) presented a series of such metaphors, including investigative reporting, architecture, geography, philosophy, and watercolor painting. Each of these disciplines was investigated by a different researcher in an attempt to find parallel and useful concepts and methods for program evaluation.

Investigative reporting was depicted as an attempt "to expose to the public those hidden conditions or behaviors that are inimical to the public interest" (Smith 1981:62). Investigative reporters collect self-report data in the field and analyze documentary files using the techniques of document tracking, key interviews, and file summaries. A program evaluator can apply these techniques to the documentation of the program and the key participants in the program.

In the context of applied linguistics, this metaphor could be realized in the following fashion.

A teacher at the Chinese Institute in New York is given 3 months of released time in order to conduct an evaluation of the Chinese as a foreign language program. He aligns himself with the institute's newsletter staff and carries out a series of interviews with students, other teachers, and institute administrators. He uses the interview data, in combination with information from the newsletter's files and documents solicited from the institute, to write a series of articles for the newsletter, ranging from the history of the language program to emerging events such as a teachers' strike. At the end of the 3 months, he compiles a report for the institute based on his investigations.

In Smith (1981:62), architecture was characterized as seeking "to define in physical form a solution to functional and psycho-social needs. Architects perform conceptual analyses of alternative forms and existing structures, critique design solutions, gather information on human needs, examine the use of building structures, and consider both professional and lay reactions to structures. In the same mode, a program evaluator can analyze alternative forms for an existing program, while collecting information on program needs and criticisms of the existing program.

The following vignette illustrates this metaphor for an evaluation in the context of applied linguistics.

The director of the Action English Academy decides to consult her friend, an architect, concerning an evaluation of the academy's ESL program, which has been requested by the agency funding its curriculum development. After visiting the program and interviewing participants, the architect will draw up a set of schematics that depict the program's physical space and its use. She will discuss her interpretations of the effects of these patterns on the instructional program, with the director providing clarifications and interpretations of her own. The two of them will then interview various teachers and students in the program to verify the initial interpretations and to arrive at possible solutions to problems they have uncovered. The director will then prepare a report that elaborates this structure-program use analysis in light of larger curriculum issues.

A geographer tries "to understand the spatial aspects of natural and social phenomena," wrote one of Smith's researchers (Smith 1981:63). This requires going into the field to collect data through interview techniques and the collection of documentary data. The geographer also makes use of statistical analysis and cartographic analysis. Operating within this metaphor, an evaluator could gather field data on the spatial aspects of a program and examine their effects on the processes of the program context.

This metaphor might be realized as follows.

The president of The Bilingual School arranges for an evaluation of his program with an evaluator who proposes a geography metaphor. The evaluator will spend 3 weeks exploring the school, taking photographs, making notes and sketches, and observing the day-to-day workings of the program. He will also interview teachers and students, asking each to draw a "map" of the program for him. The photographs, notes, sketches, and participant maps will be assembled into a visual presentation accompanied by tape-recorded conversations and the evaluator's own narrative, describing the program and making recommendations for change.

In philosophical analysis an attempt is made "to clarify the meanings of terms basic to philosophical inquiries" (Smith 1981:63). This is accomplished through the analysis of naturally occurring language use and meaning. Techniques for such analysis are: the use of clear cases, contrary cases, and borderline cases; describing contexts; using metaphors; and mapping concepts. In the context of program evaluation, the evaluator would apply these techniques to investigate program terminology as a means of clarifying a description of the program.

Using this metaphor as a guide, an evaluation in an applied linguistics context might resemble the following vignette.

The Institute for Pronunciation Improvement is applying for a grant that requires periodic evaluation reports. The evaluator they hire has received permission to develop a comprehensive list of key terms that are used as part of the instructional process. These terms will be compiled following a 4-month period of classroom observation by the evaluator. The analysis of these terms as used in the classroom will then form the basis of the evaluator's description of the program and her recommendations for program improvement.

Perhaps the most unusual, if not amusing, of Smith's metaphors for evaluation comes from watercolor painting. A watercolorist seeks "to create a representation that can become a shared message or experience" (Smith 1981:63). Although this conceptualization may not be shared by all watercolorists and artists, it is useful for the context of program evaluation. Seen in this light, the artist starts with a basic set of techniques for the use of watercolors, studies the work of others, and proceeds through a process of trial and error with color and form combinations. This requires sustained effort over time. As a metaphor for evaluation, this suggests that one approach would be a dedication of many years of study and experience with a particular type of program, refining one's ability to make evaluative interpretations over time. It also suggests the perhaps obvious need for comparative evaluation studies – looking at the program evaluation research conducted by others in similar contexts.

As an illustration of the potential use of this metaphor, consider the following vignette.

An ESL teacher has been given responsibility for developing an evaluation report for the program in which he teaches. He goes to the library and finds evaluations of similar programs reported in the TESOL literature. Taking from these studies the techniques that appear to be relevant and feasible in his setting, the teacher/evaluator plans to conduct some preliminary data collection and analysis. These preliminary findings will be presented at the local TESOL convention. Using feedback from this experience, the teacher/evaluator plans to revise the evaluation, gather more data, and reanalyze. He hopes to convince the program administrators to allow him to conduct a similar evaluation each year. Along with this continued experience, the teacher/evaluator plans to initiate a special-interest section in his local TESOL chapter, to discuss and refine methods for the evaluation of similar ESL programs with his colleagues.

This chapter has presented a variety of designs for program evaluation from the naturalistic perspective and has illustrated them with vignettes from applied linguistics contexts. Transactional designs, such as Stake's and Parlett and Hamilton's, look closely at program process and attempt to respond to the needs of the program audience(s). Goal-free evaluation seeks to get at the reality of a program by avoiding contact with the stated goals or objectives. Many other designs borrow perspectives and methods from other disciplines as diverse as the law and watercolor painting.

All of these naturalistic designs pay considerable attention to the processes, to what is happening inside a program. Some of the designs are more selective than others in terms of what is being looked at, for example, the judicial model and the geography metaphor. Although they can serve a variety of different purposes, from adjudicating specific issues to portraying the program in its entirety, they all are based on description and the interpretation of qualitative data with a naturalistic perspective on validity. To varying degrees, these models are exploratory, inductive, and holistic, allowing the evaluation findings to emerge from the data-gathering process rather than testing an a priori hypothesis.

Chapter 7 presents methods for putting these naturalistic designs into practice and for arriving at conclusions that will be useful for program evaluation. In the next chapter, however, I return to the positivistic paradigm in order to present techniques for collecting and analyzing data that come from the designs discussed in Chapter 4.

6 Quantitative data gathering and analysis

Data gathering

If, as an evaluator, you choose to make use of a positivistic, quantitative design, one of the most important concerns you will have will be identifying an appropriate test or other instrument for measuring the effect of the program. Finding the appropriate test is further complicated when the evaluation design includes a control, or comparison, group. In that case, the test needs to be appropriate for the curricula of both the program and comparison group. As we saw in Chapter 2, a test of oral/aural skills will tend to show an audio-lingual program to be superior to a grammar-translation program, whereas a test of grammar and reading skills will tend to show the opposite. Tests that do not favor one program type over another may be insensitive to the types of effects that occur in either, and result in a finding of no differences where important differences actually exist.

As introduced in Chapter 4, there are two basic types of tests that can be drawn upon for the purposes of program evaluation: norm-referenced and criterion-referenced tests. Norm-referenced tests (NRTs) are what are usually referred to as standardized tests (cf. Beretta 1986c). They are usually developed using large samples of examinees, resulting in published statistical properties that are used for comparison across groups of examinees and administrations of the test. The key element to NRTs, however, is the fact that they are developed by selecting items that are successful at maximizing variability in the total test score distribution. This means the items must be able to accentuate the differences between students, to spread out the scores on the test. The ideal item for an NRT is one that only half of the examinees get correct (assuming that most of those examinees are getting most of the other items correct, as well). If the goal of measurement is to discriminate among the students taking the test – in other words, to rank-order them – then this type of measurement is appropriate.

NRTs have been criticized, however, for their lack of sensitivity to instruction (Popham 1978; Bachman 1981, 1989; Hudson and Lynch 1984; Beretta 1986c). This insensitivity on the part of norm-referenced measurement is especially problematic for program evaluation and stems from its conception of the ideal item and its requirement of normal distribution, the bell-shaped curve. Under this approach to measurement, items that are answered correctly by most of the examinees will tend to be eliminated from the test during the statistical analyses that inform test development. This means that items that measure aspects of the program that all or most students have mastered will not be judged as useful items for NRTs. Although we would not expect students to answer these items correctly before instruction, we assume that they will be able to do so *after* instruction. If an NRT is used as the posttest in a program evaluation, it will not have sufficient items that capture this instructional effect.

Criterion-referenced tests (CRTs), on the other hand, are designed to be sensitive to instruction. This type of measurement emphasizes the content validity of the test, and selects items for their ability to measure mastery of a well-defined skill or behavior (Popham 1978). The ideal item in this case is one that discriminates between examinees who have received instruction on the skill being tested and those who have not. The purpose of a CRT is to assemble a set of items that will determine whether each examinee has mastered the skill being tested, not to be able to spread out the score distribution. An individual's score on a CRT is interpreted in relation to the *criterion*, the skill or knowledge being tested, not in relation to the other individuals taking the test. Rather than maintaining the bell-shaped curve of test score distribution, CRTs assume that the distribution will change as a result of instruction, with more scores bunching up at the high end of the test scale following a successful program.

This is not to say that there is no role for NRTs in program evaluation. Even though some have completely discounted their value for evaluation (e.g., Beretta 1986c), there are convincing arguments for their use, especially when they are used along with CRTs (cf. Sax 1974). NRTs do allow us to compare students from different program contexts, even though we need to examine the tests carefully for bias toward one type of curriculum over another. If we conduct a program evaluation and discover that the innovative curriculum group is performing better than the comparison group, we do not necessarily know that the innovative program was truly effective. The test may have shown that the program students responded better to instruction than the comparison group did, but both curricula may have been ineffective. Being able to reference the test scores to external norms, to scores achieved by students in a proven curriculum, would give us a stronger interpretation of the effect of the program being evaluated.

In addition to the type of measurement – norm-referenced or criterion-referenced – the program evaluator is also faced with the choice of test *content*. Basically, there are again two choices. The evaluator can attempt to find or construct a test that is neutral in content (i.e., favoring neither the program group nor the comparison group), or the evaluator can find or construct tests that represent the curricula of the program and the comparison group. The problems with both of these choices have already been discussed in Chapter 2. In the Pennsylvania Project, the use of the "neutral" MLA tests was ultimately found to be misleading by Valette (1969), whose content analysis demonstrated that even supposedly neutral tests can be biased toward one instructional approach or another. In the Bangalore Project evaluation, the program group did better on the tests that were specific to the content of the innovative curriculum, and the comparison group did better on the tests that were specific to the content of the traditional curriculum, leaving the evaluators without a principled way of determining whether the program group had outperformed the comparison group.

Although there is no true solution to this dilemma, the best course of action seems to be to use multiple test types. There should be tests that are sensitive to, and representative of, the curricula of both the program and the comparison groups. If the typical pattern of each group doing better on its own test emerges, the evaluator may be able to examine the relative performance on the two tests in comparison to performance on a test of more neutral content. For example, it might be found that although each group performed better on its own test, and that these differences were statistically significant, the program group's significant difference was of a greater magnitude than the comparison group's. If performance on the content-neutral test also favors the program group, to the extent that the content can be shown to be truly neutral, this would be evidence of a positive effect for the program.

Data analysis

With the true experimental designs, data analysis can be approached in a relatively straightforward manner using the analysis of variance (ANOVA). However, given the fact that most program evaluations, conducted in field settings, do not conform to the requirements of randomization, I will present techniques for analyzing quantitative data in quasi-experimental designs. The techniques that I have chosen to illustrate represent a range of statistical sophistication, so that even evaluators with extreme math phobia will, I hope, be able to find something approachable in this chapter. Furthermore, I have chosen techniques with which I have firsthand experience, primarily in the evaluation of the Reading English for Science and Technology (REST) project at the University of Guadalajara, Mexico.

Chi-square analysis

Perhaps the most accessible technique for analyzing quantitative data for the purposes of program evaluation is the *chi-square procedure.* The advantages of this technique are that it can be easily calculated by hand, and it can be used with data that do not meet the requirements of more sophisticated statistical procedures. This accessibility, however, is accompanied by a loss of ability to make claims about cause-and-effect relationships. Chi-square establishes a relationship, or dependence, between two or more variables that have been quantified as frequencies. In the case of program evaluation, the variables are the program and student achievement (as a measure of program effect). Chi-square allows us to establish whether or not there is a significant relationship, or dependence, between the program and student achievement, but it does not allow us to say for certain that the program *caused* the achievement. However, in the absence of test data that can be used with statistical procedures that can establish cause-and-effect relationships, or when used in conjunction with such procedures, chi-square can be used as a qualified indication of program effect.

The use of chi-square for program evaluation purposes requires a comparison group, a pretest, and a posttest. The students are placed into independent categories based on whether they are in the program group or the comparison group, and whether they increased or did not increase their score from pretest to posttest (Henning 1987). The independence of these categories is an important assumption of the chi-square procedure; that is, each student can be put into one and only one category: +program/+increase, +program/−increase, −program/+increase, or −program/−increase. These categories, which represent a two-by-two chi-square table, are depicted in Table 6.1.

The chi-square statistic (χ^2) is calculated from the frequencies that occur for the categories in Table 6.1. Because there are only two levels, or possibilities, for each variable in the table, a special calculation that incorporates an adjustment known as the *Yates correction factor* is used.[1] This calculation is

$$\chi^2 = [N(ad - bc - N/2)^2] \div [(a + b)(c + d)(a + c)(b + d)]$$

where N is the total number of students, program and comparison, and

1 This is the correction factor that is automatically given by statistical packages such as SPSSX and SPSSPC, despite some research (e.g., Camilli and Hopkins 1978) suggesting that it may be overly conservative, producing inaccurate estimations. If the sample size is small, resulting in expected frequencies of less than 5 in some cells, you may also consider using Fisher's exact test (Hays 1973).

TABLE 6.1 CHI-SQUARE TABLE FOR PROGRAM EVALUATION

	No gain[a]	Gain[a]
Comparison	a	b
Program	c	d
$N = a + b + c + d$		

[a]No gain: no increase from pretest to posttest. Gain: an increase from pretest to posttest.

TABLE 6.2 CHI-SQUARE TABLE FOR REST PROJECT EVALUATION

	No gain	Gain
Comparison	16[a]	37[b]
Program	8[c]	91[d]

a, *b*, *c*, and *d* represent the frequencies of students in each cell, or category, in the chi-square table.

The following example, using data from the evaluation of the REST project, can be followed like a recipe. I calculated the gain scores using the UCLA English as a Second Language Placement Exam (ESLPE) as pretest (September 1985) and posttest (February 1986).

1. Separate the students into program group and comparison group. In the REST project evaluation, there were 99 students in the program group and 53 students in the comparison group, who took both the pretest and the posttest.
2. For each student, subtract the pretest score from the posttest score (= the *gain score*).
3. If the gain score is positive, assign the student to the "gain" group; if the gain score is zero or negative, assign the student to the "no gain" group.
4. Total the number of program group students in the "gain" group and in the "no gain" group; total the number of comparison group students in the "gain" group and in the "no gain" group. The totals from this step are the frequencies, given in Table 6.2.
5. Substitute the frequencies from the table into the chi-square formula:

$$N = a + b + c + d = 16 + 37 + 8 + 91 = 152$$
$$ad = 16 \times 91 = 1456$$
$$bc = 37 \times 8 = 296$$

$$N/2 = 76$$
$$a + b = 53$$
$$c + d = 99$$
$$a + c = 24$$
$$b + d = 128$$

$$\chi^2 = \frac{152(1,456 - 2961 - 76)^2}{(53)(99)(24)(128)}$$

$$= \frac{152(1,084)^2}{16,118,784}$$

$$= \frac{178,608,512}{16,118,784}$$

$$= 11.081 \quad \text{chi-square observed}$$

$$\alpha = .05, = 3.84 \quad \text{chi-square critical}[2]$$

Notice that the chi-square observed value is greater than the chi-square critical value – in this case, we can conclude that there is a dependence between the program and student achievement (as measured by pretest to posttest gain). Reviewing the chi-square data in Table 6.2, we can see that the dependence is expressed as a greater relative frequency of program students in the "gain" group as compared to the comparison group. Although this does not imply that the program *caused* the greater achievement, the significant dependence can be taken as an indication of positive program effect.

Effect size analysis

The effect size technique makes use of a statistic referred to as the *effect size*, which involves the difference of two group mean scores divided by the standard deviation for one or the other of the groups (or a pooled estimate for the two groups combined). The use of this statistic can be found in Stallings et al. (1979), where the mean gain scores for the program and comparison groups and the standard deviation for the comparison group were used to calculate the effect size. Effect size analysis can also be used with mean scores from a posttest (cf. Dunkel 1991); however, this presumes equivalence between the program and comparison groups at pretest time.

Although it is somewhat more complex than the chi-square statistic,

---

2 The chi-square critical value is obtained from a table of such values, available in most statistics textbooks, for example, Hatch and Lazaraton (1991). The *alpha level* (α) is traditionally set at the indicated .05. This value is the *p*, or probability value, which for 1 degree of freedom – the case for all 2 by 2 chi-squares – will reference a 3.84 critical value in the chi-square table. For a more complete discussion of chi-square, see Hatch and Lazaraton (1991:406–24).

TABLE 6.3 REST PROGRAM EVALUATION: EFFECT SIZE ANALYSIS

	Mean gain score	*Standard deviation*
REST students	8.31	
Comparison group	3.49	5.25
Effect size = 8.31 − 3.49 ÷ 5.25 = 0.918		

calculation of the effect size is still relatively accessible and easy to illustrate. The recipe is as follows:

1. Subtract the pretest from the posttest scores for all students (= the gain score).
2. Calculate the mean gain score for the program group; calculate the mean gain score for the comparison group. (A mean score is equal to the sum of all student scores in the group, divided by the number of students in the group.)
3. Calculate the standard deviation of the gain scores for each group, separately.[3]
4. Subtract the mean gain score for the comparison group from the mean gain score for the program group.
5. Divide the result of 4 by the standard deviation of the comparison-group gain scores.

Steps 1 through 5 can be represented by the following formula:

$$\text{Effect size} = (\overline{X}_P - \overline{X}_C) \div s_C$$

where

$\overline{X}_P$ = program-group mean gain score
$\overline{X}_C$ = comparison-group mean gain score
s_C = gain score standard deviation for comparison group

Using this analysis, an effect size of 0.5 is considered a moderate effect for the program, and an effect size of 1.0 is considered strong. Table 6.3 presents this technique with data from the REST project evaluation. Once again, I calculated the gain scores using the ESLPE as pretest (September 1985) and posttest (February 1986). Table 6.3 shows a relatively strong effect for the REST program, using the total score on the ESLPE as a measure of student achievement.

3 For a discussion of, and formula for, the standard deviation, see Hatch and Lazaraton (1991:173–78).

Standardized change-score analysis

Standardized change-score analysis, proposed by Kenney (1975), also requires a comparison group, a pretest, and a posttest. It is especially appropriate for program evaluations where the selection to program or comparison group is based on intact groups (i.e., preexisting groups, nonrandomly assigned) and where the groups may be growing, or learning, at different rates. Although its statistical logic derives from some relatively complex mathematics, the analysis ultimately reduces to a pair of *correlation coefficients*, which can be accessed via computer.

The two correlation coefficients that need to be calculated are the correlation of treatment group (i.e., program or comparison) with the pretest and the correlation of treatment group with the posttest; or, the strength of the relationship between the group to which a student belongs and his or her scores on these tests. If the program has no effect, then we would expect these two correlations to be equivalent. On the other hand, if the program does have an effect, then the relationship between treatment group and student achievement should become stronger at posttest time, resulting in a larger coefficient than existed in the correlation of treatment group and pretest.

For example, if there is no relationship between whether a student is in the program group or comparison group and his or her score on a test, the correlation coefficient will be low. This is what we expect at pretest time – we expect no major differences in the number of program students and comparison group students who do well on the pretest. The correlation coefficient might be perhaps .20. When a program is successful, however, we expect a significant increase in the number of program students who score high on the posttest, as compared with the performance of the comparison group students. This stronger relationship between treatment group and test scores is expressed in a higher correlation coefficient – perhaps as high as .70. These two correlation coefficients are clearly not equivalent. The relationship between treatment group and test scores has become significantly stronger and, if the program students are in fact scoring higher than the comparison group at posttest time, then this is evidence that the program has had a significant effect on student achievement. This change in the correlation coefficients can be tested for statistical significance, as well, using a *t-test* developed by Hotelling (1940; Guilford and Fruchter 1978).

The recipe for this technique is as follows:

1. Calculate the correlation between treatment group and pretest scores.
2. Calculate the correlation between treatment group and posttest scores.
3. Compare the two correlation coefficients; if the posttest correlation is higher, compare the group mean scores on the posttest.

4. Perform Hotelling's *t*-test[4] to see if the two correlation coefficients are significantly different; if they are, and the program group has the larger posttest mean score, the program has had a significant effect.

I also used this technique in the REST project evaluation, from which the following data are taken. The analysis used the ESLPE as pretest (September 1985) and posttest (February 1986).

Correlation of treatment group and pretest   = .1478
Correlation of treatment group and posttest = .3897
Hotelling's *t* = 5.17   (significant at α = .05)

Thus, the REST program, using this analysis, was found to have a significant effect on student achievement, as measured by the ESLPE total score. (The group mean scores on the posttest were higher for the REST group.)

Analysis of covariance (ANCOVA)

As mentioned earlier, if students are randomly assigned to the program and comparison groups, the program effect can be measured by testing the significance of the difference in the two mean scores (program group mean and comparison group mean) with an analysis of variance (ANOVA). However, if randomization is not possible, then we need some method for eliminating the potential effect of preexisting differences between program and comparison group students on our results. One way of doing this is by design – we can select pairs of students, one from each group, who are equivalent at pretest time (i.e., who do not have preexisting differences). For example, we could use the pretest to select students from the program and comparison groups who have the same scores, and then compare the posttest scores of students in these two groups. Such *matched pairs* can be tested for significance using a *t*-test or ANOVA. The problem with this approach is that the results of the *t*-test or ANOVA are affected by a statistical property known as *regression to the mean*. Simply stated, this means that individual scores on a test from one time to the next will tend to get closer to the mean

4 The formula for Hotelling's *t*-test is

$$t_r = (r_{12} - r_{13}) \sqrt{\frac{(N - 3)(1 + r_{23})}{2(1 - r_{23}^2 - r_{12}^2 - r_{13}^2 + 2r_{23}r_{12}r_{13})}}$$

where

r_{12} = correlation of pretest with treatment group
r_{13} = correlation of posttest with treatment group
r_{23} = correlation of pretest and posttest
N = total number of students in both groups

(Guilford and Fruchter 1978:164)

of the group, regardless of the actual changes in ability. If the two groups we are trying to match have preexisting differences, they tend to represent different score distributions, with different means. When we match students from the two groups using the pretest, with their different group means on that test, and then compare them on the posttest, the comparison is confounded by the fact that the students in each pair are regressing toward different means. The students in the group with the higher pretest mean will have been selected (for matching) from the lower part of that group distribution. The students in the group with the lower pretest mean will have been selected from the upper part of that group distribution. The student scores (posttest) in the higher (pretest) group will tend to become higher, regardless; and the scores in the lower group will tend to become lower, regardless. The actual effect of the program will be lost in the statistical shuffle.

ANCOVA represents a statistical, as opposed to a design, method for eliminating the effect of preexisting differences. It actually represents a more sophisticated and precise form of matching, in which the problem of regression to the mean is significantly reduced, primarily because it uses the entire sample from both groups, rather than just those pairs for whom equivalent scores can be found. This technique combines ANOVA and *linear regression* in order to reduce the experimental error and bias in estimating the effect of the program when using quasi-experimental designs. ANOVA estimates the effect of the independent variable (the program versus the comparison group) on the dependent variable (the measure of student achievement, or posttest). ANCOVA adjusts the dependent variable (posttest) to remove the effects of another variable, called the *covariate*, which is believed to affect the dependent variable in some systematic fashion. In program evaluation, this covariate is taken to be the preexisting differences in ability between the groups, and it is measured by the pretest.

The problem with using ANCOVA to adjust for preexisting differences is that the statistical model is based on several restrictive assumptions. In fact, one of these assumptions is random selection and assignment to treatment, the very condition that we lack in the quasi-experimental design and that we are trying to correct for with ANCOVA. However, this assumption is meant to ensure that the covariate and the independent variable are statistically independent. ANCOVA can still be recommended for reducing error and bias when randomization is not employed, especially when the groups being compared are not extremely different to begin with. Furthermore, we can, and should, check to see that there is no statistical interaction between the covariate and the independent variable, before interpreting the results of ANCOVA.

There are several other assumptions underlying the use of ANCOVA,

TABLE 6.4 ANCOVA TEST FOR INTERACTION

30-APR-92	SPSS RELEASE 4.0 FOR IBM OS/MVS		
14:40:22	U C L A / O A C	IBM 3090/600J	MVS/ESA

***********A N A L Y S I S   O F   V A R I A N C E – DESIGN 1*

TESTS OF SIGNIFICANCE FOR TOTAL2 USING UNIQUE SUMS OF SQUARES

SOURCE OF VARIATION	SS	DF	MS	F	SIG OF F
WITHIN + RESIDUAL	4145.46	148	28.01		
TOTAL	6339.60	1	6339.60	226.33	000
TREAT	198.83	1	198.83	7.10	.009
TREAT BY TOTAL	27.57	1	27.57	.98	.323

4960 BYTES OF MEMORY ARE NEEDED FOR MANOVA EXECUTION.

where TOTAL 2 = DEPENDENT VARIABLE/POSTTEST
      TOTAL   = COVARIATE/PRETEST
      TREAT   = INDEPENDENT VARIABLE/REST VERSUS
                CONTROL GROUP

including the requirement that the covariate is measured without error (see Elashoff [1969] for a more complete discussion of these assumptions). As discussed in Chapter 3, the violation of the assumptions underlying a statistical model can threaten internal, or, more specifically, statistical conclusion validity. Because of this, some experts feel that the use of ANCOVA is almost never justified (e.g., Winer 1962). In certain program evaluations, the use of ANCOVA has been demonstrated to lead to underestimation of the program effect (Campbell and Erlebacher 1970). Others, however, feel that it may be used, with care given to the choice of covariate and the interpretation of results (e.g., Cronbach et al. 1975; Kirk 1982).

Tables 6.4 and 6.5 present the ANCOVA results for the REST project evaluation, using the ESLPE pretest from September 1985 (TOTAL) as the covariate, the ESLPE posttest from February 1986 (TOTAL2) as the dependent variable, and REST versus control group membership (TREAT) as the independent variable. I used the SPSS-X (Release 4.0 for IBM OS/MVS) MANOVA procedure, which is designed to test for the interaction of the covariate and independent variable. Table 6.4 presents the output from that procedure.

Since the covariate (TOTAL) by independent variable (TREAT) interaction is not significant (significance of $F = .323$), we may proceed to a test of the effect of the independent variable on the dependent variable (TOTAL2), adjusted for the covariate. Table 6.5 presents output from the SPSS-X MANOVA procedure, which is designed to test this effect.

TABLE 6.5 ANCOVA FOR REST VERSUS CONTROL GROUP

30-APR-92	SPSS RELEASE 4.0 FOR IBM OS/MVS		
14:28:59	U C L A / O A C	IBM 3090/600J	MVS/ESA

***********A N A L Y S I S   O F   V A R I A N C E – DESIGN 1*

TESTS OF SIGNIFICANCE FOR TOTAL2 USING UNIQUE SUMS OF SQUARES

SOURCE OF VARIATION	SS	DF	MS	F	SIG OF F
WITHIN CELL	4173.02	149	28.01		
REGRESSION	7675.56	1	7675.56	274.06	.000
TREAT	1062.97	1	1062.97	37.95	.000

where TOTAL2 = DEPENDENT VARIABLE/POSTTEST (ADJUSTED FOR THE COVARIATE)
TREAT = INDEPENDENT VARIABLE/REST VERSUS CONTROL GROUP

This analysis demonstrates that there was a positive effect (significant at $\alpha = .05$) for the REST program (September 1985 – February 1986) on student achievement as measured by the dependent variable (ESLPE) (significance of F for the independent variable "TREAT" = .000).

Value-added analysis

A technique called value-added analysis, developed by Bryk and Weisberg (1976), allows an evaluator to estimate the effect of a program beyond that expected as a result of natural growth. In the context of evaluating language education programs, natural growth refers to the amount of language learning that would be expected if no language program were being offered. As I mentioned in Chapter 4, this analysis is related to structural modeling and makes use of linear regression, requiring a variable that can be used to represent natural growth. One such variable is chronological age. As an indicator of growth, or maturation, in the absence of instruction, the chronological age of individual students at the time of the pretest becomes the baseline measure. The use of linear regression calculates a regression weight that expresses the degree to which the pretest score can be explained by the natural growth variable (e.g., chronological age). If we subtract the pretest score from the posttest score, the result is the *observed growth*, which includes natural growth and growth due to the program. By subtracting the natural growth regression weight (adjusted for how much time has passed between the pretest and the posttest) from the observed growth, we arrive at an estimate of how much the students achieved, or grew, because of the program alone.

In using this technique, the choice of a variable to represent natural growth is obviously critical to arriving at interpretable and defensible results. Bryk and Weisberg (1976:151) recommend using the length of foreign language study to model natural growth in the evaluation of a foreign language program. A distinct advantage of this technique is that although it can make use of a comparison group, it does not require one. In this sense, the natural growth variable is acting as a stand-in for the comparison group.

Value-added analysis can also be made more precise by including various background variables in addition to the natural growth variable to determine individual growth rates. In the evaluation of language education programs, background variables such as native language, sex, or chronological age could be used. These are incorporated into the analysis in a manner similar to that in which the natural growth variable is used: A regression weight is found for the interaction, or product, of the natural growth variable and each background variable in relation to the pretest, and these regression weights are used along with the natural growth weight to adjust the differences between pretest and posttest scores (for a more complete description of this procedure, see Bryk et al., [1980]). There is also a technique for testing this value-added estimate for statistical significance (Mosteller and Tukey [1977: chap. 8], discussed in Bryk et al. [1980:16]).

This technique, although it is appealing because it can be used without a comparison group, has not gone without criticism. Burstein (1981), for example, points out that it does not deal with certain critical measurement problems such as biases associated with measurement errors, changing metrics, and the changing structure of behavior. He does, however, agree that the technique is a useful one if it is used as part of a multiple quantitative strategies approach.

I used value-added analysis in the REST project evaluation, with the ESLPE as pretest (September 1985) and as posttest (May 1986). The results of this analysis can be depicted as follows:

Value added = posttest − pretest − natural growth estimate

where

REST posttest group mean score = 43.85
REST pretest group mean score   = 33.21
natural growth estimate   = 1.94
value added due to REST program = 8.70

I interpreted this result as a gain of 8.7 points (out of a possible 88 points on the ESLPE) by the REST students beyond what would have

TABLE 6.6 FACTORS AFFECTING QUANTITATIVE ANALYSIS

Comparison group	Yes	No
Normal distribution score data	Effect size Standard change score ANCOVA Value added	Value added
Non-normal distribution frequency data	Chi-square	

been expected of them if they had been exposed to their natural university instructional environment without the REST program. I then checked this result with the aforementioned statistical test and was able to claim that it was significant at the level of probability set for the experiment (.05).

Conclusion

When the evaluation goals and audience call for a rationalistic design, the data gathered can be analyzed using the techniques presented in this chapter. Depending on one's experience with such statistical analysis, the more sophisticated techniques (e.g., ANCOVA, value added analysis) should be readily accessible using either a mainframe computer or personal computer hardware and software. Factors other than statistical expertise that affect the ability to use these techniques are design related – availability of a comparison group – or data related – existence of interval-like score data and normal distribution. Table 6.6 indicates these factors in relation to the techniques discussed in this chapter.

In those contexts where only frequency data or non-normally distributed data and no comparison group exist, quantitative analysis is limited to nonparametric tests of the significance of pretest – posttest differences (see Hatch and Lazaraton, 1991). Without a comparison group, of course, the observed change from pretest to posttest is difficult to interpret – it may have occurred in spite of the program, or an even greater change may have resulted from an alternative program.

In those contexts where normally distributed score data exist but no comparison group is available, the evaluator may also choose to compare the program group's pretest – posttest change to published accounts of such testing in other, relevant programs. Here is a case where data from norm-referenced tests can be helpful. For example, in the REST project evaluation, the use of the ESLPE, an NRT-like exam, allowed me to compare the scores achieved by REST students with how those scores would have placed them in the UCLA ESL curriculum. I was then able to report to interested audiences (e.g., the UCLA administrators responsible for partial funding of the project) that after a 10-week period of instruction at REST, students had moved from the entry-level ESL class at UCLA to the next level (which would presume successful completion of 10 weeks' worth of ESL instruction at UCLA). Since my initial reporting, it has been pointed out that a comparison of these two curricula may not be a reasonable one (Alderson and Beretta 1992:97–98). However, I still maintain that this is the type of comparative information that, in the absence of a more directly relevant comparison, can help evaluators communicate a sense of the program's achievements to their audience.[5]

There are, of course, other techniques that can be used for analyzing quantitative data for program evaluation purposes. The use of structural modeling, a more complex form of the type of analysis presented in this chapter as value-added analysis, was mentioned in Chapter 4 (see Cordray 1986). Econometricians have also provided extremely sophisticated techniques for *selection modeling* (see Cain 1975; Rindskopf 1986), in which information about how the students were selected into the experimental program or the control group is used to analyze post-test outcomes. Another potential technique is *categorical modeling* (see Hatch and Lazaraton, 1991:509–21), which can allow the evaluator to consider important background and process variables that may not lend themselves to quantification as interval score data. It is hoped, however, that the techniques I have presented in this chapter will provide a solid basis for analyzing quantitative data in most applied linguistics program evaluation contexts. In the next chapter, I discuss the gathering of qualitative data and techniques for its analysis and interpretation.

5 The UCLA audience for the REST evaluation, for example, found the ESLPE comparative data informative, since they had a fairly good sense of the general level of proficiency indicated by scores on the ESLPE. This comparison was aided by the fact that the REST curriculum and the UCLA ESL curricula are similarly focused on English for Academic Purposes.

7 Qualitative data gathering and analysis

Overview

If the audience and goals for your evaluation have led you to choose a naturalistic design, you will need to plan on spending a significant amount of time gathering the evaluation data. These data can be recorded in a variety of ways and can describe the program from a variety of points of view. The most common methods for gathering and recording data in a naturalistic program evaluation are observation, interviews, journals, questionnaires, and document analysis. The data that are recorded by these methods can come from a variety of sources: students, instructors, administrators, evaluators, and other persons who interact with the program. Once the data have been collected, you will need to approach the analysis and interpretation of these data with the same systematicity and thoroughness required to gather them. Unlike quantitative analysis, there are no set procedures, defined in detail, for the evaluator to follow. There are, however, basic principles and guidelines that inform the analysis of qualitative data for the purposes of program evaluation. The procedures that I suggest in this chapter consist of the following stages: developing a thematic framework, organizing the data, coding the data, reducing the data, and interpreting the data. These analytic procedures are not a linear series of steps, but are accomplished in an iterative fashion – for example, they include returning to the coding stage after reducing the data.

Because the data are recorded, summarized, and interpreted in the form of words and not numbers, they may be suspect in the eyes of certain audiences. Often such data are referred to as *anecdotal*, or *subjective*, implying that they are not as meaningful or convincing as quantitative data. I hope that the discussion of naturalistic perspectives on validity has made it clear that these charges are unfair and reflect a misunderstanding of this approach to evaluation. However, naturalistic evaluation is still the "new kid on the block," as far as applied linguistics is concerned, and lingering biases need to be kept in mind when reporting results. The techniques presented in Chapter 3 for enhancing naturalistic validity provide a principled way of carrying out such eval-

uation, for explaining the nature of the data, and for justifying conclusions to evaluation audiences.

Data gathering

Observation

TRAINING

To gather evaluation data by observation is a deceptively simple task.
The famous baseball player and infamous thinker, Yogi Berra, is re-
puted to have said, "It's amazing just how much you can observe by
just sitting and watching."[1] Successful observation requires something
more than just sitting and watching. Although this is something most
qualitative researchers can agree upon, there is little information available on how observers should be trained. An exception to this rule can
be found in Levine et al. (1980), who provide a useful description of a
course in observation skills. Abilities that these researchers consider to
be important include question-generating skills, the use of flexible and
efficient note-taking and coding devices, observer frame-of-mind preparation skills, and being able to "see more to see."

The observation training techniques that Levine et al. use in their
course are instructive for evaluators who may need to do their own in-
service training. As an illustration of this potential, I offer the following
vignette from my experience with adapting the Levine et al. techniques
for use in a graduate seminar on program evaluation. The following
text may strike the reader as a radical shift in tone. In part, this is due
to the reporting of personal experience; in part, it reflects the "first-
person" nature of this type of data gathering.

I use Levine et al.'s techniques as an introduction to data gathering
through observation, the first technique being the "sudden shock" exercise. Before discussing observation techniques, I send the students out
to an environment of their choice (suggesting a public space where lan-
guage-program-like activity might occur – lecture classrooms, or an area
where students gather and interact) and ask them to "observe and take
notes." The most common complaint upon returning from this assignment is "I didn't know what to take notes on; there was so much going
on all at once!" As a class, we then discuss the various problems and
frustrations encountered in the sudden shock exercise.

As a follow-up activity, I give the students a list of questions to serve
as an observation guide.[2]

1 This quotation, like many of my other favorites, was first brought to my attention
  by Peter Shaw.
2 Adapted from LeCompte and Goetz (1982b).

1. *Who?* (How many participants? What are the individual and group identities?)
2. *What?* (What are the participants doing? Are there repetitive behaviors? Irregular behaviors? What are the resources used in activities? How are the activities organized? What is the nature of participant interaction: Roles evident? Status? Content of conversation? Form of language used? Who talks? Who listens?)
3. *Where?* (What is the physical setting like: sights, sounds, smells, tastes, and feelings?)
4. *When?* (Time of interaction? Length?)
5. *How?* (Overlaps with *what*: What is the interrelationship of events and activities? How is change initiated and managed? What norms and rules can be observed?)
6. *Why?* (Overlaps with *what* and *how*: What meanings can be attributed to activities and events?)

The students are then provided with something to observe. I have primarily used simulations – either planned, live interactions in the classroom, or videotaped excerpts from language classrooms. In the case of the videotape observation simulation, I play a 5-minute segment of the tape and ask the students to write down a list of everything there is to observe. This is followed by a 10-minute discussion of the resulting lists. Next, I ask the students to choose one or two things to focus on for the next 5 minutes of the videotape, warning them that they may need to be flexible about their original choices for focus. The students are instructed to be descriptive, not evaluative or judgmental, in their recording of what they observe. At the end of the 5 minutes, I ask several students to read from their notes. The discussion that follows generally centers on distinguishing *descriptive* notes from *evaluative* notes and on the need for greater elaboration of their notes. For example, many students will record things like the following:

The teacher was impatient with the students. . . . The students were bored. . . .

We discuss why this type of observation goes beyond describing what the observer is seeing and how the observer can change statements like "being impatient" into descriptions of what the participant is actually doing or saying that led the observer to such a judgment. This observation and discussion is repeated with an eye toward getting the students to be more descriptive in their observation and note taking. Strategies for note taking and comments about the limitations of the videotape for observation are also discussed.

In subsequent training sessions, students can be asked to practice different styles of observation recording: checklists, schedules, and field notes. Basically, these techniques vary along a continuum of structured to unstructured observation and are discussed in the following section.

STRUCTURED VERSUS UNSTRUCTURED OBSERVATION

At the structured end of the observation continuum, various forms of checklists and schedules have been developed for observing second language classrooms. It should be noted that the more structured and tally- or counting-oriented are the observation instruments, the less naturalistic is the information they provide. Such instruments may be able to tell us how often something occurred, but they will not always give us a clear idea of how it occurred. Most likely, these structured instruments will provide useful data for a naturalistic evaluation only if the categories for recording have come from more open-ended, unstructured observation. The latter type of observation provides the necessary clarity and detail in describing the characteristics of the language education program that the categories are meant to represent. In fact, most naturalistic researchers would generally eschew the use of any form of structured observation. However, the following examples have been used in evaluation efforts that I believe have paved the way for program evaluation in applied linguistics contexts to move beyond the positivistic perspective.

Ullman and Geva (1982, 1985) describe an observation instrument called the Target Language Observation Scheme (TALOS). This instrument is intended for use in observing live classroom activity (*real-time coding*), and consists of categories such as "Content Focus: Linguistic: phrase" and "Teaching Act: explain," which the observer checks as occurring during the 30-second *time on* units (the observer spends 30 seconds *time on* followed by 90 seconds *time off*, which allows for 20 observational units within a 40-minute class). The authors describe the coding categories as *low inference*, meaning that they are clearly described and should be easy for persons using the instrument to identify in actual classroom behavior.[3] There is a second part to the TALOS, designed to be completed at the end of the observation, which is a *high-inference* rating scale. The observer rates categories such as "personalized questions & comments" on a five-point scale (*extremely low* to *extremely high*). In both low- and high-inference sections of the TALOS, the categories were developed to reflect aspects of second language program implementation that previous research had suggested were important. This instrument was also designed specifically for the purposes of formative program evaluation (see Figure 7.1).

Another structured observation instrument is the Communicative Orientation of Language Teaching (COLT) scheme developed by Allen

---

3 It should be noted that Chaudron (1988) classifies the TALOS coding system as *mixed*, signifying that some of the categories are high inference.

et al. (1984). The first section of this scheme is also intended for real-time coding, but uses the classroom event, or activity, as the unit of analysis, rather than a prespecified time period. Categories are mixed low and high inference, such as (low inference) "Participant Organization: Class: Teacher–student," and (high inference) "Content: Other Topics: Broad: Imagination." The second section uses a time sampling approach for coding categories of student and teacher verbal interaction from a tape recording of the observed lesson. Categories are mixed low and high inference, such as (low inference) "Teacher Verbal Interaction: Target Language: L1," and (high inference) "Student Verbal Interaction: Information Gap: Request Information: Genuine." The categories for both sections were developed from essential second language classroom features suggested by the research literature (see Allen et al. 1990) and were meant to operationalize constructs from first and second language communication theory. This instrument was used in the Development of Bilingual Proficiency (Harley et al. 1990) project mentioned in Chapter 2 (see Figure 7.2 on pp. 114–15).

Other structured observation instruments have been used in second language classroom research as well; for example, see Moskowitz (1970), Fanselow (1977), and Bialystok et al. (1979).

These instruments all involve a relatively large number of sometimes complex categories to code, but there are other useful ways of recording observations that consist of relatively simple rating scales or checklists. One such instrument was developed by the Royal Society of the Arts and presented in an adapted form by Nunan (1989). The observer rates how accurately a series of statements reflects what happened in the observed classroom using a five-point scale (see Figure 7.3 on p. 116). Another, even simpler technique is to keep track of the occurrences of a particular classroom behavior with a tally sheet (see Figure 7.4 on p. 117).

Toward the unstructured end of the observation continuum are instruments that combine a standardized form that acts as a guide with open-ended note taking. I developed one such observation guide for use in the evaluation of the REST project (Lynch 1988, 1992). This guide included a section at the end of the form where the observed teacher could react to the observation notes, which proved to be extremely helpful in elaborating the observed lesson and clarifying ambiguities for the observer (see Figure 7.5 on p. 118).

In many program settings there will already be instruments for classroom and teacher observation in use, and it is always wise to start with these and adapt, where necessary, rather than to create something entirely new for the evaluation. There is for example the observation form that my colleagues and I at the UCLA ESL Service Courses have developed over the past several years. The form is a semistructured guide

School _____   Grade _____
French Teacher's Name _____   Date _____

c	b	10	c	b	9	c	b	8	c	b	7	c	b	6	c	b	5	c	b	4	c	b	3	c	b	2	c	b	1	Observation Unit

Who — TEACHER

To Whom:
- Large
- Small
- Individual
- Other

What-Type of Activity (Formal-Functional Focus):
- drill
- dialogue
- frame
- spelling
- translation
- paraphrasing
- free communication

Content Focus — Linguistic:
- sound
- word
- phrase
- discourse

Content Focus — Substantive:
- grammar
- culture
- integrated subject matter

Skill Focus:
- listen
- speak
- read
- write

Teaching Medium:
- text
- A.V.
- authentic materials
- draw
- poem
- song
- game
- role playing

Teaching Act:
- drill
- narrate
- explain
- discuss
- compare
- answer
- meta-comments & questions
- cognitive questions
- low level questions
- correct
- reinforce
- routine
- displine

L Use:
- L_1
- L_2

Who — STUDENT

To Whom:
- large
- small
- peer
- teacher
- other

What-Type of Utterance:
- sound
- word
- sentence fragment
- sentence
- extended disocurse
- non verbal
- no response

Type of Question:
- meta-comments & questions
- cognitive Q
- low Q
- routine Q

L Use:
- L_1
- L_2

(a)

Figure 7.1 The TALOS observation scheme: (a) the Low-Inference TALOS; (b) the High-Inference TALOS. (From Ullman and Geva 1981. Reprinted by permission.)

	extremely low	low	fair	high	extremely high
TEACHER					
Use of L_1	0	1	2	3	4
Use of L_2	0	1	2	3	4
teacher talk time	0	1	2	3	4
explicit lesson structure	0	1	2	3	4
task orientation	0	1	2	3	4
clarity	0	1	2	3	4
initiate problem solving	0	1	2	3	4
personalized questions & comments	0	1	2	3	4
positive reinforcement	0	1	2	3	4
negative reinforcement	0	1	2	3	4
corrections	0	1	2	3	4
pacing	0	1	2	3	4
use of audio-visual aids	0	1	2	3	4
gestures	0	1	2	3	4
humour	0	1	2	3	4
enthusiasm	0	1	2	3	4
STUDENTS					
Use of L_1 on task	0	1	2	3	4
Use of L_2 on task	0	1	2	3	4
student talk time on task	0	1	2	3	4
initiate problem solving	0	1	2	3	4
comprehension	0	1	2	3	4
attention	0	1	2	3	4
participation	0	1	2	3	4
personalized questions & comments	0	1	2	3	4
positive effect	0	1	2	3	4
negative effect	0	1	2	3	4
S to S interaction on task	0	1	2	3	4
PROGRAM					
linguistic appropriateness	0	1	2	3	4
content appropriateness	0	1	2	3	4
depth	0	1	2	3	4
variety	0	1	2	3	4
listening skill focus	0	1	2	3	4
speaking skill focus	0	1	2	3	4
reading skill focus	0	1	2	3	4
writing skill focus	0	1	2	3	4
formal properties	0	1	2	3	4
functional properties	0	1	2	3	4
integration with general curriculum	0	1	2	3	4

(b)

Figure 7.2 COLT observation scheme, (a) and (b). (From Allen, Swain, Harley, and Cummins 1990: 242–43. Reprinted by permission of Cambridge University Press.)

© J. P. B. Allen, M. Fröhlich and N. Spada, OISE 1983

STUDENT VERBAL INTERACTION

- Incorporation of S. Utterances: Elaboration, Expansion, Comment, Paraphrase, Repetition, No Incorp.
- Reaction Co/Mes.: Reaction, Explicit Code
- Form Restr.: Unrestricted, Limited, Restricted
- Sust. Speech: Sustained, Minimal, Ultraminimal
- Information Gap — Request Info.: Genuine, Pseudo; Giving Info.: Unpred., Pred.
- Disc.-Initiation
- Target Lang.: L_2, L_1
- Choral

TEACHER VERBAL INTERACTION

- Incorporation of S. Utterances: Elaboration, Expansion, Comment, Paraphrase, Repetition, No Incorp.
- Reaction Co/Mes.: Reaction, Explicit Code
- Sust. Speech: Sustained, Minimal
- Information Gap — Request Info.: Genuine, Pseudo; Giving Info.: Unpred., Predict.
- Target Lang.: L_2, L_1
- Communic. Features: Off talk, No talk

(b)

Directions: During or after the class you have observed or taken part in, rate the following statments according to how accurately they reflect what went on.

Key: 1 – Does not at all reflect what went on
        2 – Only marginally reflects what went on
        3 – Neutral
        4 – Describes rather well what went on
        5 – Is a totally accurate reflection of what went on

1 There were no cultural misunderstandings.		1 2 3 4 5
2 The class understood what was wanted at all times.		1 2 3 4 5
3 All instructions were clear.		1 2 3 4 5
4 Every student was involved at some point.		1 2 3 4 5
5 All students were interested in the lesson.		1 2 3 4 5
6 The teacher carried out comprehension checks.		1 2 3 4 5
7 Materials and learning activities were appropriate.		1 2 3 4 5
8 Student groupings and sub-groupings were appropriate.		1 2 3 4 5
9 Class atmosphere was positive.		1 2 3 4 5
10 The pacing of the lesson was appropriate.		1 2 3 4 5
11 There was enough variety in the lesson.		1 2 3 4 5
12 The teacher did not talk too much.		1 2 3 4 5
13 Error correction and feedback was appropriate.		1 2 3 4 5
14 There was genuine communication.		1 2 3 4 5
15 There was teacher skill in organising group work.		1 2 3 4 5
16 There was opportunity for controlled practice.		1 2 3 4 5
17 Students were enthusiastic.		1 2 3 4 5
18 General classroom management was good.		1 2 3 4 5

Figure 7.3   Classroom observation checklist. (From Nunan 1988:147–48. Reprinted by permission of Cambridge University Press.)

that is used for all supervisor observations of teaching assistants, as an integral part of our teacher development procedures (see Figure 7.6 on p. 120). These records also serve as an excellent data source for our ongoing evaluation of the ESL program.

In program settings where the qualitative evaluation design dictates the need for gathering data without any a priori decisions about what one is looking for, a more ethnographic style of observation will be appropriate. The recording of these observation data is usually referred to as *field notes.* The most important characteristic of field notes is that they are descriptive. This means that they need to be detailed and clear, and this descriptive quality needs to be distinguished from evaluative or interpretive statements. The ethnographic observer records judgments, interpretations, and his or her own reactions to what is being observed, as well. However, the most important goal of field notes is to record as thoroughly as possible what is happening in the observed context. The judgments and interpretations should follow from the descriptive observation and should be taken as working hypotheses. The following field notes are meant to exemplify this distinction between description and interpretation.

	Tallies	Total
1. Teacher asks a display question (i.e. a question to which she knows the answer)	*III*	*3*
2. Teacher asks a referential question (i.e. a question to which she does not know the answer)	*IIII*	*4*
3. Teacher explains a grammatical point		*0*
4. Teacher explains meaning of a vocabulary item		*0*
5. Teacher explains functional point		*0*
6. Teacher explains point relating to the content (theme/topic) of the lesson	*I*	*1*
7. Teacher gives instructions/directions	*HHI*	*6*
8. Teacher praises	*I*	*1*
9. Teacher criticises		*0*
10. Learner asks a question	*III*	*3*
11. Learner answers question	*IIII*	*4*
12. Learner talks to another learner		*0*
13. Period of silence or confusion		*0*

Figure 7.4   Classroom observation tally sheet. (From Nunan 1989:78. Reprinted by permission of Prentice-Hall Inc.)

Interpretation: The teacher has established a very good rapport with the students. The affective environment is very positive and supportive.

Description: T asks S1 about the homework assignment and jokes about her always being late for class. S1 smiles and says that it was S2's fault – he was asking her about the homework at the coffee shop before class. Most of the Ss laugh; T laughs and says, "I knew this assignment was going to be confusing – let's go over it now and try to clear things up."

Note that the interpretation notes might, in fact, be a valid working hypothesis based on the description notes.

Another aspect of recording detailed and clear field notes is the need to avoid labeling something that is observed without explaining why the label was chosen. For example, an observer might note:

The teacher was nervous and seemed uneasy about starting the class.

DATE: March 19, 1986   OBSERVER: Brian
TIME: 2:00–3:00   # OF STUDENTS: 14
TEACHER: CLASSROOM: Aula 20

CONTENT / LESSON EVENTS

2:13 – Text from students' math class is presented on OHP; students were assigned the text as homework; T. presents "my outline", warning students that theirs may be different because of their familiarity with the content. *

The objective of the lesson seems to be to outline the structure of the text: introduction, main ideas/points, supporting info; and then locate connectors and determine their function. After presenting her outline of the text, T. asks students for theirs (all of this has been presented in English, so far, with students responding in Spanish); one student comments on one part of the text (I don't quite hear or follow what he is saying), but it seems to wind up that he agrees with T's outline/analysis; another student also volunteers comments (in Spanish) on this part of the text; at times there seem to be differences of interpretation of the text between some of the students.

2:32 – T. goes through the text pointing out connectors (practice for tomorrow's quiz): so that, however, since, thus, and, similarly, or, when, whereas, hence. These are explained/comprehension checked primarily by translating them into their Spanish equivalents, but also by T. mentioning that certain connectors signal certain functions, e.g., a conclusion, a relation to a preceding idea, a contradiction.

T. points out that in this text, there is often a series of math equations joined only by connectors—important to understand their meaning.

2:45 — T. explains tomorrow's quiz.

2:53 – Class ends.

COMMENTS / OBSERVATIONS

*good use of OHP—the text structure is clearly marked in different colors—excellent way to discuss text.

I would have been curious to know how many of them felt they could understand the text (and to what degree) without reading the English. Along these lines, it was interesting that some admitted the text would have been difficult even if it were written in Spanish. Perhaps there could be a HW assignment where they write down or mark the parts of the text when their comprehension breaks down and why (language or concept or both?). The problem is, of course, that many students seem to habitually fail to do the HW. I think we need to discuss/explore ways of getting them to take more responsibility for doing their HW (electric-shock comes to mind), so that there can be more participation in class, e.g., have individual students come to OHP (have several unmarked text transparencies available) and explain their "outline" of the text's structure.

A question I had about the example phrasal verbs you showed them for the quiz: all of the sentences/contexts seemed to be non-science—was this by design? Were phrasal verbs chosen because they are important for scientific discourse? I guess these are naive questions, but the reason I'm trying to observe more often when I have the time is to try and get a better sense of where we're at. I realize it would be more helpful to be giving you answers (instead of more questions) but first I need to become clearer about what's going on "in the trenches."

I liked the way you brought information from your previous class (student comments on the meaning of certain equations and their interpretation of the resulting organization of the text) into this discussion, and I thought you did a very clear presentation of your text structure outline. The presentation of the connectors was excellent and should be very helpful to the students.

REACTIONS FROM T/Rs

Brian — this class was a bit unusual in that I did most of the talking . . . this was in great part due to the fact

Figure 7.5   REST observation form. (From Lynch 1992:71–72.)

that most of the students had not done their homework, which is a constant problem. I don't know how we can resolve the problem . . . I've told them that participation counts a lot, but most of them don't really care.

About the phrasal verbs . . . this was an aside. A couple of students had asked me about them and I decided to present something. P.M.'s book has no p.v.s, so I took what I could find in Azar. My idea was to present the concept so that when we encounter p.v.s in one of our texts, I can address it directly. (for example: 2 days ago, in a Heat Transfer text, we saw "setting up"). This is something that's been done only in this class.

Figure 7.5 (cont.)

    The label "nervous" needs to be explained in terms of the behavior that caused the observer to choose it. More descriptive field notes might record:

The teacher quickly shuffled through the papers on her desk, glanced up at the students, then quickly back down to the papers, shuffling through them again. She looked at her watch, then at the classroom clock, then back at her watch; took a deep breath, walked over to the blackboard, then quickly back to the papers on her desk, shuffling through them again; glanced up at the students, then at the clock; took another deep breath, walked to the class-room door and looked down the hall; came back to the front of the class and said (voice shaking a little), "Well, maybe we should start," not looking at the students.[4]

    Your strategy for recording field notes will often need to change over time, adapting itself to the observation context and changes in what you decide to focus on. The following account from Corsaro (1981: 126), observing peer interaction in an L1 preschool setting, is a good example of this.

On this first day I primarily watched the activity and attempted to hear both teacher–child and peer conversations. . . . As it turned out I recorded only a few observations relating to how long parents remain in the school with their children. . . . Later, . . . I followed a few of these [sustained peer activities] as best I could and attempted to record some of the verbal exchanges in field notes. This was difficult, however, because I did not know the children well and I had trouble hearing and understanding many of their utterances. I dropped this strategy after the first day, but then readopted it in a modified form near the end of this period of concealed observation. . . . [During the first month of school] I recorded the topic or nature of peer activities, names of the children involved, and the location, duration, and a running summary of peer episodes.

    In addition to the differences in recording observation, from struc-tured schemes to unstructured field notes, there are differences in the

---

4 These field note vignettes were patterned after Patton (1987:93–94).

ESL SERVICE COURSE OBSERVATION/FEEDBACK

Date of Observation: Class:

Teaching point(s):
_____   Instructor:
_____   Observer:

LESSON QUALITY (Achievement of objectives, organization, sequencing, pacing, use
of AV aids, etc.)

TEACHER PRESENTATION (Clarity of presentation, knowledge of material, classroom
management, speech clarity, etc.)

STUDENT PARTICIPATION (Interest level, interaction with instructor, balance of
student/teacher speech, opportunity to practice learning points, etc.)

MAJOR STRENGTHS

QUESTIONS OR UNCERTAINTIES ABOUT THE LESSON

SUGGESTIONS

Post-Observation Conference held on _____ at _____ PM

Chronological description of lesson

---

*Figure 7.6   UCLA observation form. (Developed by D. Brinton,
J. Goodwin, C. Holten, L. Jensen, and B. Lynch.)*

way that observers define their role within the context being observed.
These differences are discussed in the next section.

PARTICIPANT VERSUS NONPARTICIPANT OBSERVATION[5]

As an observer, you are immediately faced with a basic choice: Will
you actually participate in the setting you plan to observe, or will your
role be that of a nonparticipating outsider? Upon closer inspection, it
may be more accurate to think of this choice as involving various degrees of participation. True nonparticipant observation may occur only

5 I am indebted to Andrea Kahn for insights into the issue of participant versus
  nonparticipant observation gained from her unpublished manuscript (Kahn 1991)
  cited in this section and from numerous discussions concerning her M.A. thesis
  research.

in the case of someone who observes from behind a one-way mirror, or someone who uses a videotape recording of a classroom for observation data (without having been present for the recording). Although the pure form of nonparticipant observation may occasionally present itself as necessary (you may not be able to schedule live observations, but have access to recordings), some form of participant observation will most often be the preferred data-gathering strategy.

A useful way of portraying your choices is presented by Spradley (1980), who defines different types of participant observation based on the level of involvement with the setting. At one end of the continuum is *passive participant observation*, in which the observer does not actively participate in the classroom interactions and does not have a role to play other than observer. This type of observation is often labeled *nonparticipant*, and corresponds to the type of observation that normally occurs for teacher development purposes in most language programs. At the other end of the continuum is *complete participant observation*, where the observer already has an established role within the setting, such as when a teacher decides to gather observational data on his or her own classroom. Between these two ends of the continuum are two other levels of participation. *Active participant observation* occurs when the observer takes on a typical role within the setting, such as joining the class as a student. *Moderate participant observation* is defined by the observer alternating between active and passive roles within the setting. For example, an observer might take on the role of teacher's aide, occasionally participating in student group work in order to get more of an "insider" experience and occasionally staying on the sidelines to observe without being involved in the classroom interactions.

In order to choose which of these observation types will be best for the context in which you are observing, certain advantages and disadvantages should be kept in mind. When attempting complete participant observation, one advantage is that you have already solved the problem of gaining entry to the setting. You already have a legitimate role in the setting and can gather your observational data from an insider's point of view. When carrying out a naturalistic, qualitative evaluation design, this is the ideal. However, as Spradley (1980) points out, this insider's knowledge of the setting can also pose problems for naturalistic evaluation because it may prevent the observer from seeing and recording events within the setting from perspectives other than that of his or her own participant role. The complete participant observer may be overly influenced by prior knowledge and understanding of the setting and fail to observe aspects that do not conform to that understanding.

If you do not already have a role in the setting, you have the option of attempting to gain entry to the setting and do what the participants do. This active participant observation has the advantage of allowing the observer to come into the setting without preconceived notions of what it is like. The major disadvantage lies in the potential difficulty in gaining entry – will the observer be accepted and treated as an ordinary participant, or will the participants act differently in her presence? In the case of second language classrooms, the observer's proficiency in the language may be a barrier to this acceptance. If, for example, the observer is a native speaker of the language being taught, the students may identify him as an expert or another teacher, and the role of student participant may be impossible to negotiate.

Acknowledging the difficulty in gaining entry as an active participant, you may choose to move between the roles of insider and outsider. In this case, moderate participant observation, the observer has the advantage of being able to sample the role of insider while still being able to step back and observe the larger picture. The major disadvantage is the difficulty of obtaining an accurate sense of the setting from the insider's perspective. In the second language classroom context, the observer will never be able to experience the setting fully from either the students' or the teacher's perspective. The observer's identity as outsider will always tend to dominate and change the character of the interactions she is attempting to experience. The observation will, by definition, be overt, and the problem of reactivity (discussed in Chapter 3) will be of greater concern when attempting to use the data for evaluation purposes. However, if the observer is able to successfully negotiate a role such as that of teacher's aide, she may be able eventually to blend into the normally occurring classroom interactions and gain some insight into the students' and teacher's experiences.

An excellent example of how moderate participant observation can provide the best observational experience in the second language classroom context is described by Kahn (1991). Suppose that the observer is attempting to record an activity such as a paced reading. If the teacher sets the reading pace at, say, 200 words per minute, the native speaker (or highly proficient) observer who is actively participating in the activity will not be able to gain the insider's experience. The potential for frustration with the task because of its difficulty, or the feeling of competition with the other students, will be outside this observer's experience. In this case, a moderate participant observer could choose to stand apart from the activity and record student behavior – expressions, interactions with other students, comments to the teacher – in great detail. This observation experience would result in a better understanding of the activity than if the observer had actually tried to participate in it.

Finally, you may choose to observe the program setting with minimal involvement or to make use of the normally scheduled classroom observations in a program. The advantage of this passive participant approach, besides being easier to negotiate, is that it gives the observer maximum time and flexibility in deciding what to observe. The observer can spend as much time as he wants getting a general, holistic feel for the setting, and then focus on a particular behavior suggested as critical by that preliminary observation period. The observer also has more flexibility with how he chooses to observe, being able to move from the rear of the classroom to a spot near a particular student table as the focus of the observation changes, for example. The major disadvantage is that such relatively distanced observation may fail to capture a detailed description of the program experience from the participant's point of view. It may also be impossible for the participants to avoid seeing the observation as an intrusion on their classroom, even though they will usually, with time, become used to the observer's presence.

Different program evaluation contexts require different degrees of observer participation in order to gather the most useful information. In addition to considering the advantages and disadvantages of the types of observation roles discussed above, you also need to consider the question of observation *focus*, the subject of the next section.

OBSERVATIONAL FOCUS

Some discussion of the topic of observational focus has already been presented in the section on training. When pursuing a naturalistic evaluation design, there is usually a desire to obtain a holistic sense of the program and allow specific issues to evolve out of the data-gathering stage. If you are gathering data through observation, then, you will most likely need to attempt at least an initial period where the focus is extremely broad. It follows from the discussion in the previous sections that an unstructured observation instrument will be called for and that there are advantages to less active forms of participant observation for achieving the desired holistic sense of the setting.

As Patton (1987:82) points out, however: "It is not possible to observe everything." To aid in the process of deciding what to observe, he suggests *sensitizing concepts*. Rather than replacing a holistic approach with preordinate, fixed categories, these concepts act as a guide to help you manage the observational task. Essentially, these sensitizing concepts are the same as the questions in the observation guide that I presented earlier in this chapter as a training exercise.

In addition to these general sensitizing concepts, the particular evaluation context, with its particular audience and goals, may suggest areas where you will want to focus almost immediately. If, for example, an evaluation audience is expecting information that will help them decide whether to continue funding a computer-assisted instructional unit, then an obvious focus for the observation will be the use of this technology. It is important, in this case, not to focus too much too soon, however.

Too narrow a focus on student interaction with computers, for example, may lead to missing critical information on how this instruction interacts with other instructional materials.

The following represents a partial list of potential observational foci in second language classroom contexts, ordered roughly from broad to narrower focus.

- Student verbal behavior (when they speak, nature of language used, whom they speak to)
- Student nonverbal behavior (facial expressions, body language, seating patterns)
- Student use of native language
- Teacher verbal behavior
- Teacher nonverbal behavior
- Teacher use of native language
- Student–student interactions (language used, how initiated, group dynamics)
- Student–teacher interactions (language used, how and who initiates, relationship to instructional activity)
- Student questions (linguistic form, relationship to instructional activity)
- Teacher questions (linguistic form, relationship to instructional activity)
- Student questions concerning grammar
- Teacher *display* versus *referential* questions[6]
- Student responses to teacher display questions

The issues of structured versus unstructured observation, participant versus nonparticipant observation, and observational focus ultimately leave us to consider *sampling*, which is discussed in the next section.

SAMPLING

Regardless of the type of observation instrument or the observer's role, you will need to make some decisions concerning sampling. The decision concerning what to observe is the observational focus. The remaining sampling decisions involve who, when, and how often to observe.

Who   With complete or active participant observation, you may be locked into a sampling of whatever comes your way. This is sometimes referred to as *convenience sampling* (Patton 1987). With moderate participant observation, you will need to decide on defining your participant role with an eye toward which individual students or student groups you want to spend time observing. With passive or nonparticipant observation, you will have more flexibility to sample across different teachers, classrooms, or schools. Unless a particular observational

6 "A display question is one to which the questioner knows the answer, whereas a referential question is one to which the person asking the question does not know the answer" (Nunan 1989:29).

focus or evaluation goal has dictated whom you need to observe, a sampling plan will be a useful organizing tool for your data gathering. It will also help you address the issues of validity, discussed in Chapter 3. Your sampling plan may be random in nature (e.g., selecting different students for different observation periods at random) or purposeful (e.g., selecting the students with the lowest level of L2 proficiency).

When With the more active participant observer roles, you will usually be observing intensely within one classroom, whenever it is scheduled. With more passive observation, you may need to have a plan that samples across the various times of day and days of the week that the program is offered.

How Often The more passive participant observer will need to decide on the frequency of observations. A related question will be how long each observation period should be. Generally, with naturalistic evaluation designs, it is preferable to schedule as many observations as possible and, normally, to include the entire class period for each observation. The reason for this is that sampling, in naturalistic designs, is ultimately aimed at allowing the observer to experience the ongoing, day-to-day process of the program. When evaluation goals, time, or resources do not permit this ideal naturalistic sampling, the observer will want to capture as much of the program process as is possible. Table 7.1 represents a hypothetical sampling plan given time and resource constraints. The attempt is made to observe each teacher/classroom across the days of the week, across the weeks of the instructional term, and to allow for only one observational period per day (due to potential time constraints on the observer). Note that this is an example of *purposeful sampling* (Patton 1987), where the aim is to gather observational data that will reflect the maximum variation across the setting. On the other hand, it has aspects of *random sampling*, in that the observational choices of which teacher/classroom to observe on which day/week are made at random. In both cases – purposeful sampling for maximum variation and random sampling – the goal is to collect data that are representative of the overall setting.

Interviews

STRUCTURED VERSUS UNSTRUCTURED INTERVIEWS

As with observational data gathering, interviews can be carried out using different formats that vary along a structured to unstructured continuum. Depending on the evaluation goals, the specific evaluation context, and the type of qualitative design chosen for the evaluation, a

TABLE 7.1 MAXIMUM VARIATION/RANDOM SAMPLING PLAN

	Wk. 1	*Wk. 2*	*Wk. 3*	*Wk. 4*	*Wk. 5*	*Wk. 6*	*Wk. 7*	*Wk. 8*	*Wk. 9*
Level A									
T.1	M			Th, F			Tu, W		
T.2		M, Th			Tu, F			W	
T.3			M, Th			W, F			Tu
Level B									
T.4	Tu, F			M, W			Th		
T.5		W			M, Tu			Th, F	
T.6			Tu, W			M, Th			F
T.7	W			Tu, Th			M, F		

T = teacher/classroom; Wk. = week; M, Tu, W, Th, F = Monday–Friday class instructional period.

more or less structured interview format will be required. When a highly naturalistic design is guiding the evaluation and the concern is for data that are grounded in the variety of individual experiences that exist in the program, a less structured interview format will be best. If the most important concerns are getting the same information from all persons interviewed and demonstrating a comprehensive, systematic approach to data gathering, then a more structured interview is preferred.

Patton (1980, 1987) discusses three types of qualitative interview format: the informal conversational interview, the interview guide, and the standardized open-ended interview. At the unstructured end of the continuum is the *informal conversational interview,* where the interviewer attempts to engage the interviewee in a natural conversation in which the questions arise more or less spontaneously. This approach works best if the interviewer has already established some sort of relationship with the interviewee – for example, as a result of moderate to active participant observation or other legitimate contact with the program. The interview has no predetermined agenda or set of questions; instead, it allows the interaction between interviewer and interviewee to establish its own dynamic. The interviewer's job is to be sensitive to the immediate conversation and to seek clarification and elaboration of the interviewee's comments and responses. Instead of attempting to identify or confirm hypotheses expressed in terms created by the interviewer, the informal conversational approach puts a premium on discovering the interviewee's perceptions of the program in his or her own words.

The major advantage of this approach is that the interview can be tailored to the individual being interviewed. This maximizes the amount of relevant information that the interviewer can obtain from each interview. Topics that the interviewer may not have predicted can arise and be pursued, and topics already familiar to the interviewer can be developed in relation to the interviewee's understanding of them. This approach lends itself to multiple sessions and follow-up interviews to obtain the most in-depth understanding possible.

The major disadvantage of the informal conversational interview is that it requires a great deal of time. Usually, one interview per person will not be enough to gain the desired in-depth understanding. In terms of the overall evaluation, it requires still more time in order to gather comparable information across all interviewees. Finally, the analysis of these interview data is difficult and time-consuming because the interviews each generate different sets of questions and answers, making patterns more difficult to identify. An example of the informal conversation interview is given in Figure 7.7.

At the most structured end of the qualitative interview continuum is the *standardized open-ended interview*. Under this format, the exact wording and order of questions to be asked is determined in advance. Like structured observation, this form of interviewing is not acceptable to many naturalistic researchers, given the preordained set of questions to be answered by the interviewee. However, this approach to interviewing may be useful toward the end of an evaluation study, when the major themes have had the opportunity to emerge from less structured data gathering.

The obvious advantage to the standardized open-ended interview is its efficiency. The interviewer knows in advance where the interview is going and how the questions will be asked. This is especially important in evaluation contexts in which there is a limited amount of time available for data gathering, or when the people to be interviewed are available only at certain, limited times. Using this approach, the interviewer is assured of obtaining the same information across the various interviews and will usually need to conduct only one interview per person. As a result, the information collected in these interviews will be easier to compare across persons; patterns in the data will be easier to identify. This approach is especially useful when more than one person is collecting the interview data. The standardized approach increases completeness and systematicity across interviewers, avoiding the differences that might result from an unstructured format with different interviewers asking different questions of different interviewees.

The inflexibility of this format is its equally obvious disadvantage.

Interviewer: So, how's it going in your ESL class this quarter?
Interviewee: It's going fine. . . .

Interviewer: How many times have you taught the course before?
Interviewee: This is my fifth time through the curriculum, but my fourth time teaching it.

Interviewer: What did you do the time you went "through the curriculum" when you weren't teaching it?
Interviewee: I was a student teacher the first time through, and Martha Jones was the master teacher.

Interviewer: How is it teaching the same course four times? Is it repetitive?
Interviewee: Well, it probably should be, but I'm still enjoying it. I actually think I'm just now beginning to know what I'm doing. The hardest thing has been switching between the American Language Institute and the "regular university" versions of the course because of differences in the number and length of class sessions, the two kinds of students and their needs, and other practical considerations.

Interviewer: How do you keep the curriculum new for yourself as a teacher?
Interviewee: Well, there's a new group of students every time. Also, I felt lost my first time through it, and now I finally feel kind of comfortable with it. I like knowing what's coming up in three weeks. The first time I taught the course, I did not feel very well prepared, so I never really felt I had a long-term vision of what was going on. This changed this past term. The current term marks only my second time through feeling like I knew what I was doing. So I'm ready to move on to something new. I'll be teaching at a new level this summer, so that'll be a good change, I think.

Interviewer: What kinds of changes have you been making the different times you've taught the course? . . .

Figure 7.7   Informal conversational interview format. (Adapted from interviews conducted by T. Griggs, K. Thomas, and D. Babel in TESL and Applied Linguistics 225, a UCLA graduate seminar on program evaluation, Spring 1992.)

The interviewer is locked into a set of questions and an order for asking them. Spontaneity and naturalness in the interaction with the interviewee become difficult. Topics that have not been predicted in advance are not allowed to emerge or be elaborated. An example of this format is given in Figure 7.8.

Somewhere midway along this continuum of interview formats is the *interview guide*. This approach allows the interviewer to specify a range of questions to be covered in advance, but also allows the interviewer to formulate the wording of the questions as well as the order for asking them as the interview progresses. The range of questions is written out prior to the interview in the form of an outline. This outline acts as a checklist, to make certain that each interview covers the same information. Unlike the standardized interview, however, the interviewer has the flexibility to adapt the questions to the individual being interviewed and to establish a relatively natural conversational interaction.

1. What level of the ESL curriculum do you teach at?
2. How structured is the curriculum?
3. Do you know how your course fits into the overall curriculum? How?
4. Are you satisfied with the course you teach? What do you like about the course you are teaching?
5. Are the students satisfied with the content-based curriculum? What do they say about it?
6. What do the students say about the curriculum in relation to learning English?
7. How does the curriculum relate to the previous ESL learning experience of the students?
8. How much do you interact with other teachers at your level? In what capacity?

Figure 7.8   Standardized open-ended interview format. (Adapted from interviews conducted by T. Griggs, K. Thomas, and D. Babel in TESL and Applied Linguistics 225, a UCLA graduate seminar on program evaluation, Spring 1992.)

The major advantage of this approach is that it combines some of the best characteristics of the two extremes on the structured–unstructured continuum. The guide allows the interviewer to make efficient use of time and to be systematic and complete across interviews. At the same time, the interviewer can phrase the questions in response to the nature of the individual being interviewed and in response to the natural flow of the interview conversation. If a question results in an ambiguous response, the interviewer is free to probe for a better understanding.

Like the standardized open-ended interview, the interview guide has the potential for failing to encounter and pursue important topics that have not been articulated in advance. Like the informal conversational interview, there is the potential for different interviewers asking somewhat different questions of different interviewees, resulting in data that are difficult to compare and analyze. However, it is clear that the resulting data will be more systematic than that of the informal conversational approach and that the interviewer will have more flexibility than in the standardized approach. An example of this format is given in Figure 7.9. (Note that the order and wording of the interview guide questions in Figure 7.9 are meant to be adapted freely to the context of any interview in which they are used.)

INDIVIDUAL VERSUS GROUP INTERVIEWS

Most often, we think of the interview as being a one-on-one encounter, or, at least, that there is only one interviewee. There are several advantages, however, to conducting interviews with small groups of people. The most obvious advantage is the ability to sample a greater number of people within the same amount of time that a one-on-one interview might take. Suppose that you have four one-hour periods of time that you are able to arrange for gathering interview data from program par-

1. What are the goals of the REST project? Have they changed over the past year?
2. What are the means for achieving the REST goals? Have they changed over the past year?
3. What are the social climate/relations like on the REST project?
4. What are the most prominent features of the program?
5. What are the ultimate results for the program this year?
6. What are the principal causes for those results?
7. Was the REST project successful this year?
8. What were the major dilemmas/problems on the project this year? How were they coped with? How were they resolved?
9. Do you have suggestions for improving the REST project?
10. Is there anything else you want to comment on or question?

Figure 7.9   Interview guide format. (Adapted from the interview guide used in the evaluation of the REST project – see Lynch 1988.)

ticipants. You could schedule one individual interview for each hour, thereby getting information from four participants, or you could schedule small group interviews – with four to eight people in each group, for example – and increase dramatically the number of participants.

Another advantage of the group interview is that the participants can question and clarify each other's responses. In the evaluation of the REST project, I used the group interview to gather data from the students in the program. Extreme statements from certain individuals, such as, "We haven't learned anything," or "Everything about our English class is great," tended to be challenged by others in the group, and a more balanced portrait of the program emerged than might have with isolated individual interviews. Although the experienced interviewer will often be able to clarify such extreme statements in the course of a one-on-one interview, he or she does not always have the knowledge or authority to challenge or question these statements in the way that peers do. It should also be mentioned that these extreme statements are not to be ignored or discounted simply because are challenged by others in the group. During the REST project group interviews, certain individuals would cling to the intent of their original words when challenged, while clarifying their position for the other students (and the interviewer). In other cases, the individuals would indicate that they had, perhaps, been guilty of exaggeration. All of these types of cases provide a rich and dynamic set of interview data for the evaluator.

There are, of course, disadvantages to using the group interview. Certain individuals may feel uncomfortable saying anything in a larger group, especially anything that might be controversial. This will limit the range of information available to the interviewer. However, my experience with the REST project group interviews leads me to believe that you can attempt to draw out less responsive individuals with non-threatening questions. In other cases, you can attempt to read nonverbal behavior (facial expressions, gestures) that indicates, for example, a lack of agreement with what is being said. Those individuals who seem to be reticent can be approached later for follow-up one-on-one interviews, where possible.

The trade-off to being able to sample a greater number of people in a group interview is that you can cover a smaller number of questions or topics. It is also more difficult, in most cases, to manage an interview with several people than with one interviewee. Furthermore, you may not be able to probe as deeply and follow through in as much detail in the group format as you can with individual interviews. Despite these disadvantages, however, the group interview can be an extremely useful format for gathering evaluation data, especially when there are large numbers of participants to sample and when time and resources for data gathering are limited.

QUESTION TYPES

Whether the interview is group or one-on-one, structured or unstructured, the aim of gathering naturalistic interview data is to arrive at the participants' perspective on the program *in their own words*. The types of questions asked by the interviewer are critical to achieving this aim. It is easy for an interviewer to constrain or condition the response of the interviewee by the way the question is worded. For example, if the interviewer asks "Is this program helping you to learn English for science and technology?" the goal of the program has already been identified and labeled, to a certain extent, in words chosen by the interviewer that may or may not reflect the interviewee's perspective. The question also, on the surface, calls for a yes or no answer, which further constrains the response from the interviewee. You might want to rephrase this question as "What kinds of things have you learned in this program?" or "What do you think about this program?" Although such questions may seem overly general or vague, they allow the interviewee to choose his own terms and categories for communicating his experience of the program. The interviewer can also follow these questions with more specific probes, or questions designed to gather further detail or clarification on statements made by the interviewee.

Patton (1987) offers a set of question types that can help in organizing an interview. These are:

- Behavior/experience questions
- Opinion/value questions
- Feeling questions
- Knowledge questions
- Sensory questions
- Demographic/background questions

Perhaps the best way to explain these question types is to give examples of each.

- *Behavior/experience:* Tell me about what happens to you, what you do, during a typical class hour.
- *Opinion/value:* What is the most important aspect of this program for you?
- *Feeling:* Tell me about anything in the classroom that makes you feel uncomfortable.
- *Knowledge:* How are students chosen for this program?
- *Sensory:* Describe the physical environment of your classroom. What is the lighting like? the noise level? . . .
- *Demographic/background:* How many years did you study ESL before coming to this program? What type of study was that?

These question types and examples are clearly not meant to be exhaustive, but rather to provide a starting point and general checklist against which to organize the interview.

The sequencing of interview questions will depend to some extent on the format of the interview. In a standardized open-ended interview, there is a rigid order in which questions are to be asked, whereas the less structured formats allow for some flexibility in sequencing. For any of the formats, I suggest the following sequence as a guide:

1. *Casual, put-the-interviewee-at-ease question/comment:* It's a little hot today, isn't it? It may also be appropriate to explain the purpose of the interview, anonymity, etc.
2. *General questions:* What do you think of the program?
3. *Specific questions:* What was it that made you feel uncomfortable about that lesson? There will obviously be more latitude here when using less structured interviews – probes and follow-ups can be tailored to previous responses.
4. *Closing questions:* Is there anything else you can tell me about the program?
5. *Casual, wind-down questions/comments:* I want to thank you, I've really learned a lot from our conversation today.

As with the question types, this list is meant as a general guide and will have to be developed for different program and interview contexts.

The flip side of question types in the interview process is listening. Denzin (1989:43) points out that listening is the key ingredient to the successful conduct of an interview and offers the following suggestions:

1. Do not gossip.
2. Do not interrupt.
3. Share experiences.
4. Learn what to listen for.
5. Have a reason for being a listener.

Sharing experiences takes the interviewer beyond the listening role, but it is important because it helps to create a sense of trust. The interviewer who merely sits and listens, nodding occasional agreement and taking notes, can provoke an uneasy response in the interviewee. ("Wait a minute, now; here I am spilling out my innermost thoughts to this complete stranger!") If the interviewer is able to open up a bit and make personal connections with what the interviewee is saying, without shifting the focus of the interview, the process is enriched and greater rapport is achieved. This, combined with learning what to listen for – getting a sense of what each person has to contribute to the portrait of your setting – and having a reason to listen – creating an identity within your setting – improves the quality of interview data (also see Douglas 1985).

RECORDING INTERVIEWS

I have mentioned that the aim of gathering naturalistic interview data is to capture the participants' perspective on the program in their own words. This argues strongly for tape recording (audio and/or video) the interview. However, some very important data can be gathered through informal conversational interviews where a tape recorder would be inappropriate. In this case, the burden of proof is on the notes that the data gatherer writes following the interview exchange (and these should obviously be written as soon as possible after the interview).

When conducting a more formal interview, a tape recorder is a must. You should always ask permission to record from the interviewee, in advance, and explain the rationale for recording. Explaining that you want to make certain that you get down everything the interviewee has to say can add a sense of seriousness to the interview and communicate a sense of respect for the person being interviewed.

It is usually a good idea to take notes even if you are recording the interview, to remind yourself of important issues that are raised, to provide an outline for analyzing the data, and to act as a partial backup in case there are recording difficulties. The most important aspect of interviewing, however, is to be responsive and interactive with the interviewee, especially in the informal conversational format. The more your head is turned down into your notepad, the less attentive you will be to the actual interaction with the interviewee, and the less conversational the exchange will be. There will be enough for you to do in terms of attending to the interviewee's responses and formulating the next questions to ask without also attempting to get it all down in your notes.

Other techniques of data gathering

QUESTIONNAIRES

When questionnaires are used as a data-gathering technique within a naturalistic evaluation design, they are perhaps best thought of as written interviews. In evaluation contexts where time, resources, and availability of program participants for interviews are limited, an open-ended questionnaire can serve as a surrogate for the standardized open-ended interview. The discussion in the preceding section of this chapter concerning the advantages of the standardized open-ended interview format and the content of interview questions applies, for the most part, to open-ended questionnaires as well. Questionnaires are a time-efficient means of gathering data from a large number of people: They can be mailed or otherwise delivered without the need to arrange individual or group appointments. Because one set of questions is being asked, you are assured of obtaining roughly the same information across the various questionnaire respondents, and, as a result, questionnaire data are easier to analyze for patterns than data acquired by less structured techniques.

However, unlike the interview format, in which the interviewer can attempt to make certain that all questions are answered, the questionnaire format is more likely to result in incomplete data. Respondents will fail to answer certain questions, for a variety of reasons, and some questionnaires will not be returned at all. It is my experience that without a concerted follow-up effort a 25 percent (or less) return rate is typical. The potential for incomplete data poses problems for determining the representativeness of the responses. This, coupled with the potentially limiting nature of a set list of preordained questions, poses problems for validity. Like the standardized open-ended interview, it is probably best to use this data-gathering technique toward the end of an evaluation study, regardless of the design, when the major themes have already emerged from less structured data gathering. An example of an open-ended questionnaire used in the evaluation of the UCLA ESL Service Courses is shown in Figure 7.10.

JOURNALS, LOGS, RETROSPECTIVE NARRATIVES

I should emphasize that, by including these data-gathering techniques lumped together as a category of "other," I intend no demeaning of their value to naturalistic evaluation. My experience with journal data, in particular, leads me to recommend it very highly as a rich source of information about the program from a participant's point of view. It is not always possible, however, to have access to this type of labor- and time-intensive and, at times, highly personal data. At the very least, the

---

ESL Service Courses Evaluation – Student Questionnaire

In an attempt to evaluate the ESL Program, we are asking our students to provide us with information about the kind of work they are doing in their academic courses at UCLA.

II: Please answer the following questions regarding your ESL courses in as much detail as possible.

1. Describe an activity that you found to be useful and explain why.

2. Describe an activity that you found to be less useful and explain why.

3. What do you think should be added to the ESL course you are taking now?

4. What do you think should be left out of the ESL course you are taking now?

III: General comments
Please comment in more depth about any of the above statements, or any other aspect of the ESL Service Courses provided in the space below. Your comments and suggestions are very useful to us and help us evaluate and modify our courses.

Figure 7.10   UCLA student questionnaire. (Developed by A. Kahn and B. Lynch.)

evaluator or evaluation team should consider keeping journals of their daily experience with the program. Where possible, program teachers and administrators should be encouraged to keep some sort of daily or weekly record of their experiences and perceptions for use in the evaluation. It may also be possible to have students keep journals or *dialog journals* (Brinton and Holten 1989) as a normal part of the curriculum and to make anonymous use of the data.[7]

Journals can be more or less structured in the same ways that have been discussed for observation and interviews. Rather than just entering stream-of-consciousness thoughts at the end of the day, journal-writing can be guided by a set of general questions to answer or a set of informational categories to be addressed. An example of this structured journal approach was used in the evaluation of the REST project (see Figure 7.11). The teacher/researchers (T/Rs) on the project were asked to keep a journal that reflected their daily classroom experiences. The format was developed over the first few months of the project in response to the T/Rs' request for more guidance on what their journal entries should include. The journal format kept track of the curriculum

---

7 For more on the use of journals, or diaries, to gather data on the language learner's experience, see Bailey (1983) and Allwright and Bailey (1991:190–93).

NAME:			
	DATE: 1-24-86		
Curriculum module/objectives	Lesson Events		Material/media
	Teacher presentations	Student participation	
Text structure understand paragraph of function and physical description; relationship between text and diagram	*Class I.* T1 shows Ss text only from p. 51 and has them read it, looking for main ideas and the type of text (classification). T1 then asks Ss what words in text indicate physical description or description of function. T1 explains unknown words and then goes over the exercises at bottom of page. T2 has Ss read paragraph on p. 52 and then has Ss answer chart from that page. (For Class IV, over)	Ss decide its classification. Some Ss come up to OHP to fill-in the blanks, giving the pen to a new person to answer. Ss say which part of the eye has given function.	*RAM*, pp. 51–52 OHP SPAN/ENGL % 13:00–14:00 SPAN = 80 ENGL = 20 14:00–15:00 50/50

COMMENTS/OBSERVATIONS

Today, like yesterday, was strange because we did completely different things in the 2 classes. We decided to do the exercise from Class IV yesterday today because they were the ones who had originally asked to see the examples. They weren't very pleased when we told them that the (over)

Figure 7.11 REST project teacher/researcher journal (From Lynch 1992:70).

as it was developing – listing, for each lesson, the module, the materials, the type of activities and exercises, media, amount of Spanish versus English used in the classroom, what the teacher did, and what the students did. In addition, the journal format included the T/Rs' reactions to and characterizations of the program and served as a vehicle of communication between the T/Rs and project coordinators.

For the purposes of this discussion, logs can be thought of as highly structured and abbreviated journals. The major aspects of a program that the evaluator would like to keep track of can be specified, and a convenient and quick means of recording these aspects can be provided in the log format. I used this type of data-gathering technique in the evaluation of the REST project, to record daily events in the life of the program from the coordinator's point of view. The format allowed me to record journal-like "subjective impressions" and "overall comments and observations" as well as to cross-reference the log entries to other data being collected for the evaluation by including a column for "expanded description" (EX. DES.) that indicates the specific event is referred to in another data file (see Figure 7.12).

Retrospective narratives were used in the evaluation of the Bangalore Project (Beretta 1990) in an attempt to provide more information about the implementation of the project than the original evaluation design had allowed. The narratives were collected from teachers after the end of the project through a set of questions designed to guide them in their historical account of their experience. A cover letter stressed that the questions were not intended to limit the nature of their responses, but were intended to help them recall the experience of the project, which they were encouraged to describe in as much detail as possible. The following represents a sample of such a retrospective narrative:

... before I involve myself in this project I thought about this approach. I planned my time to pretask (3 minutes) and task (10 minutes). I was easily able to assess through classroom management the involvement of students and their progress which satisfied me. I introduced the new tasks on the basis of the feedback I got from the previous class. In this way I was able to increase the effectiveness. I conducted a common test both for students who learn through structural method and for those who learn through CTP. The test was constructed in such a way that no group has special advantage in this because of a particular method of teaching. (Beretta 1990:337)

As in the case of the Bangalore evaluation, this technique is especially useful when the evaluator is brought in after the implementation of the program has been completed or when the amount of time that can be spent observing and interviewing at the project site is limited.

DAILY LOG: REST PROJECT

Monday, April 7, 1986   Brian

EVENTS	BRIEF DESCRIP.	EX.DES.	SUBJ.IMPRESSIONS
1. Meeting w/ Carlos & Alfredo	Discussed lesson plan for today.	NO	We need to find a more comfortable way of helping them with their planning; seemed awkward; hard to tell how much guidance or in-class help they want.
2. Meeting w/ Alvarez	See Meeting Subfile.	YES	Quick and successful except for class times not being arranged - - vacations slowed everything up.
3. Work on Treatment File	Trying to get a description of what's been done second term.	NO	Very interesting to go through the journals - - lots of info, but how to organize? Also time consuming.
4. Trip to CIDLE	Picked up checks; Turned in AF letter to PH.	NO	New office design seems quieter; good relations with most of staff, still.
5. Trip to USIS	Met J. Roney informally, set up formal appt. 4/15; got Fulbr. travel info from Iceland.	NO	- - - - - - - - - -

OVERALL COMMENTS AND OBSERVATIONS
Everyone seemed in good spirits following the 2-week vacation; a little difficult to get back in the swing of things however. I felt like I had a full and productive day. The new USIS director seems nice enough; a little distracted at this time as he is still settling in. Rumor today from several sources that the Universidad has no money - - IA said that the work on the new classroom building has been postponed.

Figure 7.12   REST project administrative daily log. (From Lynch 1992:73.)

PROGRAM DOCUMENTS

A final data-gathering technique is to collect the available documentation for the program being evaluated. Strauss (1987:2–3) emphasizes the importance of a variety of materials as data in qualitative research. Relevant documents include program brochures, official press releases, newspaper articles concerning the program, advertisements, curriculum descriptions, policy statements, memoranda, organizational charts, and correspondence. As Patton (1987:90) points out, program documents can give the evaluator basic information concerning the activities and processes of the program and can suggest important evaluation questions to be pursued in greater detail using the other techniques suggested in this chapter.

Data analysis

Focusing

The first step in the nonlinear, iterative process that I will present here for qualitative data analysis is to *focus* the evaluation. One useful way of doing this is to develop a *thematic framework* that represents the most important evaluation questions to be answered. Following the context-adaptive model discussed in Chapter 1, the evaluator should return to the preliminary thematic framework that was developed from a consideration of the evaluation audience and goals. What are the central issues, the questions to be answered, the information that the audience needs? The preliminary thematic framework for the REST project was presented in Chapter 1. Table 7.2 provides another example, this one taken from the in-progress evaluation of the ESL Service Courses at UCLA.

In the process of gathering data, the naturalistic evaluator will have gained new insight regarding these original evaluation issues. Certain themes may need to be reconceptualized, others may have proved to be less important than originally thought, and entirely new themes may have emerged. These revised and newly emergent themes, then, constitute the new thematic framework. At this stage the evaluator will want to approach the evaluation audience(s) to present this framework as a type of preliminary feedback. Discussing this feedback with them will allow the evaluator to make further modifications to the thematic framework before proceeding to the next stage of data analysis. An example of a modified thematic framework is presented in Table 7.3 (on p. 141), with the preliminary thematic framework from Chapter 1 reprinted for ease of comparison. As will be seen from

TABLE 7.2 PRELIMINARY THEMATIC FRAMEWORK: UCLA ESL PROGRAM

1. Differences in needs between foreign and immigrant students
2. Differences in needs between transfer and freshmen undergraduates
3. The "new curriculum": What is it? *Whose* is it?
4. Student perceptions of the curriculum: Service Course philosophy versus student expectations
5. TAs: Expectations as ESL professionals versus as graduate students in TESL & AL
6. The relationship of the Service Courses to the Department of TESL & AL
7. The relationship of the Service Courses to writing programs
8. Newly-placed versus continuing students: Can the curriculum keep pace with placement?

this example, this focusing does not necessarily result in fewer themes and issues.

Organizing the data

At this stage, the evaluator needs to collect all of the data that have been gathered from various sources and instruments and begin to organize them for the next stage of analysis. I say "next stage" in recognition of the fact that, in the process of collecting the data, the naturalistic evaluator will have already begun to analyze in the sense of forming hypotheses, revising preliminary themes, and constructing categories and codes for the data. The data will generally exist as several folders and scattered, large piles of paper, and possibly audio and video cassettes. As Patton (1980) recommends, the data should first be checked for completeness. For example, are there observation data for all of the teachers that you decided to sample? As a related issue, you should check for quality: If the tape recordings have been transcribed, are the transcriptions accurate? Checking the transcriptions against the original recordings is especially important if someone unfamiliar with the data-gathering process was responsible for transcribing. The specific transcription conventions and amount of detail required may not have been communicated properly. Field notes need to be checked for legibility.

The data then need to be systematized in some way, so that the evaluator knows where everything is. This system may reflect the data-gathering techniques – for example, putting all the observational data in one file, all the interview data in another. Another system would be

TABLE 7.3 PRELIMINARY AND MODIFIED THEMATIC FRAMEWORKS: THE REST PROJECT

Preliminary thematic framework	Modified thematic framework
1. Effects of focusing instruction on reading only	1. Use of explicit grammar instruction along with reading skills
2. Effects of focusing instruction on reading skills and strategies	2. Use of team teaching
3. Effects of using authentic reading texts	3. Effects of using authentic reading texts
4. Feasibility of using Spanish versus English for instruction	4. Use of English versus Spanish in the classroom
5. Availability of classrooms	5. Effect of class size on instruction
6. Feasibility of using a "modified adjunct model" approach	6. Effects of using a "modified adjunct" approach
7. Feasibility and effects of conducting classroom-centered research	7. Use of introspection/retrospection with students as a research tool
8. Level of student proficiency in English upon entering the program	8. Teacher perception of student ability
	9. Student–teacher relations

Adapted from Lynch 1990a:32, 37–38.

to organize the data by the source – for example, all of the data gathered from students in one file, data from teachers in another. For the REST project evaluation, I created a system of files, and subfiles had been created during the data-collection phase.[8] A "treatment file" consisted of all the data relating to what actually happened in the program classrooms, with subfiles representing the two major data-collection instruments: teacher/researcher journals and observations. Another major file, an "administrative file," consisted of the daily log kept by the project coordinators and the meetings subfile (notes kept by the project coordinators). Two other files spanned the content of treatment and administration: an "interview file" and a "questionnaire file," which held data collected from students and teachers.

Once you have a complete set of data, it is extremely important to make copies. I am always reminded of the experience of the novelist Malcolm Lowry, who, after laboring for years on his great novel, *Under the Volcano*, lost his only copy of the manuscript in a fire. Fortunately, he persevered and rewrote the novel from what he remembered of the initial writing experience. As a naturalistic evaluator, you may not have the time, or the memory, to reconstruct your data should it be lost to similarly unforeseen circumstances. Several copies, housed in different

---

8 I am indebted to Harold Levine for his guidance in the construction of this system.

TABLE 7.4 EXAMPLE CODES FROM THE REST PROJECT EVALUATION

PROC = classroom process
  (subcodes): GRAM/READ = use of explicit grammar instruction versus reading skills instruction
              AUTH MATs = use of authentic reading texts

RELATs = social relations on the project (teacher–student, teacher–teacher, teacher–administrator, ...)
  (subcodes): S ATT/MOT = student attitude and motivation

STRUCT = curriculum structure, goals, outcomes
  (subcodes): ADJUNCT = attempt to use modified adjunct by coordinating with Chemical Engineering professors
              GRADING = system for grading/assessing student achievement

---

Adapted from Lynch 1992:78.

locations – at home, at the program site, with a friend – should be maintained. It is also a good idea to have copies that you can use to cut-and-paste and annotate during the later stages of analysis.

Coding the data

At this stage, the evaluator needs to read through the entire data set, using the thematic framework as a guide but being alert to new themes, patterns, and examples in the data. This first pass through the data will help the evaluator decide on a preliminary system for coding the data. *Codes* are simply abbreviated labels for the themes and patterns that the evaluator is beginning to identify. The code should be short enough to serve its purpose as a time-saving data marker, but long enough so that it is easily interpretable and distinguishable from other codes as the evaluator scans through the data. As with every aspect of qualitative data analysis, coding should be approached as an iterative process. The evaluator should work back and forth between the data and the codes, revising the latter as new patterns emerge that suggest better ways of labeling the data. This is at the heart of *grounded theory* (Glaser and Strauss 1967) and is expressed by Strauss (1987): "The focus of analysis is *not* merely on collecting or ordering a mass of data, but on *organizing many ideas* which have emerged from analysis of the data" (pp. 22–23, original emphasis). Some examples of codes used in the REST project evaluation are given in Table 7.4; for a more complete discussion of coding systems, see Strauss (1987:55–129).

The evaluator then proceeds to make several passes through the data, coding in the margins or on a separate note-taking sheet. For example, Figure 7.13 represents notes from the meetings subfile of the REST project evaluation with coding in the left margins. In the case of the teacher/ researcher journal subfile, I selected salient entries and coded them on a separate page, as shown in Figure 7.14 (on p. 145). The initial entries in the left-hand margin are the date of the journal entry and the initials (changed from the original) of the teacher/researcher, followed by the code and the selected entry notes (quotation marks indicate verbatim wording from the journal).

Classifying and reducing the data

Coding the data represents the beginning of a classification system, which is expanded in the next stage of data analysis. Although some data reduction is accomplished during the coding stage, the evaluator now needs to reduce the data further by using classification schemes such as category systems, typologies, and display matrices. The creation of a category system flows naturally from the preliminary thematic framework, the modified thematic framework, and coding. The basic idea is to look for recurring patterns in the data and to find ways of grouping those patterns and themes. For example, Table 7.5 (on p. 145) represents an initial category system for the REST project evaluation, suggested by the modified thematic framework in Table 7.3 and patterns in the data.

Another classification system that can be used to reduce the data is a typology. Typologies are normally characterized as *indigenous* or *analyst-constructed* (Patton 1980:306–11), where the former refers to ways of grouping or describing persons or phenomena that come from the participants themselves, and the latter refers to a typology created by the researcher/evaluator. Patton describes an example of an indigenous typology from an evaluation of a high school setting where the focus was on dropouts. Observation and interview data revealed that the teachers had a typology for the problem students: There were *chronics* and *borderlines*. Basically, the chronics were the students that no one seemed capable of reaching, whereas the borderlines seemed to be testing the limits of what they could get away with and would respond to teacher discipline. This typology became an important focus for the data analysis.

An example of an analyst-constructed typology comes from Bailey (1982), who examined the communicative competence of non-native speakers of English serving as teaching assistants (TAs) in math and physics at UCLA. In addition to using a coding system that reduced her data for statistical analysis, Bailey used her field notes to develop profiles for each of the TAs (native speakers and non-native speakers) she

March 20, 1986

REST STAFF MEETING

(see Agenda)
1. No general announcements
2. (See Achievement Test Development Schedule.)
We need to find out when we can give the tests and if it can be whenever we want. BL alerted T/Rs to the need for one work session per week during normal hours and at least one per week after hours.
3. *Translation*: JC: When connectors are covered + in depth reading, we get to the word level.
SM: We (the T/Rs) don't do the translation, we have the students do it. It was easier when we were just doing "general ideas" in the text to avoid translation. What we ultimately hope to do is *not* have students translate, but "think in English."
JC: Everyone will be translating to a certain extent in their minds, the words they know, then paraphrasing (different skill from translating).
MM: If the purpose of translating is to get the meaning of the sentence, are *all* sentences that difficult, to require translation? As long as it's not the norm, that it's the last thing you try, translation is okay.
JC: When we are concerned with *clarity*, not allowing for any ambiguity, you need to focus on words and translate. Maybe I'm doing this too often, however.
MM: Are we doing comprehensive reading?
JC/SM: With some of these texts + connectors, yes. We can't check on their comprehension of *ideas* being connected without some translation.

STRUCT/   MM: Continue with translation and see if it works.
CURRIC   SM: Maybe we're ahead of ourselves - - maybe we shouldn't do comprehensive reading until second year, and do only general, main-idea type reading the whole first year. We have these authentic texts, however, that the professors want *comprehensive* understanding for.
ADJUNCT   MM: After talking to the professors, these materials are only "suggested," not required + the information is summarized in "recetas de cocina" in Spanish. They *will* be reading in English after they graduate, however, in their work.
SM: But we were trying to make it more real, more relevant by using something like the "adjunct model."
MM: But at least we can give them something they will be studying (in Spanish) . . .

GRAM/   JC: We haven't dealt with grammar-based instruction; key words that get
READ   in the way of comprehension. What I'm doing now is trying to address this issue.
MM: Just that some of our students are no longer afraid of approaching a text in English is an accomplishment.

ADJUNCT   JC: But we're getting conflicting information from professors, students and ourselves. What Irma (I.Q. prof.) told me was that the students *would*
AUTH   be using/seeing that text in their content course and they would need to
MAT.   know it comprehensively (unlike what the other professor said). The first issue is the authenticity of the *task*: what are they going to do with it - - we need someone to explain this + the concepts to us. If they can do without it, . . .

Figure 7.13   REST project meeting field notes with coding.

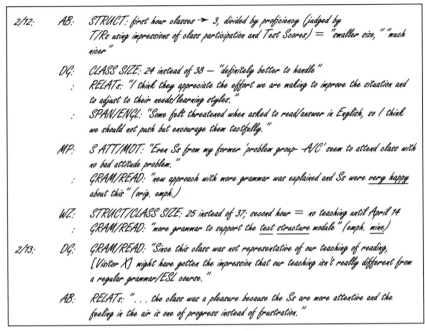

Figure 7.14 Teacher/researcher journal coding.

TABLE 7.5 PRELIMINARY CATEGORY SYSTEM FOR REST PROJECT EVALUATION

1. PROC = PROCESS: Activities, Practices, Methodology
2. STRUCT = STRUCTURE: Setting, Organization, Goals/Objectives
   (+ idea of Innovation, Program Philosophy)
3. RELATs = RELATIONS: Social Climate, Attitudes, Motivation,
   Perceptions/Judgments

PROC/STRUCT	1. Use of explicit grammar instruction along with reading skills
PROC	2. Use of team teaching
PROC/STRUCT	3. Effects of using authentic reading texts
PROC	4. Use of English versus Spanish in the classroom
STRUCT	5. Effect of class size on instruction
PROC/STRUCT	6. Effects of using a "modified adjunct" approach
PROC/STRUCT	7. Use of introspection/retrospection with students as a research tool
RELATs	8. Teacher perception of student ability
RELATs	9. Student–teacher relations

(Additional themes added to previous thematic framework)

STRUCT	10. Changes in class level and teaching assignment
PROC/STRUCT	11. Reading text and task difficulty
PROC	12. Use of student group work in class
PROC/STRUCT	13. System of grading student achievement
PROC/RELATs	14. Student attendance
RELATs	15. Student attitude and motivation

observed. From these profiles she then developed a typology that grouped the TAs into five categories: Active Unintelligible, Mechanical Problem Solver, Knowledgeable Helper/Casual Friend, Entertaining Ally, and Inspiring Cheerleader. This typology was used to help Bailey draw conclusions about native speaker/non-native speaker differences and successful/unsuccessful TA attributes.

Finally, either as an extension of category systems and typologies or as a separate method for classifying and reducing the data, the evaluator can construct *display matrices* (Miles and Huberman 1984). These displays are created by rearranging the data into meaningful categories or ordered lists, usually in the form of a matrix with intersecting columns and rows into which the data are placed. In order to facilitate the discovery of new patterns and relationships in the data, the displays should be constructed and used as a single visual unit, no matter how large that unit needs to be.

One type of display is the *effects matrix* (Miles and Huberman 1984). This matrix attempts to organize data that have been identified through the coding and category systems mentioned earlier as relating to program effects, or outcomes. These effects might be organized by time periods, by type of effects (e.g., primary changes versus side effects or unexpected changes), or by adding presumed causes or antecedent factors to create an *explanatory effects matrix* (Miles and Huberman 1984; cf. Patton's 1980: *process-outcome* matrix).

Table 7.6 represents a first attempt at constructing an effects matrix for the REST project evaluation. The rows of the matrix represent the perspectives of the different participants – teacher/researchers, students, and administrators – and within each participant row, the types of effects or outcomes – those relating to objectives (project goals), process (the methods used in the project), and relations (the social/affective climate). The columns also differentiate the types of effects – original/ intended, intervening/intermediary, and ultimate. The entries in the matrix are paraphrases or quotations from the relevant data sources (e.g., from the T/R journals for the teacher/researcher rows, from the interviews for the student rows). To enter the data systematically into such matrices, it is best to formulate *decision rules* (Miles and Huberman 1984). For the REST project effects matrix, any change or outcome that was mentioned by at least one person was selected. A positive effect was indicated by a + sign, and a negative outcome by a − sign. Double signs indicated that more than one person mentioned the effect.

This preliminary form of the effects matrix, however, did not seem to provide the best characterization and reduction of the data. There were numerous empty cells, and the matrix was cumbersome and difficult to read. The process of matrix construction continued through several more versions before the final effects matrix, shown in Table

7.7 (pp. 150–52), was created. In this process, the categories for type of effect (original, intermediary, and ultimate) were discarded because of their lack of usefulness, and the student perspective was differentiated by group (i.e., group B/beginning, group B/advanced, group A/C intermediate, and group A/C beginning) since this accounted for some important differences concerning perceived outcomes for the program.[9]

Interpretation and conclusions

The final stage in naturalistic data analysis involves interpreting the reduced data and forming conclusions. Although this is the final stage, it will usually be necessary to continue in the iterative fashion of this type of analysis – returning to the data, revising thematic frameworks, reconstructing classification systems and displays – before coming to any final conclusions. The changes made in the preliminary effects matrix for the REST project evaluation, discussed above, reflect an initial attempt to make interpretations and draw conclusions, for example. Once the effects matrix was in its final form, the interpretation and conclusions stage began again. In the remainder of this section, I will use this stage of the REST project evaluation as an example of how interpretations and conclusions can be drawn from the classified and reduced data.

Scanning the REST project effects matrix (Table 7.7), certain patterns reveal themselves rather quickly. First, you can gauge or count the number of + signs versus – signs. There are many more negative outcomes (–) under "Process/methods" than there are under "Objectives/goals." This suggests the possible interpretation that although the goals for the REST project may have been well defined or even reached, the ultimate outcomes for the ways in which those goals were approached needed some reappraisal.

Another method for interpreting the effects matrix is to scan for specific difference patterns. One example can be found under the process/methods column of the matrix, where the UCLA teacher/researchers (UCLA T/Rs) and one group of students (Ss group A/C Int.) indicated

9 These four groups – A/C Beginning, A/C Intermediate, B/Beginning, B/Advanced – represent the four classrooms of students that existed at the beginning of the REST program. The letters A, B, and C refer to the grouping of the students by the Chemical Engineering Faculty for administrative purposes. In order to establish reasonably equivalent class sizes, groups A and C were combined for REST project instruction. The labels Beginning, Intermediate, and Advanced refer to EFL academic proficiency as determined by the REST project staff. Interviews were conducted with students representing these classroom groups both before and after the classroom grouping was changed to add an A/C Advanced and the grammar component was added. Therefore, A/C Advanced and A/C Intermediate are not distinguished in this qualitative analysis.

TABLE 7.6 PRELIMINARY EFFECTS MATRIX: REST PROJECT EVALUATION (OUTCOMES/CHANGES IN THE PROGRAM AS SEEN BY THE VARIOUS PARTICIPANTS DURING YEAR 1)

As seen by	Intended/original	Intervening/intermediary	Ultimate
Teacher/researchers			
Objectives			− Mex. T/Rs are not really being trained per se, but are told "here is a class, now teach it"
Process			− Insufficient materials − Problems with classrooms and schedules
Relations			+ Good attitude from all T/Rs
Students			
Objectives		− − Skim/scan skills ineffective + Need English for career − Things taught obvious, "busy work" − Learned "casi nada" up to now	− Didn't learn as much as we could − Too much grammar + Overall, class helped us + Strats. do help with Chem. Eng. texts − Want 4 skills + Since Feb. more vocab. and grammar was good − Reading strats. ineffective − we "look at articles, don't *read* them"

Process

++ Chem. Eng. texts effective
-- Class not stimulating
- Don't understand instructions in English
++ In general, class is dynamic
-- Not enough variety

- Goals not well defined
+ Understand more English than in Sept.
- Strats. already known

-More participation/ activity for Ss;
+ Chem. Eng. articles from profs. were excellent
- Boring, going in circles
- Too much material, too fast at times

Relations

-- Treat us like children
- Frustration

- Not enough pressure from T/Rs

Administrators

Objectives

+ Provide Chem. Eng. Ss with necessary tools to be able to read articles related to Chem. Eng.
+ Stimulate research in Mex.
+ Research in reading EST
+ Develop method of evaluation
+ Teacher training

Process

- Unrealistic planning and budgeting of project by UdeG

Relations

+ "Flexible" nature of T/Rs
- UCLA and UdeG may be "awkward bedfellows"
- Culture clashes

As seen by	Objectives/goals	Process/methods	Relations/climate
UdeG Coord.	+ A curriculum framework to improve Ss ability to read EST − Ss did not "master" anything just introduced to − Did not convince Ss that they don't need to read word by word	+ Use grammar in context as a strategy for reading + Use read. strats. e.g., preview, prediction, skim, scan + Teach functions of log. connectors: rhetorical modes + Use authentic Chem. Eng. texts, but not exclusively	+ (Coord.) overall positive to Project + T/Rs hard workers − Cultural misunderstandings: T/Rs "took it personally" − Ss more demanding than most, and "a few bad apples" − T/Rs "frustrated" − T/Rs did not get along well as a group
UdeG T/B Assts.	+ Interesting curriculum, helpful to Ss	+ Well supported mat'ls., prep'd. well by UCLA T/Rs (REST) Too dependent on other Univ. depts. − Problems w/classrms and schedules − Tedious classes: too much time spent on some points; excessive repetition − Need to allow more talking and listening in English and expand grammar module	+ Good attitude – all T/Rs − lack of communication: T/R Assts. − lack of understanding (UCLA T/Rs) of Mex. S behavior
UCLA T/Rs	++ S confidence to "attack" English texts + Signif. improv't in gen. ESL prof., reading and grades in REST	+ Using texts as basis for grammar discussion ++ Give Ss more basic linguistic skills	++ UCLA support ++ Some staff members dedicated −− Lack of UdeG admin. support −− S resentment of Project and T/Rs

	+ Ss Chem. Eng. profs., now expect them to read texts in Engl., w/o translations, and do "practices" based on readings + Basic elements of a curriculum + Lots of ideas and info. for a thesis -- Not enough time for research -- Ss will not be "prof. readers" of EST in 2 years - "We didn't do enough for them" - Not able to give real training to Mex. T/Rs	+ Began to use more "4-skills" type act's for reading - Lack of materials - Lack of focus and organization - Relied too much on theory: didn't know how to implement it - "A clump of strategies": did them w/ every text - T/Rs hindered by need to all do same material same way, same rate	- REST staff "not taken seriously or taken advantage of" ? Lack of cooperation between T/Rs (1 "yes," 2 "no") -- Frustration
Ss group B/Begin.	+ Were able to use some Chem. Eng. texts (suggested by Chem. Eng. prof) in their practices – helped them + Now we can use the strategies taught + Overall, course helps us "bastante"	+Use of the OHP - Need a different system for understanding grammar - At times, too much material too fast: no time to take notes + Read. strategies do help us w/ reading	
Ss group B/Adv.	+ Used texts (English) in our "practices"	+ Use of OHP - Read. strategies approach doesn't work: "we look at articles but don't read them" - Need a review of grammar - Need more participation on part of Ss	- At times, we feel a little bored

TABLE 7.7 (cont.)

As seen by	Objectives/goals	Process/methods	Relations/climate
Ss group A/C Int.	+ Now we know how to form/write a sentence in English – Nothing well-defined in the development of the course – Very little covered first 1/2 year	+ More grammar and vocab. (since Feb.) – "going in circles": same basic activities – Reading strategies "a waste of time": already known – "Timed" factor on tests unfair	– "boring" – Lack of attend.: because not what expected/wanted: i.e., "skills" and bad schedule for English class
Ss group A/C Begin.	+ Did learn something, *not* a waste of time – Didn't learn as much as possible/hoped – Didn't know where curric. was heading	– Too much grammar: don't understand how logical connect's help us to read – Lack of dynamism in class activities: always T to S – Not enough "pressure" from Ts	– Lack of motivation – lack of attend.: due to lack of interest and to bad schedule for English class

Source: Lynch 1992:85.

that more grammar instruction was a positive outcome (UCLA T/Rs: "++ Give Ss more basic linguistic skills"; Ss group A/C Int.: "+ More grammar and vocab. [since Feb.]") However, most student groups seemed to perceive this instruction as being either incorrect (Ss group B/Begin.: "− Need a different system for understanding grammar"), insufficient (Ss group B/Adv.: "− Need a review of grammar"), or excessive (Ss group A/C Begin: "Too much grammar. . . . ").

Another difference is that the teacher/researchers and the coordinator indicated that the objectives/goals for the program had been established – the framework and the basic elements were in place. The students, however, either failed to comment or mentioned that nothing was well defined or they were not sure where the curriculum was heading.

You can also scan the matrix for specific similarity patterns. An example of this is the mention of having been able to use authentic English texts in chemical engineering, which was seen as a positive outcome by both teacher/researchers and students. The teacher/researchers also agreed with the students that there was a lack of focus and organization in terms of process/methods. A final similarity can be found concerning relations/climate. Both the coordinator and the teacher/researchers mentioned problems experienced by the teacher/researchers in getting along. This was somewhat contradicted by the opposite perception noted by one teacher/researcher (hence the "?" in the matrix). In this case, I needed to go back to the data, primarily the teacher/researcher journals, to attempt to disambiguate this outcome. Ultimately, this review of the data indicated that there were major problems among the teacher/researchers during the first year of the project, but that the teacher/researcher who indicated a positive outcome for relations/climate either refrained from mentioning these problems in journal entries, or held contradictory perceptions from the other teacher/researchers.

Ultimately, the evaluator needs to translate these interpretations into conclusions for the evaluation audience. In a sense, this process is the way in which validity is established for naturalistic research, as discussed in Chapter 3. Conclusions should always be checked across different kinds of data, data collectors, collection methods, and program perspectives. This is done, at least in part, during the data-reduction and interpretation stages, as seen in the analysis of the effects matrix for the REST project evaluation. Another technique is to look for negative cases, for evidence in the data that does not fit the pattern. Such negative cases do not necessarily eliminate potential conclusions, but rather they help the evaluator to communicate the limits of a pattern from which the conclusion is drawn. In a sense, this is similar to conclusions made in quantitative research when "outliers" are removed from the data or when the assumptions of the statistical model are not quite met.

Another technique that was presented in Chapter 3 is the search for rival explanations. There may be other ways of organizing the data, necessitating a return to the classification and reduction stage, that lead to different interpretations and other conclusions. It is a good idea to try out explanations that seem completely contradictory to the preliminary conclusions you form. Miles and Huberman (1984) suggest taking any conclusion and logically reversing it. If the conclusion is, for example, that the program is overly structured because the administration has set standards that are unreasonable, see if the data make more sense if the conclusion is reversed: for example, that the administration has set unreasonable standards because the program is overly structured.

An example of this type of conclusion verification can be found in the REST project evaluation. One interpretation that surfaced from the analysis was that the students were not attending their English classes regularly because there were bad relations with the teacher/researchers. There was ample evidence in the teacher/researcher journals, in the meetings subfile, and from observations that the teachers and certain groups of students were not getting along. There was also evidence of poor attendance in those student groups. It seemed reasonable to assume that the two were linked, even causally, and that the bad relations were antecedent to the lack of attendance. Reversing the interpretation proved illuminating, however. In fact, the English classes had been scheduled at times that conflicted with other classes that certain students were repeating. There were also student soccer games that conflicted with the hours of the English classes. Students were having attendance problems, then, but not because they were not getting along with their teachers. The bad relations between teachers and students were, rather, the result of the attendance problems, which, in turn, were due to scheduling conflicts of which the REST staff were unaware until it was too late.

In addition to the use of rival explanations, the preceding example made use of a form of multiple perspective negotiation. The evaluator discussed his preliminary interpretation, that bad relations caused poor attendance, with various participants – teacher/researchers, students, other professors in the Chemical Engineering faculty. This discussion, a negotiation of sorts across different perspectives, led to the revised conclusion. The strongest conclusions for naturalistic evaluation make use of this type of validation: techniques such as the search for negative cases and rival explanations, and multiple perspective negotiation.

In this chapter I have endeavored to provide a thorough and systematic portrayal of qualitative data gathering and analysis. Rather than just referring to a different type of data, I have presented qualitative techniques within the naturalistic research paradigm. In the next chapter, I discuss potential ways of combining quantitative and qualitative techniques, along with their attendant paradigms.

8 Combining positivistic and naturalistic program evaluation

Compatibilist versus incompatibilist perspectives

Chapters 4 and 5 presented designs and metaphors for carrying out program evaluation within two distinct paradigms for research. The possibility of mixing designs from these two paradigms entails the adoption of the *compatibilist* stance (also referred to as the *accommodationist* stance), discussed in Chapter 2. At the heart of the compatibility-incompatibility debate is the level at which the mixing of the paradigms is to take place. Are we mixing positivistic and naturalistic designs at the philosophical level, with the attendant assumptions about what is knowable and the relationship between knowledge and the knower? Or are we mixing designs at the methodological level, along with the associated assumptions about how we should conduct our inquiry?

The incompatibilist (or antiaccommodationist) will of course argue that our assumptions at one level flow logically from our assumptions at the other level. For example, if we choose to mix designs by using methods from both paradigms, without regard for the different philosophical assumptions that underlie these methods, we are merely mixing techniques, not methods. This, then, is the potential stalemate of the quantitative–qualitative debate: If you choose a paradigm, the methods that you choose can be used meaningfully only within that paradigm. From the incompatibilist perspective, it is possible to use quantitative techniques, to collect quantitative data, and to analyze it statistically within a naturalistic design. However, these techniques can provide information that makes sense – that counts as evidence – only within the naturalistic way of knowing. To the extent that this information, whether from quantitative or qualitative data, derives its sense or counts as evidence from the positivistic way of knowing, we are no longer using naturalistic methods or a naturalistic design. It is this definition of method, as opposed to data-gathering technique, that leads the incompatibilist to assert the impossibility of mixing the paradigms, even at the methodological level.

The staunch compatibilist (accommodationist) will argue that there are no important differences between the paradigms, at any level, or at least that these differences do not pose problems for mixing the paradigms at the methodological level. From this perspective, quantitative data and statistical analysis can make sense within the naturalistic way of knowing, and qualitative data and analysis can make sense within the positivistic way of knowing. How would this type of paradigm mixing actually be expressed in research? If the data collection and analysis are quantitative, then in order to make sense within the naturalistic paradigm, the researcher needs to consider various interpretations of the results. These interpretations must allow for the possibility of new hypotheses emerging, suggesting the need to collect additional data. An additional important element of such a mixed design is that the data collection and analysis must be done within the naturally occurring set of conditions for the program; the program setting cannot be manipulated for the purposes of the evaluation. The problems that such conditions cause for positivistic analysis have been discussed in Chapters 3 and 6.

The other type of mixing involves qualitative data and analysis, conducted within a positivistic design. In this case, the program setting is manipulated to the degree possible in order to arrive at an isolation of the program as a treatment. The data and analysis are qualitative, but this information is used for the purposes of deciding whether or not the differences between the program group and the comparison group were caused by the program.

Mixed strategies

If we remain open to the compatibilist perspective, several combinations of the two paradigms are possible for defining mixed designs. Patton (1980:109) has created a framework for considering these designs, which he refers to as "mixed methodological strategies." In this sense, a methodological strategy for program evaluation can be conceptualized as a *design* (as presented in Chapters 4 and 5); a type of measurement, or *data*; and a type of data *analysis*. Assuming that each paradigm – positivistic and naturalistic – has its own type of design, data, and analysis with which it is traditionally associated, the various possibilities for mixed designs can be enumerated as in Table 8.1. Note that within this conceptualization, the designs themselves are not mixed, only the type of data and data analysis with which they are combined. That is, we first choose a design, and then various combinations of methodological possibilities present themselves. A pure positivistic design assumes quantitative data and quantitative analysis; a pure naturalistic design assumes qualitative data and qualitative analysis. The mixed

TABLE 8.1 MIXED STRATEGIES

Data + analysis/ design	Quant. + qual. data	analysis	Qual. + quant. data	analysis
Positivistic		1?		2
Naturalistic		3?		4

       If we allow for the possibility of data and analysis from one paradigm being used within a design from the other, then there are two other mixed strategies:

Positivistic		X		5
Naturalistic		6		X

strategies are defined by different combinations of data and analysis within each design.

    Mixed strategies 1 and 3 are the most difficult to imagine as viable possibilities for evaluation research because whereas in most cases, qualitative data can be quantified, it is not as straightforward to turn quantitative data into qualitative data for the purposes of qualitative analysis. We can imagine taking data such as test scores and converting them into qualitative descriptions of what each score or group of scores signify in relation to the ability being tested. However, it is not immediately apparent how such a conversion would be of greater value in the evaluation than analyzing the test score information quantitatively.

    Mixed strategies 2, 4, 5, and 6, on the other hand, can be conceptualized more readily. Consider the following vignettes.

(*Mixed strategy 2*):   Students are randomly assigned to either the innovative Back-to-Nature (BTN) ESL program or to the more traditional Give 'Em the Basics (GEB) curriculum. The setting for the evaluation is strictly controlled so that conditions for the students in the two groups are exactly the same except for which curriculum they are receiving. Before instruction begins, a team of evaluators conducts in-depth interviews with all students. At the end of instruction the team conducts another set of in-depth interviews. The qualitative data from pre- and postinstruction interviews are then rated using a scale developed by the evaluation team and designed to capture the essential elements of ESL proficiency from both the BTN and GEB perspectives. The scores for students in the BTN group are then compared with the scores for the GEB group using appropriate statistical techniques in order to assess the effect of the BTN program.

    An actual example of this mixed strategy can be found in the evaluation of a university health service (UHS) organization by Trochim (1985). Staff members from the UHS participated in a brainstorming session to produce a collection of statements concerning their understanding of the UHS organization. The resulting qualitative data were then analyzed quantitatively using an unstructured sorting procedure (Rosenberg and Kim 1975), multidimensional scaling (Kruskal and Wish 1978), and cluster analysis (Everitt, 1980). These quantitative analyses produced "concept and cluster maps,' which the UHS organization used for further evaluation and planning efforts.

(*Mixed strategy 4*):   An evaluation team has been asked to come to the Panda School of Foreign Languages in Tokyo, Japan, to evaluate its EFL program. The evaluators spend several months at the school site, collecting interview and observation data from students, teachers, and administrators. These data are then categorized, and a scale is developed for each category to measure "degree of positiveness." These measures are compared across groups (students, teachers, administrators) using appropriate statistical techniques. These statistical comparisons provide the basis for a descriptive portrayal of the program.

(*Mixed strategy 5*):   IBM randomly selects 50 of its executives and then randomly assigns them to either a Total Physical Response (TPR) or a Suggestopedia (S) group for instruction in Japanese for Business Purposes. Evaluation team members interview all executives both before and after instruction. Classroom observation data are collected at regular intervals for both TPR and S classes. The data are analyzed qualitatively, that is, by looking for important themes and issues in each classroom, developing typologies, reducing the data to display matrices, and drawing conclusions. These conclusions are examined to determine which curriculum is producing the most effective student achievement.

(*Mixed strategy 6*):   An applied linguist is hired by the Pleasant Valley High School District to evaluate their French Immersion Program (FIP). The evaluator enters the school setting with a familiarity with the literature on immersion programs, but attempts to allow important variables for analysis to emerge from her observations of the FIP classrooms. Once the major variables have been identified, the evaluator constructs instruments to measure them, collects the data, and analyzes them using appropriate statistical techniques. Using these analyses, the evaluator constructs a description of the program.

Multiple strategies

It may be possible, in certain contexts, to use a combination of a mixed strategy and a pure strategy to pursue an evaluation. Fielding and Fielding (1986), for example, combined quantitative data and analysis within a naturalistic design (mixed strategy 6) along with qualitative data and analysis in their investigation of a police training program in Derbyshire, England. Quantitative data were gathered through a series of questionnaires, including one that asked police recruits to indicate agreement or disagreement, using a five-point Likert scale, with a series of statements related to police activities and attitudes. Qualitative data were gathered through in-depth interviews with a subsample of recruits.

The advantage of this approach was that the researchers were able to use the interview data to arrive at explanations for certain unclear relationships in the questionnaire data. For example, there seemed to be a contradiction in police recruit responses to questionnaire items concerning the desirability of recruiting more black officers and the desire to limit further immigration by blacks to the society. The questionnaire data indicated a tendency to favor more black police but to be opposed to further immigration. Furthermore, there seemed to be differences in recruit response depending on whether they had previously been in the military or not. The interview data revealed that prior experience with blacks in the military and, in particular, in the context of military police, led many recruits to believe that you need black police to handle black neighborhoods. Thus, the desirability of more black police recruits was not a reflection of an integrationist attitude and was not contradictory to the expressed tendency to be opposed to further black immigration.

Mixed designs

The type of mixing just discussed, in which a design from one paradigm is mixed with a type of data and/or analysis from another, is one way in which the compatibilist approach to evaluation can be conceptualized. It is also possible to attempt a truly *mixed design*, in which both positivistic and naturalistic designs are employed within the same evaluation context. One design or the other will be compromised to a certain degree, depending on the amount of manipulation of the program setting that occurs for the purposes of the evaluation. In the following section I present an example of an attempted mixed design, drawn from the REST project evaluation (Lynch 1988, 1992).

Mixed design evaluation: The REST project

In the evaluation of the REST project I attempted to combine a positivistic, quasi-experimental design using a nonequivalent control group (discussed in Chapter 4) with a naturalistic design that adapted most elements of the illumination model (discussed in Chapter 5). Quantitative test score data were gathered and analyzed using appropriate statistical techniques (discussed in Chapter 6) and interpreted following rationalistic principles concerning what counts as evidence (discussed in Chapter 4). Qualitative data were gathered using observation, interviews, journal keeping, field notes from meetings, and document analysis. These data were analyzed using qualitative techniques (discussed in Chapter 7) and were interpreted following naturalistic principles concerning what counts as evidence (discussed in Chapter 4).

Given the difficulty of implementing even one of these designs well enough to gain useful information for program evaluation purposes, why would anyone choose to attempt both of them? Before answering that question, let me admit that for many if not most evaluations, the resources available will not make it possible to attempt such a mixed design. In the preceding chapters I have endeavored to provide a sense of the potential benefits of the two paradigms and their associated methods, to enable the evaluator to choose the best approach given the specific evaluation context. However, I heartily encourage you to attempt the use of both positivistic and naturalistic evaluation whenever the context permits. In the case of the REST project evaluation, the research nature of the program and my own interest in both research paradigms made such an attempt feasible. The advantages that this attempt provided were improvements in the ability to explain contradictory or ambiguous results and to check final interpretations and conclusions.

EXPLAINING CONTRADICTORY OR AMBIGUOUS RESULTS IN THE POSITIVISTIC DATA/ANALYSES USING NATURALISTIC DATA/ANALYSES

The results of the positivistic analyses of how much the REST program students improved in their reading ability compared to the control group students were somewhat contradictory. Reading ability was measured by the reading subtest of the English as a Second Language Placement Exam (ESLPE). Two of the statistical analyses, ANCOVA and standardized change-score analysis (see Chapter 6), provided evidence that the REST students had made significantly greater gains than the control group students. Two other statistical analyses, chi-square and effect size analysis (see Chapter 6), indicated that there were either no significant differences between the groups or that the REST students were doing moderately better than the control group.

Turning to the evidence from the naturalistic design and analysis, I discovered certain possible explanations for the apparent contradiction in the quantitative analysis. First, there were references in the student interview data indicating that the REST curriculum was not always addressing the skill of reading as the students defined it. In one of the group interviews with students the following observation was made: "We look at articles, but we don't read them" (translated from the Spanish). Evidence from the teacher/researcher journals, the observation subfile, and program documents indicated that for the first 5 months of the curriculum students were being instructed primarily in how to find main ideas (skimming) and specific information (scanning), preview texts, and examine text structure. Many of the students felt that they already had skimming and scanning skills and were unhappy with the amount of time being spent on them. However, because of the generally low level of EFL ability of most of the students, there was no overt instructional attention to in-depth reading for comprehension in the first term of the project.

In addition to this evidence, some important information was gained from a closer analysis of the content of the ESLPE. The reading subtest was composed of short, two- to three-paragraph texts, requiring the students to read the text closely and carefully in order to answer the comprehension questions. These questions often required the students to make fine distinctions of meaning in relation to the text or to draw inferences beyond the text itself.

A possible explanation for the contradictory positivistic results is thus suggested by the naturalistic results. The students were being tested by an instrument that required a careful reading and understanding of each word in the text, whereas the curriculum was focused on reading skills that discouraged students from such reading. As a result, the students may have felt frustration and even resentment. In terms of the positivistic data, posttest performance may reflect a certain amount of variance that is not attributable to their reading ability (i.e., they were not really trying to answer the questions correctly because of their resentment).

How would this affect the statistical analyses? The ANCOVA analysis has been criticized for overestimating treatment effect when the program group is superior at the beginning of the evaluation. Although this was not statistically the case in the REST evaluation, the REST students did have a higher pretest mean score on all measures. This is an example of the *fan-spread hypothesis* – when the advantaged group is growing at a faster rate than the comparison group. Standardized change-score analysis is supposed to correct for this overestimation and would therefore be expected to differ from the ANCOVA results. However, in the case of the REST project evaluation, the standardized change-score results agreed with those from the ANCOVA. If the REST students were resentful of the ESLPE test after experiencing the REST curriculum, it should probably not be assumed that their posttest results reflected a higher growth rate. This might explain why the ANCOVA and standardized change-score results agreed – the fan-spread hypothesis was not in effect – and why these analyses disagreed with the others – ANCOVA and standardized change-score were both potentially overestimating the treatment effect.

EXPLAINING CONTRADICTORY OR AMBIGUOUS RESULTS IN
THE NATURALISTIC DATA/ANALYSES USING POSITIVISTIC
DATA/ANALYSES

In the analysis of the naturalistic data for the REST project evaluation, there was a certain amount of contradictory evidence concerning student perception of the role of grammar instruction in the curriculum. In the previous chapter, I commented on this in the discussion of the effects matrix and its use in qualitative data analysis. In this discussion, I will expand upon that analysis and attempt to demonstrate the possible explanation that the quantitative data and analysis provide.

As explained in Chapter 7, the REST students were identified by their group (A, B, or C) and by their level of EFL proficiency (beginning, intermediate, advanced). Students were assigned to four classrooms for the REST program based on a combination of these two factors. The naturalistic evaluation revealed that there were differences in the way these classroom groups of students perceived the instruction they were receiving, especially after the first 5 months of the program. During the second 5 months of the program, in response to student complaints and teacher suggestions, instruction on grammar (in the context of chemical engineering) was added to the curriculum. This was not, however, being experienced in a parallel fashion across the student groups. Students in group A/C Intermediate reported in their interview from the second half of the year that including more grammar was a positive aspect of the program. Students in group A/C Beginning felt that there was too much grammar and that they did not understand how knowing about such things as logical connectors would help them to read better. Students in group B Beginning expressed the need for a different system of presenting and understanding grammar. Group B Advanced wanted more review of grammar.[1] On the other hand, data from the teacher/researcher journals and the observation subfile suggested that the grammar was being included in basically the same fashion and to the same degree across the classroom groups. There were no other data from the naturalistic evaluation that seemed to account for the contradictory perceptions on the part of the students concerning grammar instruction and the apparent similarity of instruction in grammar across classrooms.

If there were important differences, either in terms of student intake

---

1 As mentioned in the preceding chapter, these four groups – A/C Beginning, A/C Intermediate, B Beginning, B Advanced – represent the four classrooms of students that existed at the beginning of the REST program. Interviews were conducted with students representing these classroom groups both before and after the classroom grouping was changed to add an A/C Advanced and the grammar component was added. Therefore, A/C Advanced and A/C Intermediate are not distinguished in this qualitative analysis.

or reaction to the grammar component, or in terms of teacher/researcher presentation across classrooms, we might expect there to be significant differences in student achievement on measures of grammar. Using ANCOVA, it was discovered that there were significant differences between the classroom groups. However, post hoc comparisons revealed that only the A/C Beginning students differed from the other student groups. This group had complained that there was too much grammar, and they did significantly more poorly on the ESLPE grammar subtest (and the rest of the achievement measures), even after controlling for preexisting differences in overall EFL proficiency. However, the A/C Intermediate students, who were the only group to express positive attitudes about the grammar component, did not do significantly better than the other groups, including the group B beginning students. The perceived differences in usefulness of grammar instruction did not appear to result in consistent differences in student achievement, and this seems to support the evidence from the journals and observations concerning the similarity of instructional presentation. Of course, the positivistic conclusions need to be made with caution, given the inevitable violations of the strict assumptions of ANCOVA. Ultimately, this example does not result in a complete resolution of the ambiguities in the naturalistic data concerning grammar instruction. We are still left to find an explanation for the contradictory perceptions from the students across classrooms.

A related example of the potential for positivistic analysis to aid in the explanation of contradictory naturalistic analyses concerns the perception on the part of teacher/researchers that there were important differences among the student academic groups in the Chemical Sciences faculty. Evidence from meeting notes indicated that there were no systematic differences among the groups (A, B, and C); the director of the faculty had assured the REST coordinators that the students were assigned randomly. However, evidence from the teacher/researcher journals indicated that the teachers perceived group B students to be academically superior to those in groups A and C, in addition to having a better attitude toward the REST program. Journal entries from the first term (October) mentioning that A/C students seemed not to understand and that they possibly had "underdeveloped cognitive skills," whereas group B students were "coming up with great answers" were typical. Later, in November, a journal entry for a group B class remarked, "The essential element of success [in this class] is the attitude of these students . . . they're my salvation!" In a classroom observation from December there is another reference to group B attempting to use more English in class, more often, and participating more than group A/C classes.

What was of interest, from a program evaluation point of view, was the extent to which perceived differences among the student groups would result in differential effects for the program in terms of student achievement. Using the ESLPE total score as a measure of student achievement, an ANCOVA and post hoc comparisons on the posttest data revealed that group B students were significantly better than the group A and group C students after adjusting for preexisting differences in EFL proficiency. Similar results were found using the multiple-choice cloze test that had been developed to measure some of the instructional goals of the REST curriculum. This tended to resolve the contradiction between the official story of student placement into groups and teacher perception of student ability in favor of the teachers' perceptions. Certainly it indicated that, regardless of how the groups were formed, the perceived difference in student attitude, speaking in English, and other classroom participation differences between group B and the other two groups was related to student achievement. Again, however, these conclusions are tempered by the fact that not all of the assumptions underlying the form of statistical analysis, ANCOVA, were met.

CHECKING ON FINAL INTERPRETATIONS
AND CONCLUSIONS

Ultimately, the larger questions of a program evaluation must be addressed and final conclusions made. Concerning the REST project's goals for improving students' ability to read English for Science and Technology (EST), the naturalistic design provided evidence that the REST students had improved only in their basic, sentence-level linguistic skills, if at all. The UdeG (Spanish acronym for University of Guadalajara) coordinator felt that the students "didn't master anything," teacher/researchers felt that the students would not be "proficient readers" by the end of the 2-year program, and students commented that "now we know how to form/write a sentence in English [at least]." The positivistic evaluation tended to support this conclusion. The ESLPE was judged to be a measure that focused to a large extent on sentence-level grammar. The student improvement evidenced by the positivistic analyses thus confirms the sentence-level-only interpretation from the naturalistic data. Where the ESLPE seemed to measure more than sentence-level linguistic skills, in the reading subtest, the positivistic analyses were less unanimous in confirming the significance of REST student gains. Evidence from the multiple-choice cloze results suggested that the REST students might also be improving significantly in more discourse-related skills such as identifying logical connectors and pronominal references. However, evidence was, in turn, contradicted by the REST final exam data, which produced group mean scores of 40 to 66 percent.

Despite these specific conclusions, there was significant overall improvement for the REST students as measured by the ESLPE and multiple-choice cloze tests. This illustrates that, depending on the design that is chosen for the evaluation, different conclusions may be drawn for the same program. For example, whereas the overall positivistic conclusions might be that the REST project was a success during its first year, the naturalistic design provided evidence that indicated that the program had not been successful from the perspectives of the teacher/researchers and the students. In particular, the level of EST reading ability that the teacher/researchers had hoped to reach was not attained, and the process and methods used in the curriculum were not judged successful by the students or, to a certain extent, by the teacher/researchers.

These contradictory final conclusions can be seen as providing checks on each other and serving to strengthen the evaluation and, ultimately, the program. As a result of the conclusions from the naturalistic evaluation, important changes were made in the curriculum for the second year that might not otherwise have been initiated (e.g., a concentration on developing basic EFL language skills during the first-year curriculum before implementing a reading-skills-only approach). On the other hand, without the more positive conclusions from the positivistic evaluation, continued support for the project might have been difficult to obtain from the supporting institutions, and the project participants would have been less likely to develop the positive attitude that was needed to move the program forward.

Mixed designs and strategies over time

Another possibility for combining strategies and designs is through multiple studies over time. McGrath (1982:70) makes the rather disheartening claim that:

... there is no one true method, or correct set of methodological choices that will guarantee success; there is not even a "best" strategy or set of choices for a given problem, setting, and available resources. In fact, from a dilemmatic point of view, *all research strategies and methods are seriously flawed.* ... Indeed, *it is not possible, in principle, to do "good"* (that is, methodologically sound) *research. (original emphasis)*

Rather than leave us with this counsel of despair, McGrath and his colleagues (McGrath et al. 1982:117) recommend a form of *triangulation* that extends across research studies:

It is through the convergence of the efforts of diverse researchers, using diverse methods and playing diverse roles in the research enterprise, that we will make progress – if, indeed, we do. Such progress requires divergence of means, but it also requires some self-conscious coordination of our collective work.

This chapter has illustrated the potential benefits of combining positivistic and naturalistic evaluation designs, along with quantitative and qualitative data and analyses. Although not all evaluation contexts will permit the use of both, I recommend multiple strategies (or multiple designs) wherever possible in order to provide the most thorough information possible and to strengthen evaluation conclusions.

9 Conclusions

In the preceding chapters I have attempted to provide the theoretical background and practical information necessary to approach the task of evaluating a language education program. I have been assuming an audience that represents a range of the interests that are presently included in the field of applied linguistics. That field, for me, remains grounded in language education; however, I believe that program evaluation motivates research that can inform most areas of inquiry being pursued by applied linguists, including areas that consciously avoid a concern for the application of findings to the language classroom (cf. Schumann 1992). If this is true, then the discussion of research paradigms, validity, and evaluation methods presented in this book should be of value to a variety of teachers,[1] researchers, and administrators.

Before elaborating on the role of program evaluation in applied linguistics research, I would like to summarize the critical issues of theory and practice that have been discussed in the preceding chapters. In order to provide a framework for this summary, I will return to the context-adaptive model (CAM) for program evaluation (Lynch 1990a) introduced in Chapter 1. For the person who is preparing to evaluate a language education program, this will serve as a checklist of concerns for the evaluation.

CAM step 1 (audience and goals): Determine the purpose of the evaluation

All program evaluation starts with a purpose, or purposes, and this is established, initially, by the audience(s) and their goals for the evaluation. As discussed in Chapter 1, there are a variety of potential audiences for any evaluation of a language education program. These audience types are schematized in Table 9.1. Sponsors are the funding

---

1 I enthusiastically embrace the notion that all teachers are researchers as well. In the field of applied linguistics, I would also like to believe that, on some level, all researchers are teachers as well.

TABLE 9.1 PROGRAM EVALUATION AUDIENCES

	Proximity to program		
Role	*Day-to-day contact*	*Occasional contact*	*No contact*
Sponsors	P	P	T
Administrators	P	S	T
Teachers	P	S	T
Researchers	P	S	T
Students	S	T	T
Evaluators	X	T	T

P = primary evaluation audience; S = secondary evaluation audience; T = tertiary evaluation audience.

agencies, the host institutions, and the collaborating institutions that have varying degrees of contact with the program. These are the parties most likely to request the evaluation and are thus a primary-level audience, along with the administrators, teachers, and researchers who are implementing the program. The primary-level audience is usually the people who receive a formal evaluation report. Teachers, researchers, and administrators who have occasional contact with the program being evaluated (i.e., who are not directly responsible for the implementation, but who work with related classrooms, departments, schools, or institutions) constitute a secondary level audience, along with the students who are participating in the program. The secondary level audiences, because of their proximity to the program, may receive an informal report on the results of the evaluation or may request a copy of the formal report. Finally, a tertiary level audience exists in the form of sponsors, administrators, teachers, researchers, students, and evaluators who have only occasional or no contact with the program being evaluated but who are interested in the evaluation results. This audience will usually request a copy of the formal report or will find accounts of the evaluation in the research literature.

These various audience types will have different goals in mind for the evaluation. My definition of evaluation, as presented in Chapter 1, focused on the judgmental nature of evaluation, but I would like to mention that evaluation can be thought of as exploratory and discovery-oriented as well. This is an important aspect of naturalistic evaluation and its notion of validity. There are legitimate goals for evaluation that involve exploring the program and describing it, rather than sitting in judgment. The increased attention to program process is part of this notion: that evaluation is interested in how a program is work-

TABLE 9.2 PRELIMINARY MATRIX FOR CHARTING AUDIENCE AND GOALS

	Goal	
Audience	*Judgmental*	*Descriptive*
Sponsor		
Administrator		
Teacher		
Researcher		
Student		
Evaluator		

ing, as well as whether or not it has achieved some sort of standard for success. Admittedly, the motivation for wanting to know how a program works usually stems from a desire to improve it, if possible. Nevertheless, description of the evaluation as exploratory rather than judgmental can help reduce the anxiety traditionally associated with such practice.

Different audiences will be interested in either judgmental goals or exploratory, descriptive goals (and sometimes both) in relation to different program characteristics. For example, an audience may wish to have judgments made concerning student achievement of program goals, student achievement in relation to other programs, student attitudes toward the program, teacher effectiveness, teacher attitudes toward the program, or the cost-effectiveness of the program. On the other hand, audiences may wish to have descriptions of the program's instructional process, the various perspectives of program participants, language use (both target language and native language, in certain contexts), the administrative process, and the type of materials being used. There is overlap, of course, between these categories. For example, student attitudes toward the program can be approached in a judgmental way (measuring the degree of satisfaction with the program) as well as in a descriptive fashion (understanding the nature of satisfaction/dissatisfaction). In order to begin to solidify the sense of why the evaluation is being done, the evaluator can keep track of the interaction of audience and goals with a matrix like that provided in Table 9.2.

As Alderson (1992) has pointed out, there may be serious disagreements over the goals of an evaluation among the various participants and audiences. These need to be reconciled, to the extent possible, through negotiation in advance of the planning and implementation of an evaluation. The important point, at this preliminary stage, is that the evaluator become aware of the range of audiences and goals. This awareness will be enhanced in the next two stages: the context inventory and development of the preliminary thematic framework. In order to begin gauging how much time you can spend on these stages, however, a relatively clear agreement needs to be reached with the sponsors concerning what the evaluation is expected to produce – the "deliverables," as Alderson puts it – and when these deliverables will be due. Beretta (1992a) refers to this as negotiating a "coherent charter" for the evaluation, including the following elements:

- Feasibility of goals
- Deadlines for reaching goals
- Form required for reporting evaluation findings
- Persons to whom findings will be reported
- The use that will be made of findings
- Priorities for goals in terms of time and resources

CAM steps 2 and 3 (context inventory and preliminary thematic framework): Determine what is being evaluated

Normally, the negotiation of the evaluation "charter" continues as you begin to gather the information necessary to establish the context inventory and the preliminary thematic framework. This is because the evaluation audiences will not always be clear themselves on what they want from the evaluation. As you examine the dimensions of the context inventory (comparison group, reliable and valid measures, evaluation expertise, timing of evaluation, selection process, students, staff, program size and intensity, instructional materials and resources, perspective and purpose, social and political climate) and develop a preliminary sense of the important themes and issues, your questions to the participants and sponsors will provide an opportunity to clarify and refine the initially stated goals, uses, and priorities for the evaluation.

Part of the answer to "what is being evaluated," of course, comes directly from the audiences and their goals for the evaluation. These goals will focus the evaluator on various dimensions of the program, such as student achievement of instructional objectives, or the process of materials development. The other part of the answer comes from the overall sense of the program and its context that the evaluator needs in order to guide the evaluation inquiry and to situate the specific evaluation questions within a meaningful and explanatory framework. Before moving to the next step, when the design of the evaluation is specified, a consideration of the dimensions of the context inventory and a formulation of evaluation themes can help to finalize this preliminary picture of what is being evaluated.

CAM steps 4 and 5 (evaluation design and data collection): Select a design and collect the data

The field of applied linguistics has definitely moved beyond the notion that the best, or only, program evaluation is an experimental (or quasi-experimental) design. This is not to say that such designs hold no place in the evaluation of language education programs, but that they should be seen as one type of evaluation strategy that may be called for by certain audiences, goals, and program contexts. Along with Alderson (1992) and Beretta (1992a), I remind evaluators of the inherent difficulties of trying to carry out experimental research in field settings, and of the limitations to what such an evaluation strategy can tell us about the programs we are investigating. These problems have been discussed in Chapters 4 and 6. On the other hand, there are difficulties with conducting a naturalistic evaluation, as well, and these have been discussed in Chapters 5 and 7. The preferred evaluation approach, as discussed in Chapter 8, is mixed strategies (e.g., quantitative analysis of qualitative data) or mixed design (positivistic and naturalistic). However, the purpose of the evaluation, the program context, and the available resources may not always allow such an approach. The following, then, is an attempt to outline some decision points, given different combinations of evaluation purposes and contexts.

Although the research on evaluation of language education programs suggests that there is a move away from reliance on strictly positivistic designs, there is still a tendency for sponsors to want *hard data*[2] (i.e., quantitative evidence such as test score improvement). This is especially true when the goals of the evaluation are primarily judgmental. In such cases, an attempt to include one of the quantitative designs presented in Chapter 4 is warranted. Depending on the availability of a comparison group (determined in step 3, context inventory), your choice of positivistic design will be constrained. Given the fact that you will rarely have the opportunity to randomly select and assign students to program and comparison groups, your choices are further constrained. Table 9.3, elaborating on the flowchart presented in Figure 1.2, can serve to direct you to appropriate quantitative designs.

When the goals of the evaluation are primarily descriptive, a naturalistic design is preferable. As discussed in Chapter 5, these designs are not constrained by contextual features such as the availability of randomization, comparison groups, and tests. The illumination model (Parlett and Hamilton 1976) is perhaps the most eclectic and broad in terms of the array of data that it pursues. As such it is well suited to a variety

---

2 As Popkewitz (1990:57) points out, the use of the terms *hard* and *soft* data "has a gendered quality that cannot be ignored in research and among researchers."

TABLE 9.3 QUANTITATIVE DESIGN CHOICES

| Comparison group? | *Randomization?* | |
	Yes	*No*
Yes	Design 1: true experiment, control group, pre- and posttest	Design 4: quasi-experiment, nonequivalent control group, pre- and posttest
	Design 2: true experiment, control group, posttest only	Design 6: Quasi-experiment, nonequivalent control group, time series
No		Design 3: Preexperimental, no control group, pre- and posttest
		Design 5: no control group, time series

of evaluation contexts, and I recommend it as a starting point for evaluators who are embarking upon naturalistic evaluation for the first time. In contexts where the evaluator or the audiences have an affinity with other disciplines (e.g., law, journalism), the naturalistic designs discussed as metaphors in Chapter 5 may be appropriate and useful.

When the goals of the evaluation are primarily judgmental and the audience is open to naturalistic evidence, the evaluator is well advised to consider naturalistic designs such as the responsive model (Stake 1975). Here the informational needs of the primary audiences, and their responses to the portrayal of findings by the evaluator, drive the design and data collection. Thus the relevance and utilizability of the evaluation findings are an integral aspect of the design.

There may be evaluation contexts in which either the audience or the evaluator calls for a goal-free (Scriven 1972) approach. Although this design avoids judgments about stated goals for the program, concentrating instead on a descriptive account of what is actually happening, it can nonetheless result in relevant information for judgmental evaluation goals as well. The main constraint on the use of goal-free evaluation is the desire on the part of the audience for an external evaluator and the availability of such a person.

Goal-free evaluation raises an issue that was discussed briefly in Chapter 1: the value of external versus internal evaluation. Alderson and Scott (1992) point out the limitations of the "Jet-In, Jet-Out Expert" (JIJOE) external evaluator: the lack of experience and understanding of the program context from an "insider's" perspective, and the natural distrust of "outsiders" and the agenda (someone else's) that they represent. Mitchell (1992) reports on the negative effects of "outsider status" in terms of local media portrayal of an evaluation. This seems to argue against the use of external evaluation, except when it is demanded by the audience. It should be noted, however, that at least one evaluation researcher (Thompson 1989) has reported on the value of external evaluators and their ability to effect change by acting as "power brokers" and behind-the-scenes negotiators. As with the decision of whether to use positivistic versus naturalistic evaluation, I recommend that, when possible, both internal and external evaluation be made part of the design. Many of the limitations of the external evaluator can be overcome by a naturalistic effort to understand the insider's perspective or by having the outsider act as facilitator for a primarily internal evaluation (see, for example, Alderson and Scott's "participatory evaluation" [1992]).

CAM step 6 (data analysis): Analyze and interpret your findings

The analysis of quantitative data is relatively straightforward and has been discussed in Chapter 6. It is important, however, to be careful in choosing the instruments that are used to measure the program effect and to address thoroughly and openly the various assumptions underlying the statistical procedures used for analysis. Too often there can be a subtle leap of faith (and interpretation) from the finding of statistical significance to a substantive conclusion, involving either a failure to address deficiencies in the data, improper labeling of variables and test instruments, or both.

Chapter 7 presented a process for analyzing and interpreting qualitative data, a process that is nonlinear, iterative, and less straightforward than quantitative analysis. I have used the term *multiple perspective negotiation* to indicate an approach designed to enhance validity (from the naturalistic perspective) and make the interpretations more relevant and understandable. Alderson (1992) has similarly suggested that interpretations be presented to evaluation stakeholders for their reactions and potential reinterpretations, as have Guba and Lincoln (1989) and Patton (1980). To the extent that program participants, "insiders," are included in this negotiation, the evaluation provides the opportunity to discover aspects of the program in a less threatening way than if the same interpretations were arrived at by an evaluator in isolation (cf. Alderson and Scott 1992:55).

CAM step 7 (evaluation report): Communicating the evaluation findings

The final product of an evaluation is a report, which can take many different forms, depending on the audience and goals. As mentioned earlier, this is something that should be negotiated and made clear at the beginning of the evaluation process. Generally, there is a formal written report, sometimes referred to as the *archive document* (e.g., Beretta 1992a), which contains a complete picture of the evaluation questions, data collected, analyses performed, and conclusions reached. There may be a need, however, for different versions of this document for different audiences.

An executive summary, highlighting the salient findings and recommending courses of action, may be needed for the primary audiences, especially sponsors. Other primary audiences, such as teachers and administrators, may require a more informal, question-and-answer format for the communication of evaluation findings. This may, in fact, become another phase of multiple perspective negotiation. Secondary audiences may need more background on the design and implementation of the evaluation and may be interested only in general conclusions. Finally, tertiary audiences will most likely learn of the evaluation through research reports published in journals such as *TESOL Quarterly, Modern Language Journal, Language Learning, Issues in Applied Linguistics,* and *Applied Linguistics.*

A central issue in the communication of evaluation findings is validity: What counts as evidence? This same issue will have emerged from the early steps in the evaluation process, based on the perspectives of the audiences and their goals. It will then have influenced the choice of evaluation design and the analysis of the data. When the evaluation has multiple audiences, as it usually does, the use of multiple strategies and mixed designs provides the evaluator with the needed variety of evidence and evaluation language. As Beretta (1992a:20) puts it: "The jargon of research might be replaced for one audience by a telling anecdote. . . ." Although this quotation seems to suggest a difference in status between positivistic language ("the jargon of research") and naturalistic language ("a telling anecdote"), I maintain that the paradigms each have their own, equally valid "jargon." In that sense, it might be more appropriate to say: "The jargon of statistical analysis might be replaced for one audience with an excerpt from an in-depth interview."

Ultimately, the concern at this stage is successful communication between the evaluator(s) and the audience(s). In order to accomplish this, the evaluator needs to return to the dimensions of the context inventory (and, presumably, an understanding of them enhanced by the evaluation experience) to be clear on such things as the sociopolitical climate surrounding the program. There may be serious and sensitive consequences to the evaluation findings. Alderson (1992:299) has pointed out that there seems to be "the inevitable compromise between 'telling the truth' and 'getting action.' " If the evaluator and/or audiences are committed to a particular course of action based on the findings of the evaluation, it may be necessary to translate the results into language that does not offend the sensibilities of teachers, students, administrators, or the community within which the program is situated. It may be important to focus on one set of data (e.g., test results showing statistically significant improvement of program students) over another (e.g., observation and interview data that suggest poor relations between students and teachers) for a particular audience and report. When the evaluator is confident that the overall findings of the evaluation support a particular course of action, such "tailoring" of the report can be seen as an honest effort toward communication. To portray all the evidence to all audiences, without such a concern, runs the risk of obscuring the intended message and ending in a misunderstanding of the evaluation's conclusions and the evidence on which they are based.

The role of program evaluation in applied linguistics research

As mentioned in Chapter 1, I believe that program evaluation can play a key role in applied linguistics research. Evaluation of language education will always have a very practical focus: to inform decisions about language programs. Although it may be possible to distinguish program evaluation from other forms of research in this way, it should not result in its isolation. There are many areas where the findings from evaluation research can intersect with and inform other applied linguistics inquiry (see Figure 9.1).

In order to accomplish an effective evaluation, program objectives, program processes, and program outcomes must all be investigated. This brings several areas of applied linguistics research into play. *Classroom-centered research* provides information for evaluating what happens inside the program – program processes – and informs second

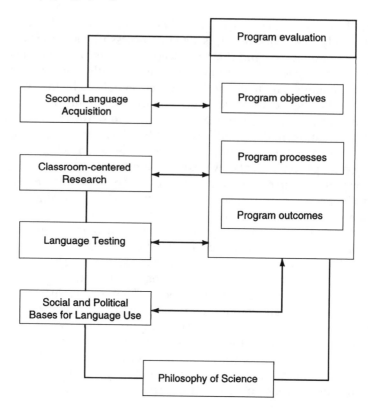

Figure 9.1 The role of program evaluation in applied linguistics research.

language acquisition (SLA) theory.[3] *Language testing* provides information for evaluating program outcomes and informs SLA theory as well as the refinement of program objectives. SLA theory, in turn, can inform program objectives and classroom methods. Sociolinguistics, or the social and political bases for language learning and use, becomes a concern in evaluation: The program objectives, processes, and outcomes need to be understood within the sociopolitical context of the program. Finally, the *philosophy of science* has been of great concern in the evaluation literature, arising from the need to seek research methodologies that look at the program from both inside and out. As discussed in

---

3 Although Beretta (1992a:19) maintains that "aspirations regarding the advancement of language learning theory will be distinctly subdued – they will be secondary to the provision of user-relevant information in the short run," I insist that program evaluation research can nevertheless make contributions to language learning theory.

Chapters 2 and 3, I feel that it is critical for applied linguistics to become clearer about the ontological and epistemological assumptions underlying its inquiry. The paradigm dialog has been articulated within the educational research literature (Smith and Heshusius 1986; Howe 1988; Gage 1989; Guba 1990a), but it has not been addressed as directly within applied linguistics. As a result, naturalistic approaches have tended to be admitted as bona fide research only to the extent that they can demonstrate conformity with the requirements for validity that come from the positivistic perspective. I argue for a serious and ongoing consideration of this dialog, not with an eye toward replacing one research paradigm with another, but in order to encourage applied linguists to be open to different approaches to research and to be clear about the philosophical basis for their inquiry.

This returns us to the questions posed in Chapter 1: What counts as evidence? What are the social and political factors that affect language learning and teaching? How can we best define and measure language abilities? What are the best research designs for our inquiry? How do learners acquire second languages? Specific program contexts, with their specific needs for evaluation, will continue to motivate research that will contribute answers to these defining questions within applied linguistics.

References

Alderson, J. C. 1992. Guidelines for the evaluation of language education. In J. C. Alderson and A. Beretta (Eds.), *Evaluating second language education*, 274–304. Cambridge: Cambridge University Press.

Alderson, J. C., and A. Beretta (Eds.). 1992. *Evaluating second language education*. Cambridge: Cambridge University Press.

Alderson, J. C., and M. Scott. 1992. Insiders, outsiders and participatory evaluation. In J. C. Alderson and A. Beretta (Eds.), *Evaluating second language education*, 25–57. Cambridge: Cambridge University Press.

Allen, J. P. B., M. Fröhlich, and N. Spada. 1984. The communicative orientation of language teaching: an observation scheme. In J. Handscombe, R. A. Orem, and B. Taylor (Eds.), *On TESOL '83: the question of control*, 231–52. Washington, D.C.: TESOL.

Allen, J. P. B., M. Swain, B. Harley, and J. Cummins. 1990. Aspects of classroom treatment: toward a more comprehensive view of second language education. In B. Harley, P. Allen, J. Cummins, and M. Swain et al. (Eds.), *The development of second language proficiency*, 57–81. Cambridge: Cambridge University Press.

Allwright, D., and K. M. Bailey. 1991. *Focus on the language classroom: an introduction to classroom research for language teachers*. Cambridge: Cambridge University Press.

Andersen, R., H. George, F. Gomes de Mateos, M. Ilomaki, B. Jacobs, R. S. Kirsner, T. Miettinen, E. Ochs, C. Pettinari, E. A. Schegloff, J. Schumann, T. Slama-Cazacu, R. P. Stockwell, R. Virrankoski, and J. Walters. 1990. Special feature roundtable: defining our field: unity in diversity. *Issues in Applied Linguistics* 1(2): 149–66.

Asher, J. J., J. A. Kusudo, and R. de la Torre. 1974. Learning a second language through commands: the second field test. *Modern Language Journal* 58: 24–32.

Bachman, L. F. 1981. Formative evaluation in specific purposes program development. In R. Mackay and J. D. Palmer (Eds.), *Language for specific purposes: program design and evaluation*, 106–16. Rowley, Mass.: Newbury House.

1989. The development and use of criterion-referenced tests of language ability in language program evaluation. In R. K. Johnson (Ed.), *The second language curriculum*, 242–58. Cambridge: Cambridge University Press.

1990. *Fundamental considerations in language testing*. Oxford: Oxford University Press.

Bailey, K. M. 1982. Teaching in a second language: the communicative competence of non-native speaking teaching assistants. Ph.D. diss., University of California, Los Angeles.

1983. Competitiveness and anxiety in adult second language acquisition: looking at and through the diary studies. In H. W. Seliger and M. H. Long (Eds.), *Classroom oriented research in second language acquisition*, 67–103. Rowley, Mass.: Newbury House.

Bechtel, W. 1988. *Philosophy of science: an overview for cognitive science.* Hillsdale, N.J.: Lawrence Earlbaum Associates.

Beretta, A. 1986a. Toward a methodology of ESL program evaluation. *TESOL Quarterly* 20(1): 144–55.

1986b. A case for field-experimentation in program evaluation. *Language Learning* 36(3): 295–309.

1986c. Program-fair language teaching program evaluation. *TESOL Quarterly* 20(3): 431–44.

1990. Implementation of the Bangalore Project. *Applied Linguistics* 11(4): 321–40.

1992a. Evaluation of language education: an overview. In J. C. Alderson and A. Beretta (Eds.), *Evaluating second language education*, 15–24. Cambridge: Cambridge University Press.

1992b. What can be learned from the Bangalore evaluation. In C. J. Alderson and A. Beretta, (Eds.), *Evaluating second language education*, 250–73. Cambridge: Cambridge University Press.

Beretta, A., and A. Davies. 1985. Evaluation of the Bangalore Project. *English Language Teaching Journal* 39(2): 121–27.

Berkowitz, L., and E. Donnerstein. 1982. External validity is more than skin deep: some answers to criticisms of laboratory experiments. *American Psychologist* 37(3): 245–57.

Bernstein, R. 1983. *Beyond objectivism and relativism.* Philadelphia: University of Philadelphia Press.

Bialystok, E., M. Frölich, and J. Howard. 1979. Studies on second language learning and teaching in classroom settings: strategies, processes and functions. Unpublished report. Toronto: Ontario Institute for Studies in Education.

Bogdan, R., and S. J. Taylor. 1975. *Introduction to qualitative research methods.* New York: John Wiley & Sons.

Boruch, R. F., and D. Rinkskopf. 1977. On randomized experiments, approximations to experiments, and data analysis. In L. Rutman (Ed.), *Evaluation of research methods: a basic guide*, 143–76. Beverly Hills, Calif: Sage.

Brinton, D. M., and C. Holten. 1989. What novice teachers focus on: the practicum in TESL. *TESOL Quarterly* 23(4): 343–50.

Brinton, D. M., A. M. Snow, and M. B. Wesche. 1989. *Content-based second language instruction.* Rowley, Mass.: Newbury House.

Brooks, N. 1961. *Language and language teaching.* New York: Harcourt, Brace, & World.

Brown, J. D. 1988. *Understanding research in second language learning: a teacher's guide to statistics and research design.* Cambridge: Cambridge University Press.

1989a. Language program evaluation: a synthesis of existing possibilities. In R. K. Johnson (Ed.), *The second language curriculum*, 222–42. Cambridge: Cambridge University Press.

1989b. Improving ESL placement tests using two perspectives. *TESOL Quarterly* 23(1): 65–84.

Bryk, A. S., A. F. Strenio, and H.I. Weisberg. 1980. A method for estimating treatment effects when individuals are growing. *Journal of Educational Statistics* 5(1): 5–34.

Bryk, A. S., and H. I. Weisberg. 1976. Value-added analysis: a dynamic approach to the estimation of treatment effects. *Journal of Educational Statistics* 1(2): 127–55.

Burstein, L. 1981. State of the art methodology for the design and analysis of future large scale evaluations: a selective examination. Report no. 177. Los Angeles: Center for the Study of Evaluation, Graduate School of Education, UCLA.

Cain, G. G. 1975. Regression and selection models to improve nonexperimental comparisons. In C. A. Bennett and A. A. Lumsdaine (Eds.), *Evaluation and experiment, some critical issues in assessing social problems*, 297–317. New York: Academic Press.

Camilli, G., and K. D. Hopkins. 1978. Applicability of chi-square to 2 × 2 contingency tables with small expected cell frequencies. *Psychological Bulletin* 85(1): 163–67.

Campbell, D. T. 1986. Relabeling internal and external validity for applied social scientists. In W. M. K. Trochim (Ed.), *Advances in quasi-experimental design and analysis. New Directions for Program Evaluation* 31: 67–77.

Campbell, D. T., and R. F. Boruch. 1975. Making the case for randomized assignment to treatments by considering the alternatives: six ways in which quasi-experimental evaluations in compensatory education tend to underestimate effects. In C. A. Bennett and A. A. Lumsdaine (Eds.), *Evaluation and experiment, some critical issues in assessing social problems*, 195–296. New York, NY: Academic Press.

Campbell, D. T., and A. E. Erlebacher. 1970. How regression artifacts in quasi-experimental evaluations can mistakenly make compensatory education look harmful. In J. Hellmuth (Ed.), *Compensatory education: a national debate*. New York: Bruner/Mazel.

Campbell, D. T., and D. W. Fiske. 1959. Convergent and discriminant validation by the multitrait-multimethod matrix. *Psychological Bulletin* 56(2): 81–105.

Campbell, D. T., and J. C. Stanley. 1966. *Experimental and quasi-experimental designs for research*. Chicago: Rand McNally.

Carroll, J. B. 1965. The contribution of psychological theory and educational research to the teaching of foreign languages. *Modern Language Journal* 49(5): 273–81.

1969. What does the Pennsylvania foreign language research project tell us? *Foreign Language Annals* 3(2): 214–36.

Chastain, K. D., and F. J. Woerdehoff. 1968. A methodological study comparing the audio-lingual habit theory and the cognitive code-learning theory. *Modern Language Journal* 52(5): 268–79.

Chaudron, C. 1988. *Second language classrooms: research on teaching and learning*. Cambridge: Cambridge University Press.

Cherryholmes, C. H. 1992. Notes on pragmatism and scientific realism. *Educational Researcher* 21(6): 13–17.

Clark, J. L. D. 1969. The Pennsylvania project and the "audio lingual" vs "traditional" question. *Modern Language Journal* 53(6): 388–96.

Coleman, H. 1992. Moving the goalposts: project evaluation in practice. In J. C. Alderson and A. Beretta (Eds.), *Evaluating second language education,* 222–46. Cambridge: Cambridge University Press.

Cook, T. D., and D. T. Campbell. 1979. *Quasi-experimentation: design and analysis issues for field settings.* Boston: Houghton Mifflin.

Cook, T. D., F.L. Cook, and M. M. Mark. 1977. Randomized and quasi experimental designs in evaluation research: an introduction. In L. Rutman (Ed.), *Evaluation research methods: a basic guide,* 103–39. Beverly Hills, Calif.: Sage.

Cordray, D. S. 1986. Quasi-experimental analysis: a mixture of methods and judgment. In W. M. K. Trochim (Ed.), *Advances in quasi-experimental design and analysis. New Directions for Program Evaluation* 31: 9–27.

Corsaro, W. A. 1981. Entering the child's world: research strategies for field entry and data collection in a preschool setting. In J. L. Green and C. Wallat (Eds.), *Ethnography and language in educational settings.* Norwood, N.J.: Ablex.

Cronbach, L. J. 1982. *Designing evaluations of educational and social programs.* San Francisco: Jossey-Bass.

Cronbach, L. J., D. R. Rogosa, R. E. Floden, and G. G. Price. 1975. Analysis of covariance in nonrandomized experiments: parameters affecting bias. *Occasional papers of the Stanford Evaluation Consortium. Stanford,* Calif.: Stanford University.

Cronbach, L. J., et al. 1980. *Toward reform of program evaluation: aims, methods, and institutional arrangements.* San Francisco: Jossey-Bass.

Denzin, N. K. 1970. *The research act.* Chicago: Aldine.

1978. *The research act: an introduction to sociological methods.* New York: McGraw-Hill.

1989. *Interpretive interactionism.* Newbury Park, Calif.: Sage.

Douglas, J. D. 1985. *Creative interviewing.* Newbury Park, Calif.: Sage.

Dunkel, P. 1991. The effectiveness research on computer-assisted instruction and computer-assisted language learning. In P. Dunkel (Ed.), *Computer-assisted language learning and testing,* 5–36. New York: Newbury House.

Eisner, E. W. 1975. The perceptive eye: toward the reformation of educational evaluation. *Occasional papers of the Stanford Evaluation Consortium.* Stanford, Calif.: Stanford University.

1992. Are all causal claims positivistic? A reply to Francis Schrag. *Educational Researcher* 21(5): 8–9.

Elashoff, J. D. 1969. Analysis of covariance: a delicate instrument. *American Educational Research Journal* 6: 383–401.

Erickson, F. 1992. Why the clinical trail doesn't work as a metaphor for educational research: a response to Schrag. *Educational Researcher* 21(5): 9–11.

Everitt, B. 1980. *Cluster analysis,* 2d ed. New York: Halsted.

Fanselow, J. F. 1977. Beyond Rashomon – conceptualizing and describing the teaching act. *TESOL Quarterly* 11(1): 17–39.

Farley, J. 1987. Justifying conclusions in naturalistic evaluations: a critical perspective. *Evaluation and Program Planning* 10: 343–50.

Feyerabend, P. 1988. *Against method.* London: Verso.

Fielding, N. G., and J.L. Fielding. 1986. *Linking data*. Beverly Hills, CA.: Sage.

Firestone, W. A. 1993. Alternative arguments for generalizing from data as applied to qualitative research. *Educational Researcher* 22(4): 16–23.

Fitz-Gibbon, C. T., and L. L. Morris. 1987. *How to design a program evaluation*. Newbury Park, Calif.: Sage.

Freedman, E. S. 1971. The road from Pennsylvania – where next in language teaching experimentation? *Audio-Visual Language Journal* 9(1): 33–39.

Gage, N. L. 1989. The paradigm wars and their aftermath. *Educational Researcher* 18(7): 4–10.

Geertz, C. 1973. *The interpretation of culture*. New York: Basic Books.

Genesee, F. 1985. Second language learning through immersion: a review of U.S. programs. *Review of Educational Research*, 55(4): 541–61.

Glaser, B., and A. Strauss. 1967. *The discovery of grounded theory*. Chicago: Aldine.

Green, P. S. 1975. *The language laboratory in school*. Edinburgh: Oliver & Boyd.

Greene, J. C. 1987. Justifying conclusions in naturalistic evaluations: a practical perspective. *Evaluation and Program Planning* 10: 325–33.

Greene, J. C., and C. McClintock. 1985. Triangulation in evaluation: design and analysis issues. *Evaluation Review* 9(5): 523–45.

Guba, E. G. 1978. Toward a methodology of naturalistic inquiry in educational evaluation. *CSE Monograph Series in Evaluation No. 8*. Los Angeles: Center for the Study of Evaluation, University of California, Los Angeles.

(Ed.). 1990a. *The paradigm dialog*. Newbury Park, Calif.: Sage.

1990b. The alternative paradigm dialog. In E. G. Guba (Ed.), *The paradigm dialog*, 17–27. Newbury Park, Calif.: Sage.

Guba, E. G., and Y. S. Lincoln. 1982. Epistemological and methodological bases of naturalistic inquiry. *Educational Communication and Technology* 30(4): 233–52.

1989. *Fourth generation evaluation*. Newbury Park, Calif.: Sage.

Guilford, J. P., and B. Fruchter. 1978. *Fundamental statistics in psychology and education*, 6th ed. New York: McGraw Hill.

Guthrie, G. P. 1982. An ethnography of bilingual education in a Chinese community. Unpublished Ph.D. diss., University of Illinois at Urbana-Champaign.

Habermas, J. 1988. *On the logic of the social sciences*. Cambridge, Mass.: MIT Press.

Harley, B., P. Allen, J. Cummins, and M. Swain (Eds.). 1990. *The development of second language proficiency*. Cambridge: Cambridge University Press.

Hatch, E., and A. Lazaraton. 1991. *The research manual: design and statistics for applied linguistics*. New York: Newbury House.

Hays, W. 1973. *Statistics for the social sciences*, 2d ed. New York: Holt, Rinehart & Winston.

Henning, G. 1982. Growth-referenced evaluation of foreign language instructional programs. *TESOL Quarterly* 16(4): 467–477.

1987. *A guide to language testing*. Rowley, Mass.: Newbury House.

Hilton, M. 1969. A scientific experiment? *Audio-Visual Language Journal* 7(2): 97–101.

Hotelling, H. 1940. The selection of variates for use in prediction, with some comments on the general problem of nuisance parameters. *Annals of Mathematical Statistics* 11: 271–83.

House, E. R., S. Mathison, and R. McTaggart. 1989. Validity and teacher inference. *Educational Researcher* 18(7): 11–15, 26.

Howe, K. R. 1988. Against the quantitative-qualitative incompatibility thesis: or dogmas die hard. *Educational Researcher* 17(1): 10–16.

Hudson, T. D., and B. K. Lynch. 1984. A criterion-referenced measurement approach to ESL achievement testing. *Language Testing* (2): 171–201.

Jacobson, P. L. H. 1982. Using evaluation to improve foreign language education. *Modern Language Journal* 66: 4–291.

Kahn, A. 1991. Considerations on the role of participant observation in program evaluation. Unpublished ms. Los Angeles: UCLA.

Keating, R. F. 1963. *A study of the effectiveness of language laboratories: a preliminary evaluation in twenty-one school systems of the Metropolitan School Study Council.* New York: The Institute of Administrative Research, Teachers College, Columbia University.

Kenney, D. A. 1975. A quasi-experimental approach to assessing treatment effects in the nonequivalent control group design. *Psychological Bulletin* 82(3): 229–34.

Kirk, R. E. 1982. *Experimental design: procedures for the behavioral sciences.* Monterey, Calif.: Brooks/Cole.

Kruskal, J. B., and M. Wish. 1978. *Multidimensional scaling.* Beverly Hills, Calif.: Sage.

Laudan, L. 1977. *Progress and its problems.* Berkeley, Calif.: University of California Press.

Laudan, R., and L. Laudan. 1989. Dominance and the disunity of method: solving the problems of innovation and consensus. *Philosophy of Science* 56: 221–37.

LeCompte, M. D., and J. P. Goetz. 1982a. Problems of reliability and validity in ethnographic research. *Review of Educational Research* 52(1): 31–60.

———. 1982b. Ethnographic data collection in evaluation research. *Education Evaluation and Policy Analysis* 4: 317–400.

Levin, L. 1972. *Comparative studies in foreign-language teaching.* Stockholm: Almqvist and Wiksell.

Levine, H. G. 1985. Principles of data storage and retrieval for use in qualitative evaluations. *Educational Evaluation and Policy Analysis* 7(2): 169–86.

Levine, H. G., R. Gallimore, T. S. Weisner, and J. L. Turner. 1980. Teaching participant-observation research methods: a skills-building approach. *Anthropology & Education Quarterly* XI(1): 38–54.

Levine, M. 1974. Scientific method and the adversary model: some preliminary thoughts. *American Psychologist* 29(9): 661–77.

Lightbown, P. M., and R. H. Halter. 1989. Evaluation of ESL learning in regular and experimental programs in four New Brunswick school districts. Unpublished report. Montreal: Concordia University.

Lincoln, Y.S. 1990. The making of a constructivist: a remembrance of transformations past. In E. G. Guba (Ed.), *The paradigm dialog*, 67–87. Newbury Park, Calif.: Sage.

Long, M. H. 1983. Inside the black box: methodological issues in classroom research on language learning. In H. W. Seliger and M. H. Long (Eds.),

Classroom oriented research in second language acquisition, 3–35. Rowley, Mass.: Newbury House.

1984. Process and product in ESL program evaluation. *TESOL Quarterly* 18(3): 409–25.

Lynch, B. K. 1988. Toward a context-adaptive model for the evaluation of language teaching programs. (Ph.D. diss., University of California, Los Angeles, 1987). *Dissertation Abstracts International* 48: 2264A.

1990a. A context-adaptive model for program evaluation. *TESOL Quarterly* 24(1): 23–42.

1990b. Two commentaries on Brian K. Lynch's "A Context-Adaptive Model of Program Evaluation": The author responds . . . . *TESOL Quarterly* 24(4): 764–67.

1991. The role of program evaluation in applied linguistics research. In Special feature roundtable: language education, language acquisition: working perspectives of four applied linguists. *Issues in Applied Linguistics* 2(1): 84–86.

1992. Evaluating a program inside and out. In J. C. Alderson and A. Beretta (Eds.), *Evaluating second language education*, 61–99. Cambridge: Cambridge University Press.

Mark, M. M. 1986. Validity typologies and the logic and practice of quasi-experimenation. In W. M. K. Trochim (Ed.), *Advances in quasi-experimental design and analysis. New Directions for Program Evaluation* 31: 47–66.

Marottoli, V. 1973. The success of private language schools: a lesson to be learned. *Foreign Language Annals* 6(3): 354–58.

Mathison, S. 1988. Why triangulate? *Educational Researcher* 17(2): 13–17.

Maxwell, J. A. 1992. Understanding and validity in qualitative research. *Harvard Educational Review* 62(3): 279–99.

McFee, G. 1992. Triangulation in research: two confusions. *Educational Research* 34(3): 215–19.

McGrath, J. E. 1982. Dilemmatics: the study of research choices and dilemmas. In J. E. McGrath, J. Martin, and R. A. Kulka, *Judgment calls in research*, 69–101. Beverly Hills, Calif.: Sage.

McGrath, J. E., J. Martin, and R. A. Kulka. 1982. Some quasi-rules for making judgment calls in research. In J. E. McGrath, J. Martin, and R. A. Kulka, *Judgment calls in research*, 103–118. Beverly Hills, Calif.: Sage.

McKerrow, K. K., and J. E. McKerrow. 1991. Naturalistic misunderstanding of the Heisenberg Uncertainty Principle. *Educational Researcher* 20(1): 17–20.

McLean, L. D., H. H. Stern, G. Hanna, and A. H. Smith. 1978. Evaluation of the bilingual exchange programs: an interim report. Toronto: Ontario Institute for Studies in Education.

Miles, M. B., and A. M. Huberman. 1984. *Qualitative data analysis: a sourcebook of new methods*. Beverly Hills, Calif.: Sage.

Miller, S. I., and M. Fredericks. 1991. Postpositivistic assumptions and educational research: another view. *Educational Researcher* 20(4): 2–8.

Mitchell, R. 1992. The "independent" evaluation of bilingual primary education: a narrative account. In J. C. Alderson and A. Beretta (Eds.), *Evaluating second language education*, 100–36. Cambridge: Cambridge University Press.

Moskowitz, G. 1970. *The foreign language teacher interacts.* Chicago: Association for Productive Teaching.

Mosteller, F., and J. W. Tukey. 1977. *Data analysis and regression.* Reading, Mass.: Addison-Wesley.

Nespor, J. K., and J. W. Garrison. 1992. Constructing "relevance": a comment on Miller and Fredericks's "Postpositivistic assumptions and educational research." *Educational Researcher* 21(3): 27–28.

Newton-Smith, W. 1982. Relativism and the possibility of interpretation. In M. Hollis and S. Lukes (Eds.), Rationality and relativism, 106–22. Oxford: Basil Blackwell.

Nunan, D. 1988. *The learner-centered curriculum.* Cambridge: Cambridge University Press.

1989. *Understanding language classrooms: a guide to teacher-initiated action.* Englewood Cliffs, N.J.: Prentice-Hall.

Owens, T. 1973. Education evaluation by adversary proceeding. In E. House (Ed.), *School evaluation: the politics and process.* Berkeley, Calif.: McCutchan.

Palmer, A. 1992. Issues in evaluating input-based language teaching programs. In J. C. Alderson and A. Beretta (Eds.). 1992. *Evaluating second language education,* 141–166. Cambridge: Cambridge University Press.

Parlett, M., and D. Hamilton. 1976. Evaluation as illumination: a new approach to the study of innovatory programs. In G. V. Glass (Ed.), *Evaluation studies review annual,* vol. 1. Beverly Hills, Calif.: Sage.

Patton, M. Q. 1980. *Qualitative evaluation methods.* Beverly Hills, Calif.: Sage.

1986. *Utilization-focused evaluation,* 2d ed. Beverly Hills, Calif.: Sage.

1987. *How to use qualitative methods in evaluation.* Beverly Hills, Calif.: Sage.

Pearsol, J. A. 1987. Justifying conclusions in naturalistic evaluations: an interpretive perspective. *Evaluation and Program Planning* 10: 335–41.

Pennycook, A. 1990. Towards a critical applied linguistics for the 1990s. *Issues in Applied Linguistics* 1(1): 8–28.

1991. A reply to Kanpol. *Issues in Applied Linguistics* 2(2): 305–312.

Peshkin, A. 1993. The goodness of qualitative research. *Educational Researcher* 22(2): 2327.

Phillips, D. C. 1990. Postpositivistic science: myths and realities. In E. G. Guba (Ed.), *The paradigm dialog,* 31–45. Newbury Park, Calif.: Sage.

Popham, W. J. 1978. *Criterion-referenced measurement.* Englewood Cliffs, N.J.: Prentice-Hall.

Popkewitz, T. S. 1990. Whose future? Whose past?: notes on critical theory and methodology. In E. G. Guba (Ed.), *The paradigm dialog,* 46–66. Newbury Park, Calif.: Sage.

1992. Cartesian anxiety, linguistic communism, and reading texts. *Educational Researcher* 21(5): 11–15.

Reichardt, C. S., and T. D. Cook. 1979. Beyond qualitative versus quantitative methods. In T. D. Cook and C. S. Reichardt (Eds.), *Qualitative and quantitative methods in evaluation research,* 7–30. Beverly Hills, Calif.: Sage.

Rindskopf, D. 1986. New developments in selection modeling for quasi-experimentation. In W. M. K. Trochim (Ed.), *Advances in quasi-experimental design and analysis. New Directions for Program Evaluation* 31: 79–89.

Rosenberg, S., and M. P. Kim. 1975. The method of sorting as a data-gathering procedure in multivariate research. *Multivariate Behavioral Research* 10: 489–502.

Sax, G. 1974. The use of standardized tests in evaluation. In W. J. Popham (Ed.), *Evaluation in education: current applications*, 243–308. Berkeley, Calif.: McCutchen.

Scherer, G. A. C., and M. Wertheimer. 1962. Extended classroom experimentation with varied sequencing of the four skills in German instruction. Final report, contract no. SAE 8823. Washington, D.C.: U.S. Office of Education.

Schotta, S. G. 1973. Student evaluations and foreign language programs: a case study. *Foreign Language Annals* 6(4): 500–18.

Schrag, F. 1992a. In defense of positivist research paradigms. *Educational Researcher* 21(5): 5–8.

——— 1992b. Is there light at the end of this tunnel? *Educational Researcher* 21(5): 16–17.

Schumann, J. H. 1992. Training applied linguists for the future. *Issues in Applied Linguistics* 3(1): 132–34.

Schwandt, T. R. 1990. Paths to inquiry in the social disciplines: scientific, constructivist, and critical theory methodologies. In E. G. Guba (Ed.), *The paradigm dialog*, 258–76. Newbury Park, Calif.: Sage.

Scriven, M. 1967. The methodology of evaluation. In R. W. Tyler, R. M. Gagne, and M. Scriven (Eds.), *Perspectives of curriculum evaluation*, AERA Monograph Series on Curriculum Evaluation, No. 1, 39–83. Chicago: Rand McNally.

——— 1972. Pros and cons about goal free evaluation. *Evaluation Comment* 3. Los Angeles: Center for the Study of Evaluation.

Searle, J. R. 1983. *Intentionality*. Cambridge: Cambridge University Press.

Shadish, W. R., Jr., T. D. Cook, and A.C. Houts. 1986. Quasi-experimentation in a critical multiplist mode. In W.M. K. Trochim (Ed.), *Advances in quasi-experimental design and analysis. New Directions for Program Evaluation* 31: 29–46.

Smith, J. K. 1987. Commentary: relativism and justifying conclusions in naturalistic research. *Evaluation and Program Planning* 10: 351–58.

——— 1988. The evaluator/researcher as person vs. the person as evaluator/researcher. *Educational Researcher* 17(2): 18–23.

——— 1990. Alternative research paradigms and the problem of criteria. In E. G. Guba (Ed.), *The paradigm dialog*, 167–87. Newbury Park, Calif.: Sage.

Smith, J. K., and L. Heshusius. 1986. Closing down the conversation: the end of the quantitative-qualitative debate among educational inquirers. *Educational Researcher* 15(1): 4–12.

Smith, N. L. (Ed.). 1981. *Metaphors for evaluation: sources of new methods*. Beverly Hills, Calif.: Sage.

Smith, P. D., Jr. 1970. *A comparison of the cognitive and audiolingual approaches to foreign lanaguage instruction: the Pennsylvania foreign language project*. Philadelphia: The Center for Curriculum Development.

Spradley, J. P. 1980. *Participant observation*. New York: Holt, Rinehart & Winston.

Stake, R. E. 1967. The countenance of educational evaluation. *Teachers College Record* 68: 523–40.

1975. *Evaluating the arts in education.* Columbus, Ohio: Charles E. Merrill.
Stallings, J., M. Needels, and N. Staybrook. 1979. How to change the process of teaching basic reading skills. Technical report. Menlo Park, Calif.: SRI International.
Strauss, A. L. 1987. *Qualitative analysis for social scientists.* Cambridge: Cambridge University Press.
Thompson, R. J. 1989. Evaluator as power broker: issues in the Maghreb. In R. F. Conner and M. Hendricks (Eds.), *International innovations in evaluation methodology. New Directions for Program Evaluation* 42: 39–47.
Trend, M. G. 1979. On the reconciliation of quantitative and qualitative analyses: a case study. In T. D. Cook and C. S. Reichardt (Eds.), *Qualitative and quantitative methods in evaluation research.* Beverly Hills, Calif.: Sage.
Trochim, W. M. K. 1985. Pattern matching, validity, and conceptualization in program evaluation. *Evaluation Review* 9(5): 575–604.
Turner, J. 1991. An adaptive model for the development of measures of student achievement in content-based language programs. Ph.D. diss., University of California, Los Angeles.
Ullman, R., and E. Geva. 1981. *The target language observation scheme (TALOS): handbook.* Toronto: Modern Language Center, Ontario Institute for Studies in Education.
1985. Expanding our evaluation perspective: what can classroom observation tell us about core French programs? *The Canadian Modern Language Review* 42(2): 307–23.
Valdman, A. 1969. Evaluation of PDE/FL research projects. In P.D. Smith (Ed.), A comparison study of the effectiveness of the traditional and audiolingual approaches to foreign language instruction utilizing laboratory equipment. Final report. project no. 7–0133, grant no. OEC-1–7-070133-0445. Washington, D.C.: U.S. Office of Education.
Valette, R. M. 1969. The Pennsylvania Project, its conclusions and its implications. *Modern Language Journal* 53(6): 396–404.
van Lier, L., J. Povey, B. K. Lynch, and J. Schumann. 1991. Special feature roundtable: language education, language acquisition: working perspectives of four applied linguists. *Issues in Applied Linguistics* 2(1): 77–94.
Webb, E. J., D. T. Campbell, R. D. Schwartz, and L. Sechrest. 1966. *Unobtrusive measures in social sciences.* Chicago: Rand McNally.
Wiley, D. E. 1969. A methodological review of the Pennsylvania foreign language research project. *Foreign Language Annals* 3(2): 208–13.
Winer, B. J. 1962. *Statistical problems in experimental design.* New York: McGraw-Hill.
Wolf, R. L. 1975. Trial by jury: a new evaluation method, 1. *Phi Delta Kappan* 57(3): 185–87.

Author index

Page numbers in italics indicate tables or figures. Page numbers followed by *n* indicate references to footnotes.

Subject index

Page numbers in italics indicate tables or figures. Page numbers followed by *n* indicate references to footnotes.